FAILING GRADES

FAILING GRADES

The Federal Politics of Education Standards

Kevin R. Kosar

LYNNE
RIENNER
PUBLISHERS

BOULDER
LONDON

The account expressed herein is that of the author alone and should not be attributed to any other person or to any institution (especially the Congressional Research Service). Any errors are the responsibility of the author alone.

Published in the United States of America in 2005 by
Lynne Rienner Publishers, Inc.
1800 30th Street, Boulder, Colorado 80301
www.rienner.com

and in the United Kingdom by
Lynne Rienner Publishers, Inc.
3 Henrietta Street, Covent Garden, London WC2E 8LU

Library of Congress Cataloging-in-Publication Data
Kosar, Kevin R., 1970–
　　Failing grades : the federal politics of education standards / by Kevin R. Kosar.
　　　　p. cm.
　　Includes bibliographical references and index.
　　ISBN 1-58826-388-6 (hardcover : alk. paper)
1. Education—Standards—United States. 2. Education and state—United States.
3. School failure—Political aspects—United States. I. Title.
LB3060.83.K69 2005
379.1'58'0973—dc22

　　　　　　　　　　　　　　　　　　　　　　　　　　　　　　　2005011304

British Cataloguing in Publication Data
A Cataloguing in Publication record for this book
is available from the British Library.

Printed and bound in the United States of America

The paper used in this publication meets the requirements
of the American National Standard for Permanence of
Paper for Printed Library Materials Z39.48-1992.

5　4　3　2　1

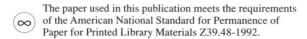

To my mother, Shirley R. Kosar, who never ceases to amaze me;
to my family, a source of support and encouragement always;
and to my wife, Laura H. Kosar, simply because

Contents

Tables and Figures

Tables

Figures

Acknowledgments

I am indebted to Lawrence M. Mead, Diane S. Ravitch, and Joseph P. Viteritti, who taught me so much about public policy and education policy and politics. Thanks also go to Stephen Greenwald, president of Metropolitan College of New York, who hired me as a lecturer and special adviser and in doing so gave me the opportunity to teach and learn from graduates both of New York City's high schools and of secondary schools around the globe.

I also thank the following individuals who so kindly took the time to speak and correspond with me regarding this subject: Francie Alexander, Lisa Bos, Kay Casstevens, Wilmer Cody, Denis Doyle, Richard Elmore, Lawrence Feinberg, Ray Fields, Chester E. Finn Jr., William Galston, Scott Hamilton, John F. Jennings, Brian Jones, Krista Kafer, Edward J. Kealy, Victor F. Klatt Jr., Phyllis McClure, Bruno V. Manno, Mark Musick, Mark Reckase, Lauren Resnick, Andrew Rotherham, Thomas Sawyer, Thomas Skelly, Gerald Sroufe, Marc Tucker, Herbert J. Walberg, and Thomas Wolanin.

—*Kevin R. Kosar*

Introduction

President George W. Bush signed the No Child Left Behind Act on January 8, 2002. Just a few months before, the nation had received dismaying news about its schools. The Organization for Economic Cooperation and Development (OECD) published a study of the reading abilities of 16- to 25-year-olds in thirty nations. It revealed that 59 percent of Americans could not read well enough to "cope adequately with the complex demands of everyday life."[1]

Sadly, there was nothing new about this news. In fact, the bad news about American educational achievement has been coming for at least two decades. To take a few recent examples: in November 1999, the National Center for Education Statistics released the results of the National Assessment of Educational Progress (NAEP) civics examinations. Almost 75 percent of the 22,000 US students who took the assessments scored below proficient. A year earlier, the US Department of Education released the final results of the Third International Mathematics and Science Study (TIMSS). American 17-year-olds, vis-à-vis their counterparts in twenty other countries, finished nearly last in both science and math. They outscored only students from Lithuania, Cyprus, and South Africa.

The No Child Left Behind Act (NCLB) is the most recent federal effort to do something about educational underachievement, a push that began in the early 1980s. Like America 2000, Goals 2000, and the Improving America's Schools Act (IASA) of 1994, NCLB aims to remedy under-achievement by raising education standards in the schools. To this end, under NCLB the federal government is authorized to spend $100 billion over six years. The result of all this spending is that by 2014 all children are to be able to read and do math proficiently.

Like America 2000 and the other standards-raising proposals before it, NCLB is predicated on a very commonsensical notion about student learning; in short, that students will learn to the level at which they are taught. If schools are to produce high-achieving young adults, then schools must teach them a rigorous curriculum and test them to see that they have learned what was taught. Thus, NLCB declares, "all children" deserve to attend schools with "challenging State academic achievement standards."

Yet, many readers will be astonished to learn that the No Child Left Behind Act does not create education standards for US schools, nor does NCLB require states to create high standards for the schools. Like the federal standards policies that came before it, NCLB provides states with more funding for schooling but wields little federal power to ensure that standards are raised. The key to standards-based reform—high standards—has been all but overlooked by federal policy. How can this be?

The answer is politics. Despite the best efforts of quality schools advocates, standards-raising policy proposals have repeatedly run into political resistance from the left and the right. President George H. W. Bush's America 2000 was repudiated outright by Congress. President William J. Clinton's Goals 2000 and Improving America's Schools Act were weakened to inefficacy, and President Clinton's plan for "voluntary national tests" was rejected by Congress.

Meanwhile, President George W. Bush, well aware of the troubles his predecessors encountered, did his best to create a proposal that was designed to raise standards while being as inoffensive as possible to the political left and right. The president got his law, and members of Congress on both sides of the aisle were pleased. Liberals got what they wanted: more money for schools. Conservatives, meanwhile, saw control over school curricula remain firmly in the control of states and localities. High standards, once again, were left behind.

The Structure of the Study

This book was written with the intent of carrying out three tasks. First, I argue that using federal power to raise education standards is a good idea. Second, I show how politics have inhibited efforts to forge a federal standards policy, leaving the nation's schools to follow peculiar and ineffective policies. Third, I give some suggestions for improving the situation. Although politics tend to prohibit the enactment of a robust form of federal education standards policy, there are ways to improve the No Child Left Behind Act to increase the chances that standards will be raised. The particulars of how this is done are discussed in the following section. Readers interested in getting straight to the story may leap ahead to Chapter 1. Scholars and education policy analysts may desire to read on.

This study undertakes both a policy analysis and a political analysis.

Chapters 1 and 2 execute the policy analysis and consider two questions: *Are students in the United States generally underachieving?* and *If so, should the federal government do something to improve the situation?* Both questions are answered in the affirmative. Chapter 1 examines student achievement and concludes that student academic achievement is low and has been low for at least thirty years. It is not merely the nonwhite and the poor who are learning less than they might; it is the vast majority of children. Chapter 2 makes the case for federal action to raise education standards, arguing that higher educational achievement would be good for the United States and showing that states have had great difficulty raising standards themselves. Thus, the federal government is justified in stepping in.

Chapters 3 through 6 undertake the political analysis, focusing on the period 1980 through 2004. Here, the reader is introduced to the two main political forces that have inhibited the enactment of federal standards policy: *antistatism* and *liberalism*. As Chapter 3 briefly describes, both these ways of thinking about the federal role in schooling have deep roots antedating the twentieth century. Antistatism, as used here, refers to the distrust of federal involvement in the public schools.[2] Antistatists usually oppose bills that seek to increase the federal role in education. For a number of reasons, antistatists hold that schools are the responsibility of states and localities and that the federal government should not meddle in them. Liberals views matters quite differently. Liberals believe that states and localities cannot be trusted to provide good schooling to all children. Moreover, liberalism holds that the federal government is more trustworthy than state and local governments. Accordingly, liberals have favored the federal government making policy to improve schooling for the dispossessed and discriminated against.[3]

Obviously, neither of these two ways of thinking about the federal role in schooling is especially congenial to federal standards reform, and this antipathy would have consequences. In the 1980s and 1990s, as Chapter 3 shows, the United States found itself in an education crisis. A number of major studies, including the famed governmental report *A Nation at Risk: The Imperative for Educational Reform*, took the public schools to task. Schools were described as rudderless and all too happy to promote students from grade to grade without requiring them to learn much. Test scores were sinking. The movement for federal education standards reform grew in response to this crisis, gathering support from a wide swath of interest groups and the American public. Civil rights advocates, business people, and most Americans—whom this study terms the quality schools advocacy (QSA) movement—favored using federal power to raise education standards in the schools.

But when it came time to make federal policy, the standards movement ran head-first into antistatism and liberalism. Chapters 3, 4, and 5 tell this story. After describing the origins of antistatism and liberalism, Chapter 3 examines the first major effort at national standards policy—America 2000—which President George H. W. Bush announced in the spring of 1991. America 2000 quickly became bogged down in Congress. Democrats did not want to give the president, who was seeking reelection the following year, an education victory. However, the debates about America 2000 also revealed that the political left and right were uncomfortable with this new idea of using federal power to raise standards. America 2000 was stymied.

By the time President Clinton offered up his Goals 2000 proposal in 1993, both the far right and the hard left had found their voices. As Chapter 4 details, antistatists denounced federal standards policy proposals as encroachments on state and local prerogatives, and liberals decried standards as punitive and unfair to poor and nonwhite children who attended underfunded schools. Goals 2000 passed Congress and became law, but it was so weakened by changes demanded by the left and the right that it did little to raise standards.

Much the same can be said for President Clinton's Improving America's Schools Act of 1994, which Chapter 5 examines. Initially, IASA too promised to wield federal power to raise education standards in the public schools and to improve student achievement. It too faced a rough time in Congress and emerged far less effective than it might have been. As his presidency wound down, Clinton took one last shot, offering up a bill that would create voluntary national tests (VNTs). These tests would measure how well students were learning a rigorous curriculum. VNTs went nowhere. Members of Congress on the left and the right voted against funding VNTs, and that was that.

Chapter 6 concludes the political analysis with a study of the politics of the No Child Left Behind Act. After years of butting heads, the far right and hard left were weary. With an eye toward recapturing the White House in 2000, Republicans rethought their politically unpopular antistatist position on education. Liberals, whose party (the Democrats) had been committed to standards by President Clinton, were reluctant to attack standards head on. With education topping the list of voter concerns, liberals and antistatists backed off and allowed NCLB to pass. Antistatists, who might have opposed NCLB, raised objections but then grudgingly went along because their president had made standards-based education reform a centerpiece of his campaign. Liberals, meanwhile, saw George W. Bush as a president who was desperate to pass an education reform package and therefore amenable to compromise. Both sides got a deal they could live with: liberals got a law that promised more funding for schools, and antistatists kept the federal government from exerting direct influence over school standards and assessments and won the right for some children to exercise limited school choice. The nation, meanwhile, got school reform that promised education standards for all children but does little to ensure that children receive a rigorous education.

Chapter 7 concludes the study. My analysis shows that although a robust exercise of federal powers to raise standards is desirable, politics will not permit it. The die has been cast for the federal role in education: the federal government will spend more money on the schools, and it will urge them to teach all children to high standards. Yet control over curricula will remain in state and local hands. The No Child Left Behind Act and the Improving America's Schools Act affirmed this. Therefore, the book closes by providing a number of suggestions for incremental reforms to the current law. These changes aim to improve the federal standards policy we have but recognize that the standards policy that would be best is precluded by politics and is unlikely to become reality anytime soon.

Methodology

The approach of the political analysis in this book is both analytical and qualitative.[4] It models the federal politics of education as elitist and largely divided along ideological (and party) lines.[5] The focus, then, is on those at the top (presidents, members of Congress, and members of the federal education policy network); this study examines their debates, their policy prescriptions, and the policies they made.[6]

The study argues that education was, until the 1980s, a two-sided dispute: the left pushed for increased federal involvement in the schools, and the right blocked such efforts as best it could. But, as with other issue areas, this stable left-right argument was crosscut with the emergence of a crisis in the early 1980s. This crisis, the achievement crisis, transformed the fight by widening the conflict.[7] No longer were the battles about education over the schooling of poor and nonwhite children; in the 1980s, all children and the nation were declared to be "at risk." This new crisis drew in new stakeholders to the political debate, creating a new "third way" coalition—the Quality Schools Advocacy movement—that believes the federal government has a legitimate role to play in public school but that the fundamental problem of the schools is not money but performance. Congress initially refused to budge, and it remained split along the antistatist-liberal divide. Goaded by voters, the QSA movement, and standards-promoting presidents, the left and right in Congress gave ground. Neither side, though, capitulated entirely. The result was legislation that symbolically affirmed support for higher standards in the public schools.

To substantiate this interpretation of the politics of federal education and explain the type of federal standards policy that has been produced, the book employs a qualitative methodology. In short, I utilize primary and secondary source documents to construct a historical narrative of the congressional, presidential, and issue network debate disputes surrounding a number of major federal standards proposals. Source materials include Congressional hearings transcripts;[8] floor debates; author-conducted interviews of persons in the education issue network; presidential speeches, platforms, and public statements; education laws and regulations; and many secondary sources, including *Congressional Quarterly*, *National Journal*, *Education Week*, and writings by persons in the education issue network.[9]

The resultant book, in outward appearances, is less scientific than much current political science research. It contains no regression analyses or rational choice framework (both of which are quite popular among empirical political scientists). This more qualitative approach may frustrate scholars who prefer crisply delineated models and mathematical explanations of political behavior.

That said, I still view this as a work of political science, a field of research that, it has been written, should "make roughly probable empirical and logical cases for and against claims about political questions that many people can be persuaded to regard as substantively important."[10] How one achieves this depends on the subject being studied. To understand education policy one needs to examine the politics that produce it. Federal education politics are messy and ideologically charged. The people involved tend to hold strong beliefs that are part and parcel of larger worldviews about liberty, equality, and the course of US history. To understand what these political actors do and why, one must listen to their words and, as best as one can, examine their deeds. When possible, speaking with them (and those who know them) can better clarify the logic of their actions.

Of course, one can never get at the whole truth, but I hope that this text provides the reader with a plausible explanation of why we have the federal standards policies we have and why they are less than optimal. It is an interesting but frustrating story, and my intent is that the policymaker, policy analyst, and concerned citizen will come away from the book with the desire to work with our elected officials to improve standards policy and educational achievement in the United States.

Notes

1. Organization for Economic Cooperation and Development, *Knowledge and Skills for Life: First Results from the PISA 2000*.

2. *Antistatism* may strike the reader as a peculiar term for an ideology that places greater trust in state government than in national government. The term, though, has long been used; it emerged as a negative to the term statism, which, ini-

tially, was used to refer to states (as in nation-states) where all political power rested with the central government (e.g., the Soviet Union, Nazi Germany).

3. Obviously, there are many variants of liberal thinking. The use of *liberal* to refer to those who favor increased federal spending on the public schools in this study is not meant to deny or diminish the differences between liberals; rather, it serves to emphasize a viewpoint they share that is key to the politics that produced the education policy we now have.

4. The methodology of policy analysis is simple and straightforward and does not require explanation.

5. Sundquist, *Dynamics of the Party System: Alignment and Realignment of Political Parties in the United States*; and Baumgartner and Jones, *Agendas and Instability in American Politics*.

6. An issue network is "a political subsystem . . . marked by its loose amorphous character and the inclusion of many policy experts," politicians, and interest groups. Adapted from James E. Anderson, *Public Policymaking: An Introduction*, p. 322.

7. On the transformation of political conflicts, see Schattschneider, *The Semi-Sovereign People: A Realist's View of Democracy in America*.

8. Members of Congress are allowed to revise their actual floor comments before they are published in the *Congressional Record*. It seems unlikely, though, that they would often have reasons to use this privilege to alter the nature of their support or objections to policy as voiced in hearings or on the floor. Moreover, they have only a week to exercise this privilege, so any revision of history would have to be done promptly. As for the congressional hearings used as data, they are limited to those held in Washington before the standing committees charged with considering said bills. Hearings held outside Washington are excluded because they often are ritualistic exercises or involve fact collection instead of position expression.

9. I recognize that this method does risk overemphasizing the philosophical and policy considerations over the more mundane matters of "who gets what." Moreover, for simplicity's sake, terms like *congressional preferences* are used. This might imply that the preferences of all members of Congress have been assessed. This is not the case. Not all members of Congress have taken an interest in every subject. Only a small number tend to speak on any one issue, and this holds true for education.

10. Rogers M. Smith, "Should We Make Political Science More of a Science or More About Politics?" p. 201.

I

Student Achievement:
A Rising Tide of Mediocrity?

In 1983, the government report *A Nation at Risk: The Imperative for Educational Reform* was released to the public. It declared:

> Our Nation is at risk. Our once unchallenged preeminence in commerce, industry, science, and technological innovation is being overtaken by competitors throughout the world. . . . The educational foundations of society are being eroded by a rising tide of mediocrity that threatens our very future as a Nation and a people.[1]

As proof of this "rising tide of mediocrity," the report claimed, among other things:

- International comparisons of student achievement reveal that on nineteen academic tests American students were never first or second and, in comparison with other industrialized nations, were last seven times;
- The College Board's Scholastic Aptitude Tests (SATs) demonstrate a virtually unbroken decline from 1963 to 1980. Average verbal scores fell over fifty points and average mathematics scores dropped nearly forty points.[2]

Despite its generally gloomy take, *A Nation at Risk* did explain that "the average citizen today is better educated and more knowledgeable than the average citizen of a generation ago—more literate, and exposed to more mathematics, literature, and science."[3] In fact, more Americans were graduating from high school and a greater percentage were attending and graduating from college. However, the slide in test scores, along with the growth in the percentage of high school and college graduates, implied that "the average graduate of our schools and colleges today is not as well-educated as the average graduate of 25 or 30 years ago, when a much smaller proportion of our population completed high school and college."[4] Rising high school and college enrollments had led to a slippage of educational and graduation standards.

In recent years, critics such as David Berliner, Bruce Biddle, and Gerald Bracey have pooh-poohed this assessment. They say the test score decline was a "manufactured crisis." They argue that the test score data "provide no evidence whatever . . . of a recent decline in the school achievement of the average American student"[5] and have charged that those who claim American students score worse than their international peers are spurious and those who say so are engaging in "a political exercise, not an intellectual one."[6]

Who is right? Is there a "rising tide of mediocrity"? This chapter considers the data on student achievement.[7] It argues that the critics are partly right, that claims of a massive slide in education are often overstated, especially in light of the test scores of recent years. However, the critics are wrong that the evidence is equivocal. "The achievement crisis is real."[8] American students generally are learning at low levels.

Student Achievement: Test Scores

Assessing the level of educational achievement in the United States is no simple matter. Public schools have been asked to educate children in any number of things, many nonacademic and difficult to measure. Still, it seems reasonable to posit that first and foremost, public schools exist to provide students with an education, here defined as the possession of knowledge and skills.

An enormous amount of data on student educational achievement exists, much of it in the form of standardized test scores. Unfortunately for researchers interested in assessing the state of education nationwide, the tradition of local and state control has made for a great diversity of examinations. States and localities have been free to choose which examinations they will employ. Thus, fourth-grade student reading scores from, say, Ohio are not readily comparable with those in New York.[9]

However, three sources of data can be utilized to gain insight on the educational attainment of children in the United States. First, some examinations have been administered to nationwide samples. These include the SAT I, the American Collegiate Test (ACT), the National Assessment of Educational Progress (NAEP), and the First National Assessment of History and Literature (NAHL).[10] The former three have been administered for three decades or more. Second, there is the Third International Mathematics and Science Study (TIMSS), which provides data on the achievement levels of American youth vis-à-vis their international counterparts. Finally, there are opinion surveys of individuals who work with the graduates of US high schools—college professors and employers.

For the purpose of this inquiry, standardized educational tests can be divided roughly into two types. *Aptitude tests* measure student skills, such as quantitative reasoning, analytic reasoning, and so forth; *achievement tests* measure student knowledge of subject area content.[11] Of course, these categories are not discrete. Both types of tests presume a minimal level of both skills and content familiarity, such as knowledge of the English language and the ability to count and recognize mathematical symbols.[12] The American College Test is an aptitude test. An example of the sort of questions one finds on the ACT is: "A vendor has 14 helium balloons for sale: 9 are yellow, 3 are red, and 2 are green. A balloon is selected at random and sold. If the balloon sold is yellow, what is the probability that the next balloon, selected at random, is also yellow?"[13]

The SAT I is, likewise, an aptitude test. It is designed to discern student ability for college course work by measuring "verbal and math reasoning abilities."[14] A sample SAT I verbal test question is:

> The question that follows consists of a related pair of words or phrases, followed by five pairs of words or phrases. Select the pair that best expresses a relationship similar to that expressed in the original pair.
> synchronize:movements
> 1. sublimate:goals
> 2. realize:dreams
> 3. prolong:intervals
> 4. remit:payments
> 5. harmonize:voices[15]

On both tests, all the information required to correctly answer the question is provided. Student success is contingent upon the ability to use the information given.[16]

Achievement tests such as the National Assessment of Educational Progress and the First National Assessment of History and Literature, in contrast, measure student knowledge of subject material. Thus, these exams mostly oblige students to recognize and understand significant persons, places, events, and ideas. So what do the test scores indicate?

Aptitude Test Scores: ACT

The ACT consists of 215 multiple-choice questions covering four skills areas: science-reasoning, math, reading, and English (that is, grammar and prose). It is administered five times each year to high school students who choose to take it (mostly college-bound sophomores and juniors).[17] The

ACT is scored on a scale of 0 to 36, though typically nobody scores below 8. Composite scores are derived by counting the number of correct answers for each section, then scaling them to a 1 to 36 scale and thereafter averaging the results and rounding to the nearest whole number. In 2003, nearly 1.2 million high school students took the test.[18]

ACT composite score data are available for most years from 1967 to 2002, as shown in Figure 1.1.[19] In 1983, when *A Nation at Risk* was published, the available ACT data displayed a modest slide in composite scores, from a high of 19.7 in 1967 to a nadir of 18.3. Since then, the scores have crept upward. From 1999 to 2001, ACT scores were at their highest, 21.0, sliding to 20.8 in 2003.

However, the data are not as promising as they might appear. For one, in 1990 the ACT was revised and made slightly easier.[20] Therefore, statisticians at ACT note that due to rescaling, someone who scored an 18.4 on 1982's ACT would have likely scored nearly two points higher on the 1990 version (20.3). Thus, in the years immediately before rescaling (1987 to 1989), test-takers scored between 18.6 and 18.8. Come 1990, average composite scores jumped to 20.6. Since then, composites have been flat.

Beyond the question of trends, though, is the matter of performance level. A score of 26 on the ACT is considered "high performing."

Figure 1.1   ACT Scores, 1967–2002

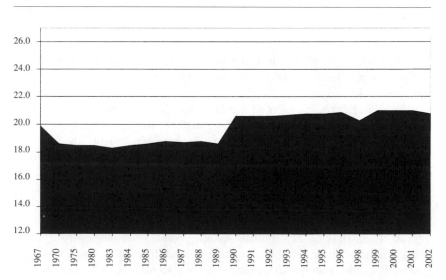

Source: ACT Inc.

Historically, only a small percentage of students taking the ACT have post-ed high-performing scores. In 1967, 14 percent of test-takers scored 26 or above. In 1996, on the rescaled exam, 13 percent did. Significant numbers also are performing at low levels. In 1996, 21 percent scored a composite of 15 or less. In 2002, 64 percent scored a 22, meaning they would have difficulty with this simple math question:[21]

> Rachel estimated the dimension of her rectangular room by heel-to-toe between opposite walls, and counting the number of shoe lengths between the walls. Rachel's shoes are each about 9 inches long, and she finds that the dimensions of her room are 14 shoe lengths by 20 shoe lengths. Which of the following is the closet estimate of the dimensions of her room in traditional feet (12 inches)?
> A. 126 by 180
> B. 18 2/3 by 26 2/3
> C. 14 by 20
> D. 10 1/2 by 15
> E. 8 by 10

ACT scores, like so many other assessments, show disparities between black and Hispanic test-takers and white and Asian examinees. Table 1.1 exhibits ACT English, mathematics, and science scores for 2003.

Black and Hispanic students performing at these levels of English will likely struggle to "identify the main theme or topic of a straight-forward piece of writing."[22] Blacks scoring at this level on mathematics are not likely to be able to "solve routine two-step or three-step arithmetic problems" or "determine the probability of a simple event."[23]

On the whole, then, ACT composite scores have remained flat over the past three decades. The 1970s saw them decrease mildly, and the 1980s and 1990s saw them rise to roughly previous levels. Generally, these students are scoring far below high performance, despite the fact they are a self-selected group who take the exam in hopes of scoring well enough to be granted entrance to the college of their choosing. And Hispanics and blacks perform worse than their low-performing peers.

Table 1.1   ACT Composite Scores by Race/Ethnicity, 2003

	Black	Hispanic[a]	White	Asian
English	16.2	18.1	21.3	20.7
Math	16.7	18.9	21.3	22.9
Science-Reasoning	17.2	19.0	21.6	21.5

Source: Data provided by ACT Inc.
Note: a. Does not include those who identified themselves as Mexicans.

Aptitude Test Scores: SAT I

SAT I scores are calculated somewhat differently from ACT composite scores. For each section of a student's exam, the multiple-choice questions answered incorrectly are subtracted from the total number of right answers. No points are added or subtracted for unanswered questions. The raw score for each section is then converted into a 200 (lowest) to 800 (highest) scaled score, using a statistical process called equating, to give a score for both the verbal and mathematical sections. The composite score—the sum of the verbal and mathematical scores—ranges between 400 and 1600.[24]

Over the past three decades, SAT math scores have risen slightly (see Figure 1.2). They fell from a peak of 517 in 1969 to the low 490s by the late 1970s and early 1980s and rebounded to 519 in 2003. The math portion of the SAT, perhaps surprisingly, only requires knowledge of introductory geometry and introductory algebra, subjects students should have studied by ninth grade.[25] In order to answer the math questions, memorization of the principles is insufficient. Students must be able to use these concepts to solve problems. Thus, the College Board credits the rise in SAT math to the growing numbers of SAT-takers who are enrolling in advanced mathematics courses. In 1992, 33 percent of seniors took precalculus and 20 percent took calculus. In 2002, 45 percent studied precalculus and 25 percent took calculus. It is not the knowledge gained from these courses that has helped pupils score higher, but the continued utilization of simpler math skills.[26]

As Figure 1.3 exhibits, SAT verbal scores are down. They dropped from 542 in 1967 to the low 490s in the late 1970s and early 1980s before inching back to 507 (in 1996 to 2003). Speaking to the decline in verbal scores, the College Board notes that from 1992 to 2002, "participation in high school English composition course work has declined significantly from 81 percent a decade ago to 67 percent today. Grammar course work participation has also dropped off from 85 percent in 1992 to the current level of 71 percent."[27]

Of a possible 1600, the average composite SAT score in 2004 was 1026, off the high of 1059 in 1976 and 1968.[28] Figure 1.4 shows composite SAT scores from 1967 to 2002. As with the ACT, SAT scores show a racial disparity (see Table 1.2).

Paul Marx points out that students who score below 500 in the verbal portion of the SAT I are unlikely to correctly answer questions such as:

Fill in the missing word:

Everyone in town knew that he would _____ questions about his past; they were used to seeing him fall silent if asked anything about himself. Is the missing word "evade," "enjoy," "project," or "digress"?

Figure 1.2   SAT Math Scores, 1967–2002

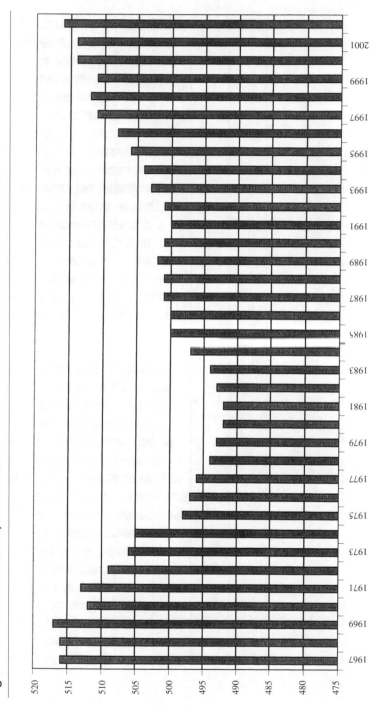

Figure I.3 SAT Verbal Scores, 1967–2002

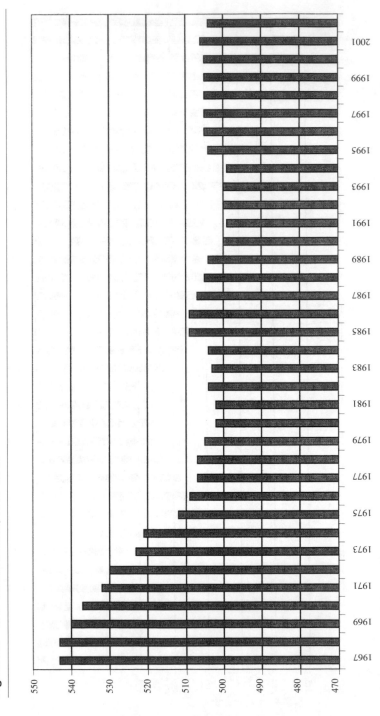

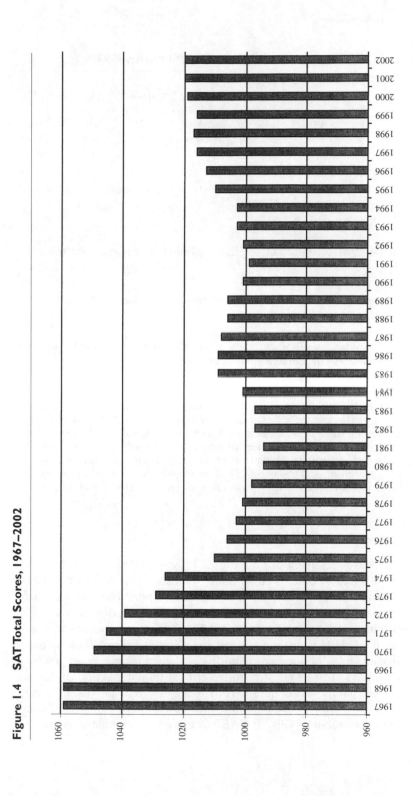

Figure 1.4　SAT Total Scores, 1967–2002

Table 1.2   SAT Composite Scores by Race/Ethnicity, 2002

	Black	Puerto Rican	Mexican	Other[a]	White	Asian
Verbal	431	456	448	457	529	508
Math	426	453	457	464	534	575
Total	857	909	905	921	1063	1083

Source: Data provided by College Board.
Notes: a. Includes those who identified themselves as Latin American, South American, Central American, Latino, or Other Hispanic.

Said students also would not see the relationships between the following words:

> venerate: disdain; script: director; stethoscope: physician; and irrigation: water.

This is not esoterica. These are words "we need to know to function as educated citizens."[29] The College Board concurs:

> The vocabulary on the SAT I is fairly demanding; it is the vocabulary students will need to access the realms of knowledge in the realms of literature, science, and the arts. On the other hand, this vocabulary is not as thorny as it often is made out to be. One never finds words like "pastinaceous" on the SAT (of the nature or relating to the parsnip). Indeed, some of the most difficult words on recent SAT's have been words such as congeal, sycophant, and collusion. These are exactly the kinds of words one needs to know in order to express ideas vividly, forcefully, and precisely.[30]

Content Exam Scores—NAEP

The National Assessment of Educational Progress (NAEP), also known as the Nation's Report Card, is an especially rich source of data on the state of student academic achievement.[31] The federally funded National Center for Educational Statistics (NCES) has administered NAEP exams to students in grades four, eight, and twelve since 1969.[32] Though mostly content examinations, the NAEP exams are not fact recollection exams. They include a significant number of questions requiring students to apply their knowledge in short essays. Test-takers also utilize critical thinking skills. On the science exams, pupils answer questions by using materials provided "to make observations, perform investigations, evaluate experimental results, and apply problem-solving skills."[33] NAEP exams contain both multiple-choice questions and constructed response questions (which require students to write from one sentence to a few paragraphs). Following is an example of a multiple-choice question for students of twelfth-grade civics:

> Which statement about the making of United States foreign policy is accurate?
> A. State governments, through their ability to negotiate independent trade agreements, have preeminent authority in making foreign policy.
> B. The Senate, because of its power of treaty ratification, has more power in setting foreign policy than does the President.
> C. The Supreme Court, because it can rule on the constitutionality of executive actions, dominates foreign policy.
> D. Congress and the courts have some authority over foreign policy, but the President and the State Department have the greatest authority.

A typical constructed-response question for fourth-graders requires that students read a short story from *Highlights Magazine for Children* about a man and his nephew catching blue crabs. Students are then asked to answer: "Do you think it would be fun to catch blue crabs? Using information from the passage, explain why or why not."

There are three sorts of NAEP exams: NAEP long-term, NAEP standard, and NAEP state-level. We will review the NAEP long-term and standard assessment results here. NAEP scales the long-term assessment results from 1 to 500. Figures 1.5, 1.6, and 1.7 provide long-term scoring trends within these three subject areas for the past three decades.

Reading Scores: Figure 1.5 indicates that reading scores have been mostly flat, with 9- and 13-year-olds showing small gains, from 208 to 212 and 255 to 259 respectively. Seventeen-year-olds' reading scores rose 2 points to 288. The slight gains for 9- and 13-year-olds were statistically significant; the increase for the 17-year olds was not.[34]

Mathematics Scores: Generally, mathematics scores have been flat (see Figure 1.6). However, all three of the age groups have made slight but statistically significant gains. The largest gains were among 9-year-olds, whose scores rose from 219 to 232 between 1973 and 1999. Thirteen-year-olds saw their scores climb from 266 to 276, and 17-year-olds saw the smallest gains, from 304 to 308.

Science Scores: The trends in science for 9-, 13-, and 17-year-olds are mixed. The scores of 17-year-olds showed a statistically significant decrease. The scores of 13-year-olds rose to the level they were previously, and the 9-year-olds have shown modest significant gains (see Figure 1.7).

On the whole, of the nine NAEP long-term test score trends (three for each subject area at each grade level), six show gains, two show no change, and one (the scores of 17-year-olds on the science examinations)

Figure 1.5   NAEP Reading Scores, 1971–1999

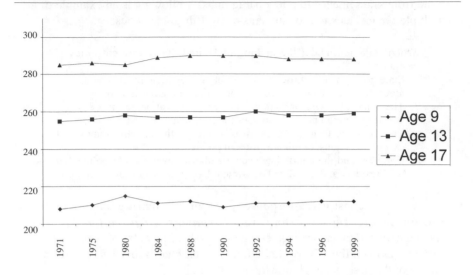

Figure 1.6   NAEP Mathematics Scores, 1973–1999

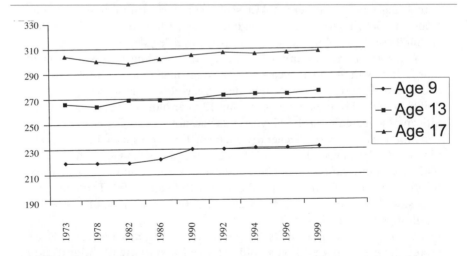

decreased.[35] Gains, unfortunately, have been small and slow in coming.[36] These scores prompt a further question: At what level of competency are students performing?

Unlike the long-term NAEP, which shows trends in achievement, the standard NAEP assessments indicate the levels of student performance relative to grade level. The National Assessment Governing Board (NAGB),

Figure 1.7   NAEP Science Scores, 1971–1999

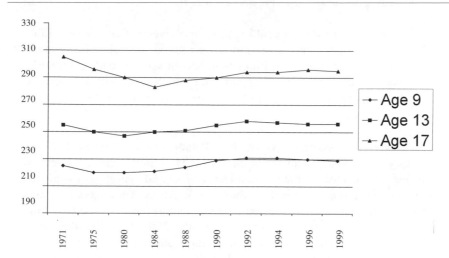

which oversees the NAEP—with the help of researchers, teachers, testing experts, and members of the general public—developed a scale of four broad achievement levels: below basic, basic, proficient, and advanced.[37] The achievement levels of proficient and advanced represent what the developers conclude are the skill and knowledge levels appropriate to that grade.[38]

A brief description of the standard NAEP exams (reading, mathematics, science, civics, US history, geography, and writing) follows. Tables 1.3 through 1.9 provide the percentages of students scoring at each level of achievement.[39]

NAEP Reading Assessments. The NAEP reading assessments were administered to over 30,000 students in 1998. The assessments measure student ability to read. Students are expected to comprehend the texts and use them to engage in vicarious experiences and acquire and apply information.[40] Correspondingly, examinees read texts appropriate to each task: literary, informative, and task-instructive. For a high school senior to score at the proficient level, his or her work must exhibit that he or she can read a passage and

> show an overall understanding of the text, which includes inferential as well as literal information. When reading text appropriate to twelfth-grade, they should be able to extend the ideas of the text by making inferences, drawing conclusions, and making connections to their own personal experiences and other readings. Connections between inferences and

the text should be clear, even when implicit. These students should be able to analyze the author's use of literary devices.[41]

Few American students could read at or above proficiency (see Table 1.3). Significant percentages of students scored at the below-basic level. For example, more than one-fifth of high school seniors reading literature could not "explain the theme, support their conclusions with information from the text, and make connections between aspects of the text and their own experiences."[42]

NAEP Mathematics Assessments. The NAEP mathematics assessments measure student knowledge and skills in five areas: number sense, properties, and operations; measurement; geometry and spatial sense; data analysis, statistics, and probability; and algebra and functions. The 47,000 students who took the exams were expected to possess conceptual knowledge of the material. More than half the questions in the 2000 NAEP mathematics assessments were constructed response questions, which demanded that students display their understanding of mathematical procedures and ability to solve problems.

More than 70 percent of examinees at all three grade levels failed to perform proficiently.[43] Nearly three-fourths of all eighth-graders struggled with basic arithmetic. Only 16 percent of high school seniors performed at or above a proficient level, meaning they could "analyze and interpret data in tabular and graphical form" (see Table 1.4).[44]

NAEP Science Assessments. The NAEP science examinations cover earth, life, and physical sciences. Approximately 49,000 pupils took these assessments in 2000. Students were obliged to exhibit their knowledge of scientific facts, processes, and reasoning.

Less than one-fifth of twelfth-graders scored proficiently, and about

Table 1.3   NAEP Reading Proficiency, 2002

	Percentages of Students Scoring at				
Grade	Below Basic	Basic	Proficient	Advanced	Advanced/ Proficient
4	38	31	24	7	31
8	26	41	30	3	33
12	23	37	34	6	40

Note: The 2003 NAEP reading scores for fourth- and eighth-graders showed nearly no change.

Table 1.4   **NAEP Mathematics Proficiency, 2000**

	Percentages of Students Scoring at				
Grade	Below Basic	Basic	Proficient	Advanced	Advanced/ Proficient
4	31	43	23	3	26
8	34	38	22	5	27
12	35	48	14	2	16

one-third of eighth- and fourth-graders did. Thus, most twelfth-grade students could not explain why the sun appears larger in January than in July or explain how mountains form. Over a third of eighth-graders would likely struggle to explain why water is critical to living organisms, and just 4 percent could be expected to explain why sounds echo in an auditorium (see Table 1.5).[45]

NAEP Civics Assessments. In 1998, the NAEP civics assessment was administered to 22,000 students. The exam was 60 percent multiple choice, 30 percent short-answer questions, and 10 percent short essays. Questions asked students at the fourth grade, for example, to identify a photo of the Statue of Liberty and to note that it represents liberty (as opposed to strength, equality, or intelligence), whereas twelfth-graders were, for example, to explain what Justice Learned Hand meant when he said,

> I often wondered whether we do not rest our hopes too much upon constitutions, upon laws and upon courts. These are false hopes; believe me, these are false hopes. Liberty lives in the hearts of men and women; when it dies there, no constitution, no law, no court can save it.[46]

None of the questions were straight factual queries or arcana (e.g., What year was the Wilmot Proviso proposed and what were its main components?).

Table 1.5   **NAEP Science Proficiency, 2000**

	Percentages of Students Scoring at				
Grade	Below Basic	Basic	Proficient	Advanced	Advanced/ Proficient
4	34	37	26	4	30
8	39	29	28	4	32
12	47	34	16	2	18

About 77 percent of high school seniors, who had or soon would have the right to vote, scored below proficient. As Table 1.6 shows, similarly large percentages of students in grades four and eight also scored at the basic or below basic levels.[47]

NAEP United States History Assessments. More than 29,000 students took the NAEP US history assessments in 2001. As with other NAEP exams, to score proficiently, a student's responses must demonstrate "competency over challenging subject material." An example of a question asked of eighth-graders is:

> What was the most significant factor that led the American colonists to form the First Continental Congress in 1774?
> A. Religious conflict inside the colonies
> B. The desire of the colonists to write a Constitution to replace the Articles of Confederation
> C. Colonial frustration with laws passed by the British government
> D. The desire of the colonists to stop the war between Britain and the colonies

Of the subject areas tested by NAEP, student results were worst in US history (see Table 1.7). The vast majority of all students (80 to 90 percent),

Table 1.6   NAEP Civics Proficiency, 1998

	Percentages of Students Scoring at				
Grade	Below Basic	Basic	Proficient	Advanced	Advanced/ Proficient
4	16	57	26	1	27
8	16	56	27	1	28
12	22	55	22	1	23

Table 1.7   NAEP US History Proficiency, 2001

	Percentages of Students Scoring at				
Grade	Below Basic	Basic	Proficient	Advanced	Advanced/ Proficient
4	33	49	16	2	18
8	36	48	15	2	17
12	57	32	10	1	11

including those in their final year of high school, scored below proficiency. For example, just 36 percent of twelfth-grade students correctly answered that the Progressive Era (1890 to 1920) was characterized by "a broad-based reform movement that tried to reduce the abuses that had come with modernization and industrialization."

NAEP Geography Assessment. The NAEP geography assessments were taken by 25,000 students in 2001 (see Table 1.8). Students were asked to utilize maps and cartographical charts to locate nations, climate regions, topography, natural resources, and trade routes. Though the exams did demand some recall of facts, they mostly required students to understand the maps and charts they were reading and draw conclusions from them.

Three-fourths of high school seniors had difficulty using a climate map to locate tropical areas or explain the reasons for international trade in petroleum oil. Few eighth-graders were able to understand why early civilizations cropped up around the Fertile Crescent, and over a quarter could not locate Lake Superior on a map.[48]

NAEP Writing Assessment. Recently, concerns over statistical reliability led the NCES to temporarily abandon the long-term writing achievement study. However, the results of the 1998 standard writing assessments remain valid.[49]

This essay exam was taken by 160,000 students in grades four, eight, and twelve. Unlike the other standard NAEP exams, this was mostly a skills test. Students were not presumed to have familiarity with any subject material (except grammar and the basic elements of composition). Their writing was graded on the basis of the skills demonstrated, such as being able to write persuasively, to construct logical narratives, and to use details to support and illustrate their essays.

At all grade levels, only about one-fourth of all students scored at or above proficiency (see Table 1.9).[50] Among them, only a tiny percentage displayed advanced writing abilities.

Table 1.8   NAEP Geography Proficiency, 2001

	Percentages of Students Scoring at				
Grade	Below Basic	Basic	Proficient	Advanced	Advanced/ Proficient
4	26	53	19	2	21
8	26	44	26	4	30
12	29	47	23	1	24

Table 1.9   NAEP Writing Proficiency, 1998

	Percentages of Students Scoring at				
Grade	Below Basic	Basic	Proficient	Advanced	Advanced/ Proficient
4	31	47	21	2	23
8	30	48	20	2	22
12	35	39	22	4	24

Source: National Center for Educational Statistics, *NAEP 1998 Civics Report Card Highlights*, p. 8.

The Standard NAEP Exams: Summation.   In every subject area measured—reading, mathematics, science, civics, US history, geography, and writing—the majority of students failed to score at a proficient level. With the exception of civics, in every subject area 25 percent or more of students at all grade levels scored below basic, meaning they lacked rudimentary grasp of the skills and knowledge expected at that grade level.

The scores of all students are disappointing. However, the scores of blacks and Hispanics are especially troubling. As with the ACT and SAT, blacks and Hispanics scored significantly lower than their under-performing white and Asian peers.[51] For example:

- Less than 40 percent of black students and less than 50 percent of Hispanic pupils could read at or above the basic level. On average, their reading scores were 30 points less than their white peers. For 13- and 17-year-olds, this gap has grown in recent years.
- In mathematics, only 5 percent of black pupils scored at or above proficiency.
- In science, black fourth-grade students scored 36 points below their white peers; in twelfth grade, they score 31 points lower.
- In geography, black and Hispanic pupils scored 20 to 30 points lower than whites and Asians.

Disturbingly, this glaring affront to the American yearning for racial equality—the black/Hispanic versus white/Asian test score gap—appears in all subject areas and at every grade level.

First National Assessment of History and Literature

The First National Assessment of History and Literature (NAHL) was administered in 1987, a time when scores on the ACT, SAT, and NAEP exams were climbing.[52] Nearly 8,000 17-year-old students participated in the exam, and most (78 percent) were enrolled in history that year.[53] The objective of the assessment was to determine if students nearing completion of their high school studies knew certain major facts about history (especially US) and literature. The test was funded by the National Endowment for the Humanities and created by a core of scholars and public school educators, with assistance from the experts from NCES/NAEP. The exam questions were multiple-choice with four possible answers. None of the answers was designed to trick students, nor was the choice "I don't know" available. By sheer probability, students should have answered 25 percent of all questions correctly.

On average, students got 54.5 percent of the questions right on the history portion of NAHL. Students were strongest in the areas of maps and geography, and science and technology, averaging 70 percent correct (which amounts to just a whisker better than a D+ on most grading scales) and worst (under 50 percent) on questions on the prenational and colonial eras and on the period from Reconstruction through World War I. Only 32.2 percent were able to place the Civil War in the time period from 1850 to 1900. Just 40.1 percent knew the purpose of the Federalist Papers was to encourage the ratification of the US Constitution. Forty-one percent mistakenly identified these essays by John Jay, Alexander Hamilton, and James Madison as seeking to "establish a strong, free press in the colonies."[54]

In literature, the national average was 51.8 percent correct. Student knowledge peaked on rudimentary questions about William Shakespeare's works (e.g., identify the play that holds the famous line, "To be, or not to be"). Students correctly answered less than 50 percent of the questions on plays and playwrights, literature involving women or blacks, and four other areas of literature.[55] Only 35.5 percent answered that George Orwell's novel *1984* was about "a dictatorship in which every citizen was watched in order to stamp out all individuality." A little less than half (47.9 percent) ventured that *1984* was about the destruction of humankind by nuclear war.[56]

TIMSS

The most extensive international comparison of US students' education is the 1995 Third International Mathematics and Science Study (TIMSS) and the 1999 follow-up thereto, the TIMSS-Repeat (TIMSS-R).[57] Thirty-three thousand American students participated in the 1995 examinations, and 9,000 took part in the TIMSS-R assessments. Over half a million students at the fourth-grade, eighth-grade, and final year of secondary schooling from forty-one nations participated in the TIMSS and TIMSS-R math and science examinations.[58]

The results of the 1995 assessments were generally disappointing. At the fourth-grade level, American pupils performed on par with their international peers in mathematics and better than most in science. Only Korea and Japan scored higher in science.[59] However, eighth-grade Americans scored lower in mathematics than a majority of other nations. They earned a 500; the international average was 513. US pupils ranked behind sixteen other countries in science, but their score of 534 was well above the international average of 516.[60] It should be noted, though, that the average science score was dragged low due to the particularly poor scores of Kuwait (430), Columbia (411), and South Africa (326). If these scores are removed, the average becomes 526, making US students a little above average. Among twelfth-graders (see Table 1.10), American math and science scores were low. In both science and mathematics knowledge, American high school seniors failed to meet international standards of adequacy. Their grasp of mathematics did not extend beyond material found in the average American ninth-grade math class, or, to put it comparatively, in the average

Table 1.10   TIMSS Average Science and Mathematics Scores, General Knowledge Performance, Grade 12, Select Countries, 1995

Science		Mathematics	
Nation	Average	Nation	Average
1. Sweden	559	Netherlands	560
2. Netherlands	558	Sweden	552
3. Iceland	549	Denmark	547
4. Norway	544	Switzerland	540
5. Canada	532	Iceland	534
6. New Zealand	529	Norway	528
7. Australia	527	France	523
8. Switzerland	523	New Zealand	522
9. Austria	520	Australia	522
10. Slovenia	517	Canada	519
11. Denmark	509	Austria	518
12. Germany	497	Slovenia	512
13. France	487	Germany	495
14. Czech Republic	487	Hungary	483
15. Russian Federation	481	Italy	476
16. United States	480	Russian Federation	471
17. Italy	475	Lithuania	469
18. Hungary	471	Czech Republic	466
19. Lithuania	461	United States	461
20. Cyprus	448	Cyprus	446
21. South Africa	349	South Africa	356

Source: TIMSS, *Overview and Key Findings Across Grade Levels,* 1995.

international seventh-grade math curriculum. TIMSS also revealed that "the average scores of US physics and advanced mathematics students were below the international average and among the lowest of the 16 countries that administered the physics and the advanced mathematics assessments. The US outperformed no other country on either assessment."[61]

The TIMSS-R assessments were administered to eighth-graders alone in 1999. As Table 1.11 indicates, the United States again ranked far behind the leaders.[62] In both subject areas (mathematics and science), the United States scored slightly above the international average.

The 1995 TIMSS exams found that between the fourth and twelfth grades, American students went from the upper echelon of achievement to the middle of the pack (in eighth grade) and toward the bottom of the rankings. On the basis of the 1995 tests, researchers were unable to conclude why this was the case. Possibly, American fourth-graders did well because they had more rigorous elementary schooling than did eighth- and twelfth-graders. Perhaps they were the beneficiaries of recent school reforms. The TIMSS-R exams, though, cast serious doubt on this hypothesis. Students who had ranked so highly in fourth grade were, four years later, now middling. The cause was straightforward: during those four years Americans had learned less than most of their international peers.[63]

Student Achievement: Opinion Surveys

Surveys of those who teach or employ high school graduates provide further evidence on student achievement levels. In 1998, Public Agenda, a nonpartisan public interest organization, interviewed 252 individuals responsible for hiring decisions and 257 college professors at two- and four-year colleges who had taught freshmen or sophomores in the past two years. They found,

> The chief concern of employers and professors, however, continues to be basic academic skills. Ratings in this area have not improved or have even declined slightly over the past year. In fact, ratings of graduates' skills have improved, if only modestly, on only one of eleven measures—the ability to use computers. . . . Employers and college professors say they consistently come across young people unprepared for the adult world of work or college. More than six in ten employers (64 percent) say most high school graduates do not have the skills necessary to succeed in the workplace.[64]

Also learned was that

> some employers have taken steps to implement their own "standards and assessments." One-fourth say they require new hires to take written exams to show mastery of skills in math or writing; and one-fifth say they have

Table 1.11   TIMSS-R Average Science and Mathematics Achievement Scores of Eighth-Grade Students, by Nation, 1999

Science		Mathematics	
Nation	Average	Nation	Average
1. Chinese Taipei	569	Singapore	604
2. Hungary	552	Korea, Republic of	587
3. Japan	550	Hong Kong	582
4. Korea, Republic of	549	Japan	579
5. Netherlands	545	Belgium-Flemish	558
6. Australia	540	Netherlands	540
7. Czech Republic	539	Slovak Republic	534
8. England	538	Hungary	532
9. Finland	535	Canada	531
10. Slovak Republic	535	Slovenia	530
11. Belgium-Flemish	535	Russian Federation	526
12. Slovenia	533	Australia	525
13. Canada	533	Finland	520
14. Hong Kong	530	Czech Republic	520
15. Russian Federation	529	Malaysia	519
16. Bulgaria	518	Bulgaria	511
17. United States	515	Latvia	505
18. New Zealand	510	United States	502
19. Latvia	503	England	496
20. Italy	493	New Zealand	491
21. Malaysia	492	Lithuania	482
22. Lithuania	488	Italy	479
23. Thailand	482	Cyprus	476
24. Romania	472	Romania	472
25. Israel	468	Moldova	469
26. Cyprus	460	Thailand	467
27. Moldova	459	Israel	466
28. Macedonia, Republic of	458	Tunisia	448
29. Jordan	450	Macedonia, Republic of	447
30. Iran	448	Turkey	429
31. Indonesia	435	Jordan	428
32. Turkey	433	Iran	422
33. Tunisia	430	Indonesia	403
34. Chile	420	Chile	392
35. Philippines	345	Philippines	345
36. Morocco	323	Morocco	337
37. South Africa	243	South Africa	275
38. International Average	488	International Average	488

Source: Reproduced from NAEP's online website at http://nces.ed.gov/timss.

programs to teach basic skills that employees should have learned in high school. Three in ten report they have had to simplify jobs because of the lower quality of recent applicants.[65]

The next year, Public Agenda queried more employers and professors and came up with similar results. Thirty-two percent of employers and 39 percent of college professors said high school graduates "have the skills needed to succeed in the work world/college," meaning the majority did not. Public Agenda also found that

- 80 percent of employers and 78 percent of professors rated graduates' spelling and grammar as poor or fair.
- Just 31 percent of employers and 16 percent of professors rated their basic math skills as excellent or good.
- A little over 30 percent of employers and 27 percent of professors say that schools in their communities do an excellent or good job of educating, in contrast to 92 percent of teachers.[66]

Further research lends credence to the perceptions of the professors. The federal government's National Center for Education Statistics reports that 35 percent of students entering public four-year colleges and universities had to take at least one remedial course.[67] Researchers found that low test scores and inadequate coursework had obliged about three in ten first-year college students to enroll in at least one remedial education course. This costs American colleges and universities nearly $1 billion a year to do what high schools ought to have done.[68] Gallup and other polls have repeatedly shown that American 17-year-olds have a weak grasp of basic history and geography and only a slight knowledge of eminent public figures: "Only 8% knew that Rubens was a painter . . . 37% who wrote 'A Midsummer Night's Dream' . . . half that Montana bordered Canada or that Mt. Everest was the highest mountain in the world."[69] The disappointing picture portrayed by test scores, then, appears to match the perceptions of those who teach, interview, and employ American high school graduates.

Crisis, What Crisis?

Test scores are a lightning rod of controversy. Researchers and the public have debated their use passionately. Should standardized tests be used to determine which students belong in special education and which do not? Ought students who fail an exam be required to take summer school, repeat the school year, or be kept from graduating? And should the performance of principals and teachers be graded on the basis of student test scores? These "high stakes" issues dominate the politics of standardized tests.[70]

But these arguments focus on the *use* of test scores. In contrast, there are far fewer debates on the *accuracy* of the test scores. Some have expressed concern that standardized tests do not measure the entirety of intelligence, creativity, and other intellectual attributes.[71] This is, assuredly, true. But it is also of little relevance, for the question here is not about the intelligence we do not measure (e.g., creativity) but the knowledge and skills we do measure.

Few scholars seriously contest the value of using test scores to assess the state of student achievement in the United States. A few, though, have, and their critiques have received much coverage in the media. The most prominent critics of test scores are Berliner, Biddle, and Bracey, and, to a lesser extent, Jianjun Wang. Their objections are considered in the next two sections.

Objection #1: Trends vs. Absolute Scores, or What Decline?

Berliner and Biddle have contested the interpretation that educational achievement as measured by test scores has been on the slide.[72] On this point they are correct. At the time of the writing of *A Nation at Risk*, the available data did show a clear decline in test scores. However, after 1983, ACT, SAT, and NAEP scores have mostly recovered. Berliner and Biddle have a sanguine interpretation of this trend. They say the data show that American education is no worse than ever.[73]

This is true, yet the data also indicate that, for the most part, student skills and knowledge are low. Excepting fourth-graders' scores on the TIMSS science test, none of the aforementioned scores indicate that most students in grades four, eight, or twelve are scoring highly. Even among students considering college, the average ACT score was far below "high performing." And a Department of Education review of the NAEP math achievement data found that most high school seniors have less than "a firm grasp of seventh-grade content" in math.[74] Thus, while Berliner and Biddle are correct that jeremiads about falling test scores are not accurate, decades of test scores indicate that American students generally learn at low levels across the curriculum.

Interestingly, Berliner and Biddle do not take issue with this larger point. They admit student underachievement is a problem, and probably a longstanding one.[75] Curiously, they seem to want to dismiss it by justifying it. In discussing the First National Assessment of History and Literature, Berliner and Biddle note that the poor showing by students on NAHL was not surprising since many adults do not know what the Seneca Falls Declaration was or why Andrew Carnegie was a significant historical figure.[76] They then cite Dale Whittington's study, which argues that compared to students from previous generations, today's young Americans know as little about history as their forebears.[77]

On this point, Berliner and Biddle also are correct. There is little evidence there was a golden age of American learning when most children were schooled to high standards.[78] But what are we to take from this? That Americans have been and always will be little educated, so why worry about it? *Pace* Professors Berliner and Biddle, the great majority of the public and education policymakers are worried; and Chapter 2 shows they should be.

Objection #2: The TIMSS Scores Should Not Be Trusted

Bracey and Wang have raised questions regarding the validity of the results of the 1995 TIMSS exams, the former questioning the sampling of students, the latter arguing that some of the science questions were poorly written.[79]

Wang's article is interesting insofar at it argues that some of the questions on the 1995 TIMSS exams were ambiguous and allowed for more than one correct answer. Unfortunately, Wang only examined a small number of questions on the exam, drawn from those that were released to the public. Thus, it is unclear how many other questions were like this. Furthermore, Wang does not argue that these findings have implications for the rankings of the countries. Presumably, a poorly drafted question that tripped up Americans would also trip up Slovenians or Italians.

Bracey's criticisms are a little stronger. He advances a barrage of complaints. Unfortunately, most are not well developed; his arguments have appeared in opinion columns in popular periodicals rather than research journals, and they unleash a barrage of criticisms that verge on the reckless.[80]

Bracey's strongest arguments are variants of "it's apples and oranges." Bracey says the TIMSS exams improperly compare US students with foreign students. The first difference, claims Bracey, is that other countries are more selective in whom they educate at the secondary level. The United States, meanwhile, educates all children, not solely the most talented. Therefore, foreign students who sat for the TIMSS exams were not representative of their nations' populations. They were an elite, so, of course, they outscored American students.

This is not true. In the past, the United States did educate more of its students to higher grade levels. But that has changed. The OECD shows that as a percentage of population at the typical age of graduation (which varies across nations), most countries that participated in the TIMSS exams graduate an equal if not a higher percentage of their children from secondary school.[81] Thus, of the nations that outscored the United States on the TIMSS exams, all had equal or higher percentages of their students in secondary schooling.[82]

Bracey tries to substantiate this claim by noting that the percentage of 18-year-olds enrolled in secondary school differs from nation to nation. For example, 32 percent of 18-year-old Australians are in secondary school whereas 83 percent of 18-year-old Germans are. Bracey does not attempt to explain this variance. Clearly, a number of factors could be at work: national policies that allow for early graduation, the age at which children start school, and so forth.[83] However, Bracey fails to develop this criticism, so it remains unclear if there is anything to it.

Bracey also takes issue with the age differences between the students taking the TIMSS exams. Table 1.12 shows the age differences between examinees. Bracey's critique is interesting but, again, underdeveloped. He asserts that older students are bound to do better than younger ones, presumably because they have spent more time in school. Thus, Iceland's students dramatically outscored US students because they were just over 21 years of age whereas US students were an average of 18.1 years of age. But there is no clear correlation between age and performance. New Zealand and Australia far outscored the United States, and their students were actually younger (17.6 and 17.7 years old, respectively). Russian Federation students scored slightly better than US students in science and math and were only 16.9 years old on average. Of those nations whose students scored better than the United States, most students were less than a year

Table 1.12   TIMSS Average Science Scores and Student Ages, 1995

Nation	Science Average	Age
Sweden	559	18.9
Netherlands	558	18.5
Iceland	549	21.2
Norway	544	19.5
Canada	532	18.6
New Zealand	529	17.6
Australia	527	17.7
Switzerland	523	19.8
Austria	520	19.1
Slovenia	517	18.8
Denmark	509	19.1
Germany	497	19.5
France	487	18.8
Czech Republic	487	17.8
Russian Federation	481	16.9
United States	480	18.1
Hungary	471	17.5
Lithuania	461	18.1
Cyprus	448	17.7
South Africa	349	20.1

Source: Reproduced from NAEP's website at http://nces.ed.gov/timss.

older. And interestingly, South Africa's students, who performed far worse than Americans, were almost two years older.[84] One finds similar results on the mathematics tests (see Table 1.13).

Moreover, Bracey claims age is a key causal factor between achievement differences, but he fails to distinguish between age and schooling. The age at which children start school varies from nation to nation. In the United States, the average age at which test-takers started school was six years. Thus, American high school seniors taking TIMSS had about twelve years of schooling. In Denmark, Norway, Slovenia, and Sweden, though, test-takers did not begin school until age seven on average. Thus, after twelve years of schooling, these students were age nineteen. Yet, as Tables 1.12 and 1.13 show, all these nations scored higher than the United States.

Bracey's claim also posits that more time spent in secondary schools will produce higher test scores. Because the overall average age of TIMSS examinees was 18.7 whereas that of the US students was 18.1, the argument is that if only US students had half a year more schooling, these differences in performance would be bridged.[85] This seems like wishful thinking in light of the often large disparities in scores. Furthermore, whether an extra few months of schooling would produce higher scores presupposes

Table 1.13   TIMSS Average Mathematics Scores and Student Ages, 1995

Nation	Mathematics Average	Age
Netherlands	560	18.5
Sweden	552	18.9
Denmark	547	19.1
Switzerland	540	19.8
Iceland	534	21.2
Norway	528	19.5
France	523	18.8
New Zealand	522	17.6
Australia	522	17.7
Canada	519	18.6
Austria	518	19.1
Slovenia	512	18.8
Germany	495	19.5
Italy	476	n/a
Russian Federation	471	16.9
Lithuania	469	18.1
Czech Republic	466	17.8
United States	461	18.1
Cyprus	446	17.7
South Africa	356	20.1

Source: Reproduced from NAEP's website at http://nces.ed.gov/timss.

that US pupils would be taking math and science courses that increased their knowledge. The facts indicate that this presupposition is extremely questionable. Because US high schoolers enjoy huge latitude in selecting their courses, a minority of students take academic courses, and even fewer opt for academically challenging versions thereof. Specifically, compared to their international peers, fewer US students in their final year of schooling took math courses (66 percent US vs. 79 percent foreign) and science courses (53 percent US vs. 67 percent foreign). As for advanced course taking, "the percentage of high school graduates who took the most rigorous mathematics curriculum (Advanced Placement [AP] calculus, [regular] calculus, and calculus/analytic geometry)" was 12 percent in 1998; "the percentage who took both chemistry and physics" was 19 percent; and in 1997, just 131 students per 1,000 twelfth-graders took AP exams.[86]

TIMSS and TIMSS-R are not the only studies that found US students to be performing unimpressively against their international peers. Six earlier international math and science assessments showed similar results to TIMSS.[87] A 1998 review of these examinations concluded that "American students—and the schools they attend—are generally functioning less effectively than they should or could."[88] And the evidence to support the TIMSS conclusions continues to grow. For example, the Organization for Economic Cooperation and Development (OECD) recently tested the reading, mathematics, and science skills of more than one-quarter of a million 15-year-olds in twenty-eight nations. The PISA (Programme for International Student Assessment) results were similar to the TIMSS: in all three subject areas, American student scores put them in mid-pack.[89] And in another study of the literacy of 16- to 25-year-olds in thirty nations, the OECD concluded that 59 percent of Americans could not read well enough "to cope with the complex demands of everyday life."[90] Berliner, Biddle, Bracey, and Wang have raised some interesting questions about test scores, but the great preponderance of evidence indicates that US students are not performing well against their international peers.

Conclusion

The testing data presented in this chapter do not indicate that American students on average are learning to advanced levels. The data show the opposite to be the case: few are. Most students are low achieving, and many black and Hispanic students are achieving at especially low levels.

A Nation at Risk claimed there was a "rising tide of mediocrity." Currently, test data indicate that the average 8-, 13-, and 17-year-old students of today achieve at roughly the same level as they did thirty years ago. Test scores did slide, and they have since recovered. Moreover, we can take comfort that American fourth-grade students score better than their international counterparts in science and mathematics.

Yet, we ought not confuse trends with levels. The data strongly suggest that student achievement is low and has been for quite some time. After twelve years of public education, America's youth lack mastery of many rudimentary skills and much basic knowledge. Not only have the content examinations including TIMSS, NAEP, and the NAHL indicated this, so have polls of those adults who work firsthand with high school graduates: employers and college instructors. In this case, *A Nation at Risk* was correct in its most fundamental judgment: there is a wave of mediocrity. But it is not rising; it has been high for at least three decades.

Notes

1. National Commission on Excellence in Education, *A Nation at Risk*, p. 5.
2. Ibid.
3. Ibid., p. 11.
4. Ibid., p. 11.
5. Berliner and Biddle, *The Manufactured Crisis*, p. 34. Bracey, Biddle, and Berliner have said that a conservative cabal is fabricating a "myth" of failing public schools for the sake of creating an excuse to privatize education.
6. Bracey, "Tinkering with TIMSS."
7. Chapter 3 considers school curricula, the other component of this issue.
8. Stedman, "The Achievement Crisis Is Real."
9. To further illustrate the diversity of data: in the past decade New York state and New York City have changed the tests they use. For example, see New York City Board of Education, *Chancellor's 60-Day Report*.
10. The College Board has ceased using SAT as an acronym for Scholastic Aptitude Test.
11. Aptitude, strictly speaking, is a blend of both innate ability and acquired skills. Ward and Murray-Ward, *Assessment in the Classroom*, pp. 214–215.
12. On this ambiguity see Mehrens and Lehmann, *Measurement and Evaluation in Education and Psychology*, pp. 305–318; on standardized tests and their use for evaluating achievement, pp. 289–394.
13. The American College Test website, http://http://www.act.org/aap/STRAT/4SampleTests.html.
14. The College Board website, http://www.collegeboard.com.
15. Ibid.
16. Again, such questions clearly presuppose that a student possesses content knowledge, in this example, the definition of the words in the question.
17. ACT website, http://www.act.org.
18. Ibid.
19. All ACT data courtesy of ACT Inc. and retrieved from http://www.act.org.
20. Ibid.
21. Taken from ACT Inc., *Standards for Transitions Guide—Mathematics*.
22. ACT Inc., *Standards for Transitions Guide—English*.
23. ACT Inc., *Standards for Transitions Guide— Mathematics*.

24. All information and data on the SAT comes from the College Board's website, http://www.collegeboard.com. The College Board is responsible for creating and administering the SAT.

25. As will be seen later, students in other nations are routinely introduced to these courses long before their junior and senior years in high school.

26. The College Board, "10-Year Trend in SAT Scores Indicates Increased Emphasis on Math Is Yielding Results."

27. Ibid.

28. PSAT scores for high school juniors follow a similar trend. Math scores are for the most part steady, but verbal scores peaked around 1970 and slid thereafter. PSAT data provided by the College Board Inc.

29. Marx, "Why We Need the SAT," p. B11.

30. College Board, *What Does the SAT Measure and Why Does It Matter?* p. 7. On the value of the SAT as a predictor of collegiate success, see Camera and Hezlett, "The Effectiveness of the SAT in Predicting Success Early and Late in College."

31. For an overview of NAEP and its history, see Jones and Olkin, eds., *The Nation's Report Card.*

32. *The NAEP Guide.*

33. NAEP, *The Nation's Report Card.*

34. All NAEP long-term data drawn from Campbell et al., *NAEP 1999 Trends in Academic Progress.*

35. However, the miniscule gains seen are perhaps disappointing in light of the growing IQs and per-pupil spending. On rising IQ scores, see Nessler, "Rising Test Scores and What They Mean."

36. Loveless and DiPerna, *How Well Are Students Learning? Focus on Math Achievement*, pp. 7–9.

37. For further details, see Greenwald et al., *NAEP 1998 Writing Report Card for the Nation and States*, pp. 10–13; see also the legislation that created NAGB and reauthorized it, PL 100-97 (1988), National Assessment of Educational Progress Improvement Act (20 USC 1221), and Improving America's Schools Act (20 USC 9010).

38. These proficiency levels are based upon the NAEP frameworks of knowledge for each subject area.

39. All data come from the National Center for Educational Statistics (NCES).

40. National Assessment Governing Board, *NAEP Reading Framework*, chapter 2.

41. Ibid., appendix A.

42. Ibid.

43. This is especially disturbing in light of a recent finding that argues that the NAEP fourth- and eighth-grade mathematics examinations are too easy. Loveless, *How Well Are American Students Learning?*

44. National Assessment Governing Board, *Mathematics Framework for the 1996 and 2000 National Assessment of Educational Progress*, appendix A. It is worth noting that the 2003 NAEP mathematics scores for fourth- and eighth-graders showed a slight increase.

45. NAEP Science Grade 12 and Grade 8 item maps. These generally unimpressive results are mirrored by society. A National Science Foundation study found that "few people in the United States understand the scientific process and many believe in mysterious psychic powers and may be quick to accept phony science reports." Quote from Associated Press, "Survey Finds Few in US Understand Science."

46. Weiss et al., *The Next Generation of Citizens.*

47. A survey of adult Americans finds low levels of knowledge of the rudiments of the US Constitution. Columbia Law Survey, *Americans' Knowledge of the Constitution.*

48. NAEP Geography Grade 12 and Grade 8 item maps. These results are similar to those found by a geography quiz given by *National Geographic* magazine. It found that only 13 percent of Americans between 18 and 24 years of age could locate Iraq on a map. National Geographic, *Roper Geographic Survey 2002.*

49. See Phillips, Acting Commissioner of the National Center for Education Statistics, "Statement on Long-Term Trend Writing NAEP."

50. Greenwald et al., *NAEP 1998 Writing Report Card for the Nation and States,* p. 25.

51. There is, of course, a class element to the score discrepancies. For example, poor, rural, and inner-city students tend to score worse than suburban students in all areas. Yet, the racial disparities remain across class and geographic categories. See individual NAEP test results at http://nces.ed.gov and, more generally, Jencks and Phillips, *The Black-White Test Score Gap.*

52. What follows is drawn from Ravitch and Finn, *What Do Our 17-Year-Olds Know?*

53. Ibid., p. ix.

54. Ibid., pp. 46–74.

55. Ibid., pp. 85–98.

56. Ibid., p. 104.

57. *Highlights from TIMSS, Overview and Key Findings Across Grade Levels,* p. 1. Thirty eight countries participated in the TIMSS-R examinations.

58. Ibid., p. 1.

59. Ibid., pp. 2–3.

60. Ibid., pp. 4–5.

61. Ibid., p. 9.

62. Reproduced in full from http://nces.ed.gov/timss/timss-r/.

63. For the most extensive analysis of the TIMSS and TIMSS-R data to date, see Schmidt et al., *Why Schools Matter: Across National Comparison of Curriculum and Learning.*

64. Public Agenda, *Reality Check 1999.*

65. Ibid.

66. Public Agenda, as reported in Education Week, *Quality Counts 1999.*

67. National Center for Education Statistics, *Remedial Education at Degree-Granting Postsecondary Institutions in Fall 2000.*

68. Breneman and Haarlow, "Remedial Education: Costs and Consequences," in *Remediation in Higher Education: A Symposium,* pp. 4–20. For the earlier study, see Breneman, "Remedial Education: Its Extent and Cost," pp. 359–383.

69. Ravitch and Finn, *What Do Our 17-Year-Olds Know?* pp. 81–82.

70. For a summary review of the critiques of the use of standardized tests to make high-stakes decisions, see Phelps, *Why Testing Experts Hate Testing*; and Orfield and Wald, "The High Stakes Testing Mania Hurts Poor and Minority Students the Most," pp. 38–40. See also late Senator Paul Wellstone's bill S.2348 (June 19, 2000), which would constrain states' use of standardized tests in making grade promotion and graduation decisions; and Luntz and Laszlo-Mizrahi, "American Voters Overwhelmingly Give High Stakes Test an 'F'."

71. E.g., FairTest, The National Center for Fair and Open Testing, "The ACT: Biased, Inaccurate, Coachable, and Misused."

72. Berliner and Biddle, *The Manufactured Crisis.*

73. Ibid., pp. 13–64.

74. Mullis, et al., *The State of Mathematics Achievement.*

75. Berliner and Biddle, *The Manufactured Crisis,* pp. 13–64.

76. Ibid., pp. 16–19.

77. Ibid., pp. 33–34; Whittington, "What Have 17-Year-Olds Known in the Past?" pp. 759–780.

78. Stedman notes that "in the middle of World War II, the *New York Times* surveyed seven thousand students in thirty-six colleges and found 'a striking ignorance of even the most elementary aspects of United States history. . . . The test involved straightforward questions of basic material. . . . The *Times* found that only 16% of students could name two contributions by Thomas Jefferson." Stedman, "An Assessment of the Contemporary Debate Over US Achievement," p. 81; see also Hofstadter, *Anti-Intellectualism in American Life,* p. 304.

79. Bracey, "Tinkering with TIMSS: A Response to Pascal Forgione," pp. 32–35; Wang, "A Content Examination of the TIMSS Items," pp. 36–37.

80. For example, Bracey finds it baffling that if only 75 percent of American 17-year-olds graduate, somehow 87 percent of our 25- to 34-year-olds have diplomas. The answer, obviously, is that diploma holders have General Equivalence Degrees. Bracey has also suggested that a high advanced math score by Cyprus might be the result of cheating. See Bracey, "TIMSS Rhymes with Dim, as in Witted"; and Bracey, "Tinkering with TIMSS."

81. Organization for Economic Cooperation and Development, *Education at a Glance,* 1996, table R11.1.

82. Takahira et al., *Pursuing Excellence,* appendix A 5.14.

83. In some participating nations, students do not start school until age seven and do not graduate until age nineteen or older. Thus it is not surprising that they have higher percentages of their 18-year-olds enrolled.

84. All age data taken from Takahira et al., *Pursuing Excellence,* chapter 4 and appendix A5.17 and A5.19.

85. All scores taken from Calsyn et al., *Highlights from TIMSS,* pp. 8–9.

86. US Department of Education, National Center for Education Statistics, *The Condition of Education 2000,* indicators 27 and 14. And this is to say nothing of the long-noted senior slump, wherein effort levels of graduating American students slide. Remarkably, Bracey raises the senior slump as a possible cause for American underachievement, attempting, it seems, to have it both ways.

87. See National Center for Education Statistics, "International Mathematics and Science Assessments."

88. Stevenson and Lee, "An Examination of American Student Achievement from an International Perspective."

89. OECD, *Knowledge and Skills for Life: First Results from the PISA 2000*; and OECD, *Learning for Tomorrow's World.*

90. OECD, *Education at a Glance—OECD Indicators,* chapter F.

2

The Case for Federal Policy to Raise Education Standards

The previous chapter presented data that suggests that American students are not learning as much as they might. This chapter offers reasons for federal governmental action to remedy this problem, considers the merits of the policy of establishing high academic standards to raise educational achievement, and reviews and answers some of the prominent critiques of using standards to improve achievement.

Why Low Achievement Is a Policy Issue

There are numerous reasons why academic underachievement is a problem in need of a governmental policy response. For one, a nation-state's economic health is becoming increasingly linked to the education levels of its citizens.[1] Of course, there is no simple causal relationship between rising education levels and, say, the value of the stock market or the appearance of recessions; other variables come into play.[2] But we should not confuse the business cycle with long-term economic development.[3]

The positive relationship between education and economic growth was discerned at least as early as the early 1960s.[4] The wealth-generating bases for nations' economies are shifting, as they have been for centuries. In the seventeenth century, Holland (now the Netherlands) was powerful thanks to its innovations in finance, capital markets, and well-developed trade relationships. Germany's economy grew in the late nineteenth century as it developed its technical schools and related manufacturing industries.[5] Today, first-world nations are evolving toward knowledge-based businesses. This is reflected in the shifting demands employers have for employee skills. Although the labor market's demand for unskilled labor remains large, its need for highly educated workers has been growing steadily over the past few decades.[6] Thus, recent surveys reveal high employer discontent with the educational skills of recent high school graduates.[7] The needs of the new economy have also helped spur discussion to reform high school. No longer should it be thought of as the end of schooling for most individuals. Rather, secondary schooling should be better integrated with the demands of postsecondary education.[8]

The increasing interdependence of nations' economies has brought them into more direct competition to create high-wage jobs. Industries that pay these wages are fostered by and attracted to places with highly skilled and learned workers. Yet, there are indicators that the education levels of American workers are sliding relative to other countries. A recent Organization for Economic Cooperation and Development literacy survey found, among other things, that 59 percent of Americans tested could not read well enough to "cope adequately with the complex demands of everyday life." Craig Wurtzel, education analyst for the OECD, noted, "Thirty years ago, the United States was the undisputed leader in educating its population. The United States has not only lost the lead for participation in education, but the U.S. has been overcome by countries doing a better job in regards to quality."[9] Thus, the United States has good reason to formulate policy to educate its workers better than its international competitors.[10]

A second reason to be concerned about academic underachievement is that the health of the US system of representative democracy is contingent, in part, on the education level of the citizenry. Longstanding low levels of citizen knowledge, especially on the workings of government and American political history, are a potential threat to the system's well-being.[11] The nexus between voter knowledge and the quality of representatives and executives in political office is readily apparent. Citizens' ability to comprehend government action and judge its legitimacy is in part contingent on their knowledge of previous governmental policymaking, the Constitution, and so forth. Widespread ignorance on these matters enables government to make policy unconstrained by principle or prudence.[12] It is troubling that as governance of the United States has grown more complex (think stem cells and homeland security), politicians are increasingly dumbing down their communications with the public. Candidates in the 2000 election spoke to the public at the sixth- and seventh-grade level.[13]

Furthermore, representative democracy requires some direct citizen involvement. As a recent study explains,

> In the world of American politics, citizens are asked to undertake a wide array of civic activities: select qualified representatives . . . for local, state, and national offices; serve as a pool from which representatives are selected; reward and punish office holders for their past performances; vote directly on policy issues through initiative[s] and referenda; fill the thou-

sands of voluntary, appointed, and bureaucratic civic roles required for the machinery of campaigns, elections, and government to work effectively; help shape local, state, and national political agendas through numerous outlets, from public opinion polls to public demonstrations to direct contact with public officials; . . . navigate government bureaucracies for information, goods, and services; attend local government and civic meetings; and more. Furthermore, the explosion of new technologies and the growing popularity of such new political forums as instant polls, interactive media, electronic town meetings, and talk show politics have all expanded the opportunities for civic participation.[14]

Many of these activities require that citizens not only have the desire to participate but also the knowledge and knowledge-gathering skills to understand the complexities involved and deliberate on what is best.[15] In addition, whether citizens will participate in public affairs is strongly correlated with their education level. A review of the research on civic engagement concludes that

> Education is the most reliable predictor of participation in public life. The probability that Citizen Jones will vote in elections, give money to political candidates, petition government for favors, or join voluntary associations in his community is strongly related to his level of educational achievement. . . . The central role that education plays in promoting an active civic life has been demonstrated and reinforced by five decades of research in political science.[16]

Thus, the higher the educational attainment, the more probable it is that a citizen will vote (see Table 2.1).

Beyond these macroscopic or systemic justifications, which begin with the question of what is good for the American state and, by implication, good for citizens, there are microscopic reasons for judging low student achievement to be a public policy problem in need of governmental action.

Table 2.1   Voting in the November 2000 Presidential or Congressional Elections

Education Level	Percentage Reporting to Have Voted
Ninth to twelfth grade, no diploma	38.0
High school graduate	52.5
Some college/associate degree	63.1
Baccalaureate degree	75.4
Advanced degree	81.9

Source: US Census Bureau, Current Population Survey, November 2000, http://www.census.gov.

Specifically, education benefits individuals and their offspring.[17] Lower achievement is correlated with a host of ills: crime, poverty, and teenage pregnancy.[18] Education levels also show positive relationships to individual health and competent management of personal finances.[19]

There also is a relationship between learning and earning. On average, adults age eighteen and over without a high school diploma earned $16,124 in 1998; those with a high school diploma earned $22,895; those who possessed a baccalaureate degree (BA or BS) earned $40,478; and those with an advanced degree, $63,229.[20] A host of variables such as cognitive ability, race, family structure, and opportunity may muddy this apparently clear correlative relationship.[21] However, when social scientists have controlled for these noneducative factors, the majority of studies still show a relationship between higher learning and higher earning.[22]

That said, public policy should not be merely a matter of the utilitarian calculation of benefits. Guidance should also be taken from fundamental principles of the republic, such as equality. Despite gains, inequality in wealth and political participation and power remain. This is especially troubling because this inequality strongly correlates with race. As was noted in Chapter 1, black and Hispanic pupils score twenty to thirty-five points lower on NAEP exams than their white peers; in addition, the average black twelfth-grader reads at the same level as the average white eighth-grader.[23] In light of the tie between education and individual well-being (financial and otherwise), it is imperative for reducing inequality that the achievement of poor and minority students be raised.[24]

Second, because the United States is a democratic republic, governmental policy should bear some relation to citizens' preferences. On the subject of education, there is abundant evidence that Americans question the efficacy of the public schools and want the federal government to enact standards reform to remedy underachievement.

In terms of determining the public mind on the subject of the public schools, the most obvious source of data is the public opinion poll. Though far from ideal, it provides the best available information. Polling data has revealed:

- The public tends to have a moderately high regard for the schools their children attend. However, their opinions of public schools in general are much lower. Those citizens expressing a "great deal of confidence" decreased from 58 percent in 1973 to 40 percent in 1995.[25] In 1997, 69 percent of Americans polled said they would give American schools a grade of C or less.[26]
- The public sees a relationship between education and America's well-being. When asked in 1982, "In determining America's

strength in the future—say, 25 years from now—how important do you feel each of the following factors will be?" 84 percent of respondents said "developing the best educational system in the world." In 1991, 89 percent gave this same response.[27]

- The public believes education and personal income are related. Citizens see education as "an economic issue," and many felt "that in today's world there is no way to get ahead without a college degree."[28]
- The public's opinion on the spending priorities of government is quite clear. Public support for education spending by government rose from sixth on national priorities in 1973 to first by 1999.[29] Some 87 percent of Americans said that increased education spending was either a top or high priority.[30]
- Even when there were state and federal budget surpluses, pollsters found that more citizens wanted the money spent on schooling than returned to taxpayers.[31]
- Although studies have shown that Americans have a tendency to support increased government spending but at the same time want their taxes cut, this view does not appear to hold with regard to education.[32] In seven out of nine polls between 1969 and 1986, the majority of Americans said they would be willing to vote for more taxes if the public schools said they needed more money.[33] Despite the recent economic downturn, voters remain adamant: they do not want education funding reduced.[34]

These are striking numbers. They indicate that Americans want more spending on education, increased federal action to improve the schools, and are willing to pay for it.

For all the talk of a backlash against standards and testing, parents remain firmly in favor of using tests as a diagnostic tool for assessing student achievement, and for publicly releasing schools' performances thereon as a way of shaming low-performing schools into reforming.[35] And years of polling data demonstrate that citizens are particularly attracted to the idea of national education standards and assessments. A review of the polls concludes that support for academic standards is

- "at a consensus level among the general public";
- "shared by all groups in the population," regardless of race, religion, or age; and is "not easily shaken," even when told that raising standards may deny some youngsters promotion or diplomas;
- based on a conviction that standards will help all students learn; and
- corresponds with deep-seated public concerns and values.[36]

Thus, the public believes that education is critical to individual and collective well-being. Americans want the federal government to improve it, and they favor high education standards.[37]

How Higher Standards Can Raise Achievement

Standards—What Standards?

Policy should not be made on the basis of public polls alone. The public supports standards, but is standards-based reform smart policy? The answer is yes.

Before considering the relationship of high standards to achievement, the term *education standards* must be defined. Generally speaking, a standard is a model or benchmark, and it is used to judge the adequacy or quality of something else. In education, there are content standards, performance standards, and opportunity-to-learn standards. *Content standards* are the knowledge and skills that students are expected to master at each grade level. *Performance standards* are the levels of mastery of the standards that one must reach to be certified as, say, proficient, advanced, and so forth.[38] *Opportunity-to-learn standards,* meanwhile, are those resources necessary to carry out learning to the standards (e.g., textbooks that focus on the standards, teachers able to teach to the standards, etc.).

Standards-based education reform generally adheres to the following four principles:[39]

- Both content standards and performance standards must be set high—that is, high enough to challenge most students, but not so high that most students could not possibly meet them.
- Content standards must be specific but not trivial. They should clearly stipulate the general capabilities and subject content a student must master. For example, Figure 2.1 provides Kentucky's standard for eleventh-grade geometry and measurement.
- Performance standards must measure students' mastery of the content standards absolutely, not relatively. Therefore, criterion-referenced exams (which measure student knowledge of the standards) are preferred over norm-referenced exams (which measure student knowledge of standards vis-à-vis other students).
- These standards must apply to all students, excepting those with substantial learning or behavioral disabilities.

Among educators and policymakers, the notion of establishing standards to raise achievement is not particularly controversial (though later in this chapter the objections of the rare few are considered). There has been

---

**Figure 2.1   Eleventh-Grade Geometry and Measurement
Standard for Kentucky**

Concepts
Students should understand:
   algebraic transformations, transformations in geometric systems;
   spatial relationships such as between-ness, perpendicularity, and paral-
      lelism;
   the structure of standard measurement systems (English, metric);
   ratio measures such as slope and rate;
   trigonometric measures (sine, cosine, tangent, degrees).

Skills
Students should be able to:
   use transformations on figures and numbers;
   describe elements which change and elements which do not change
      under transformations;
   construct geometric figures using a variety of techniques (e.g., straight-
      edge and compass, paper folding, three-dimensional models);
   use methods of indirect measurement (e.g., shadow method or mirror
      method for finding the height of a tree);
   use Pythagorean Theorem.

Relationships
Students should understand the following relationships:
   how properties of geometric shapes relate to each other;
   how trigonometric ratios relate to right triangles;
   how algebraic procedures and geometric concepts are related;
   how position in the plane can be represented using rectangular coordi-
      nates.

Source: Achieve, Inc., www.achieve.org.

---

concern expressed over attaching consequences to education standards. For example, will students who do not meet the standards be held back or denied their diplomas? Will teachers and principals lose their jobs should their pupils fail to reach the standards?[40] And can schools meet education standards without increasing their spending on material resources, such as books, computers, and improved infrastructure?[41]

However, beyond these high-stakes questions, there is a powerful logic to standards-based reform: children will not learn to high levels unless they are taught challenging curricula. As one recent text on standards notes, "decades of educational research" on the "principles of learning" show that the premises behind establishing high standards—that achievement is more a factor of student effort, that achievement at high levels requires high expectations—are sound.[42] The basic behaviorist logic behind them is compelling. Again, to raise achievement, the level of skills and knowledge students are taught must be raised, and this can be done through establishing challenging education standards. Doing this will "maximize the probability of good teaching or worthwhile content to all students."[43] And the children will respond. There is widespread confidence that if students are taught more challenging subject material, they will learn it.[44] Students themselves are undaunted at being tested on tougher material.[45]

Raising Standards to Improve Student Achievement

In 1998 a scholarly paper noted, "since state and local standards are a relatively recent phenomenon, it is not surprising that there has been virtually no research done on their relationship to student achievement."[46] Clearly, there is some truth in this. As the evidence indicates, most states have failed to develop and implement good standards. In this case, providing evidence for the power of standards to raise achievement is no simple matter.

Proving that standards work is especially difficult due to their nature. Unlike computers or smaller class sizes, standards are not concrete objects. In and of themselves they are text on paper, words that say what students should know at the end of a particular grade level. Sitting on policymakers' desks or tucked within the file cabinets of state education departments, standards cannot affect educational achievement. Standards can alter what students learn only if they are implemented in classrooms and measured by tests, and these activities presuppose larger plans of accountability.[47] Effective standards must be embedded within systems of self-assessment, self-correction, and the flexible allocation of resources.[48] Figure 2.2 shows a typical standards-based feedback system.

As Figure 2.2 indicates, a state government creates the education standards, both the content and the performance levels to which they expect schools to educate their students. The schools adopt the standards and teach the students toward them. Assessments measure student progress toward the standards and teacher success in teaching the standards. Assessments are key: they provide the systemic feedback to teachers, school administrators, and state policymakers of how well students are learning.[49] Assessments also empower state policymakers to see which schools are performing well and which are not, thus enabling them to shift their resources and efforts to those schools where children are learning least (this, it must be noted, would be a major change; traditionally, states have distributed money to school districts based on criteria other than school outputs/student achievement). Assessments also enable parents to see how well their children are doing relative to other children and other schools. A standards-based educational system, then, speaks to policymak-

Figure 2.2   A Standards-Based Feedback System

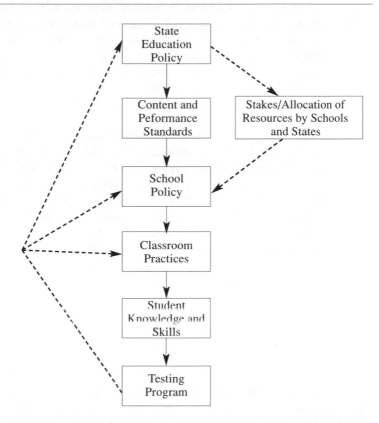

Source: Adopted and adapted from Stecher and Barron, *Quadrennial Milepost Accountability Testing in Kentucky,* p. 4.

ers, administrators, and teachers about educational achievement first and foremost.[50]

Though few states have successfully implemented fully functioning standards-based reforms, a number of individual cases can be examined. However, because standards reform must be systemic to be effective, trying to isolate the effects of implementing standards is extremely difficult. The best that can be done is to examine cases where standards-based reforms were implemented and test scores increased subsequently.

School-Level Successes

At the school level, examples of the implementation of standards and subsequent rises in student academic achievement abound[51]:

- On assuming the office of principal at Pasadena High School in the mid-1980s, Judy Codding found that only two of the 110 mostly minority, incoming ninth-grade students were sufficiently learned in math to begin schooling in geometry and Algebra II. She implemented a two-year, high-standards math program for the majority of the pupils. The results: far more of those who took the standards-based math course passed the Stanford math achievement test (71.4 percent) than those who took the traditional math course (47.3 percent).[52]
- A study of twenty-one high-performing schools in areas where 75 percent or more of the children are eligible for free or reduced-priced lunches found that each school had high academic standards and assessments thereon. Among children in poverty, 58 percent of low-income fourth-graders scored below the "basic" level on the 1998 NAEP reading test, and 61 percent of eighth-graders scored below the basic level in mathematics. Nevertheless, students in these schools scored equal to or higher than 65 percent of their peers nationwide across all demographic groups.[53]
- A study of 366 high-performing elementary and secondary schools in poor districts in twenty-one states found that each school was "unusually focused on high academic expectations for their students" and that standards undergird the characteristics that enable them to outperform similar schools.[54]

There is some evidence that district-level standards-based reform in San Antonio (TX), Philadelphia (PA), and Memphis (TN) has resulted in test score increases.[55] Schools in the Mount Vernon district of New York state saw their test scores leap after they instituted a curriculum for each grade based on state standards. At Mount Vernon's Lincoln Elementary School in 1999, 61 percent of fourth-graders met state standards. By 2001, 91 percent did.[56] But what of standards reform on a larger level?

A team of researchers undertook a massive analysis of the Third International Mathematics and Science Study (TIMSS) data.[57] They examined test results for 9-, 13-, and 17-year-olds, math and science standards and textbooks submitted by participating nations, and teachers' professed goals for learning and time allocation within subject areas. The objective was to determine if school curricula affected student achievement. Not surprisingly, they found that curricula matter. Students who were taught more, learned more. "In case after case, some significant relationship was found between achievement gains and curriculum." The socioeconomic status of students also had an effect on student test scores. However, in terms of variables that are readily manipulated by public policy, "content standards are the primary vehicle for policy impact on what teachers teach."[58]

A number of states, such as Maryland, Massachusetts, and North Carolina, and Virginia, Kentucky, and Texas have implemented standards-based reform competently.[59] This chapter will focus on Kentucky and Texas, highlighted for two reasons. First, both Kentucky and Texas have done an especially good job at enacting all the main components of standards reform (e.g., clear, high-content standards and aligned assessments, state policy responses to underachievement). Second, these states' standards reforms have been the subject of a number of major studies by respected outside researchers.

However, some caveats are warranted. First, disentangling the effects of standards from other policy variables is complex. Again, in each instance standards have come embedded in larger standards-based reform (more spending, more teacher training, etc.). Second, standards-based reform is, as noted previously, only getting started. Therefore, student gains on test scores are likely, in part, a function of students and teachers learning how to take the new tests. Thus, it might mean that in the first few years of standards reform, scores dip (as students confront the new tests), then climb quickly for a few years (as students and teachers figure out what the exams cover), but then plateau (as other variables begin to inhibit further improvement). In order to see the effects of standards in the long run, there is no choice but to wait and watch. Nevertheless, even if test score gains are influenced by other policy variables and do plateau, standards and aligned assessments are an essential component of reform. Again, without standards, it is difficult to isolate which variables (socioeconomic background, teacher training, curricula, etc.) are causing underachievement in individual schools and school districts and to do something to improve the situation.

Kentucky. In 1990 the Kentucky Education Reform Act (KERA) was signed into law.[60] This legislation dramatically altered the education system. The act had been impelled by the Kentucky Supreme Court's finding the previous year that the school funding system was inadequate and unconstitutional.[61] KERA built upon the 1984 School Improvement Act, which gave the state the power to take over schools that failed to meet state attendance, dropout, and academic performance rates. KERA added power to this statute by creating KIRIS (the Kentucky Instructional Results Information System), which was redesigned and renamed the Commonwealth Accountability Testing System (CATS) in 1998.

KIRIS/CATS is the bedrock of Kentucky's reforms. It is a system of academic standards, aligned assessments, and direct feedback to schools. Students are tested at most grade levels, and schools' aggregate scores are monitored closely. Kentucky assesses its students with two types of examinations, the Kentucky Core Content Test (KCCT), which measures student learning to state standards, and the Comprehensive Test of Basic Skills

(CTBS), a nationally administered set of norm-referenced examinations. School scores on the exams are published and made easily available to both the media and the public. Schools showing improvement can qualify for financial rewards, of which teachers themselves may receive a portion. Those schools that consistently post flat or falling scores are subject to review, supplementary assistance, and, if necessary, reorganization.[62]

Research on Kentucky's reforms indicates that the implementation of standards has affected instructional practices and that achievement has subsequently climbed. A 1996 study found that both principals and teachers in Kentucky tend to believe that test-based accountability has pushed them to focus on the content and skills that are assessed.[63] A principal of a once-failing primary school said of Kentucky's reforms,

> I should mention that the Kentucky Education Reform Act (KERA) has made a big difference to Kennedy [Elementary School]. It got everyone focused on results, and in particular on results as measured by Kentucky's new statewide assessment. The incentives have made a big impression on our staff. . . . We actually live in the environment that KERA created.[64]

Subsequent research has found that KIRIS/CATS has made teachers focus their instruction on the subjects contained on the exam rather than what they might prefer to teach.[65] At some grade levels, teachers sought more professional development on subjects that were due to be tested that school year or the next. At most tested grade levels, teachers tended to allot large amounts of their preparation time toward devising lessons and activities that prepared students for exams.[66]

Since the reforms were initiated, Kentucky's pupils have exhibited gains on a number of assessments. On Kentucky's KCCT examinations, scores in reading, mathematics, science, and social science have improved, sometimes dramatically.[67] In 1993, for example, 32.4 percent of elementary school students met state reading standards. In 1998, 58.4 percent did. Even in the poorest sections of Kentucky, such as Wolfe County, where 90 percent of children have free or reduced-price lunches, achievement has climbed.[68] Kentucky's students have also shown improvement on the NAEP reading, mathematics, and science exams. Its fourth- and eighth-graders had modest but significant gains and ranked among the top improving states in the United States.[69] Kentucky has also seen positive results on the CTBS. Recently, Kentucky's third-, sixth-, and ninth-graders have, for the first time since 1998, matched or exceeded the national average on the examination in reading, writing, and mathematics.[70]

Among older students, upon whom one would expect the effects of reform to be lighter, the picture is less clear but apparently positive. On Kentucky state tests, high schoolers are scoring higher than they were before reform was implemented. The number of secondary students emboldened to take the ACT and Advanced Placement exams (the latter, if passed, can qualify students to receive college-level coursework credits) has climbed.[71] In 1995, 63 percent of them took the ACT; in 1999, 68 percent did, and the scores held steady. Among Advanced Placement exam-takers, the number choosing to take the exams rose 32 percent from 1995 to 1999. Despite the swell in the numbers taking these exams, the proportion who passed the exam slid only from 71.4 percent to 68.4 percent.

Texas. After a high-profile committee chaired by H. Ross Perot published a report urging education reform, Texas began reforming its school system in 1984. The state government enacted legislation that brought numerous changes, including rules requiring student athletes to maintain certain grade levels in order to play sports, and new tougher teacher certification tests. Texas also created a mandatory curriculum (called Essential Elements) and aligned assessments. The Texas Educational Assessment of Basic Skills (TEAMS) exams tested students in grades one, three, five, seven, nine, and eleven on reading and mathematics.

In 1990, TEAMS was replaced by the Texas Assessment of Academic Skills (TAAS). The TAAS exams on reading, writing, and math skills are administered to students in grades three through ten and are tougher than the old TEAMS exams.[72] In recent years, the tests have been administered to more grade levels and have been aligned with the state's education standards, now known as Texas Essential Knowledge and Skills (TEKS). Texas standards have received favorable reviews from the American Federation of Teachers, the Council for Basic Education, and the Thomas B. Fordham Foundation. The latter bestowed an "Honor Roll" rating on Texas because its education standards and accountability system were judged "solid" and "strong" respectively.[73] As with Kentucky, test scores are made readily available to the media and public, and schools meeting improvement goals on these exams can qualify for cash rewards. Schools twice falling short of improvement goals may be reorganized or closed by the state. The Texas Education Agency distributes TEKS study guides to teachers, and anyone may download TEKS guides from the Internet.[74] These guides lay out clearly to students, teachers, administrators, and parents the skills and knowledge that the TAAS exams will assess.

In terms of results, from 1994 through 2002 Texas students showed dramatic gains on the TAAS reading, mathematics, social studies, and writing assessments.[75] Among tenth-graders, for example,

- In 1994, 75 percent passed the reading examination; in 2002, 94 percent did.
- In 1994, 55 percent passed the mathematics examination; in 2002, 92 percent did.

These results appeared for younger students as well. Among fourth-graders:

- In 1994, 57 percent passed the mathematics examination; in 2002, 94 percent did.
- In 1994, 73 percent passed the reading examination; in 2002, 92 percent did.

Like their peers in Kentucky, Texas lower-income and nonwhite students are also showing gains in achievement. For example, in Houston, Worsham Elementary School's enrollment is nearly 90 percent Hispanic and impoverished. However, in 2000, 98 percent of its Hispanic third- and fourth-graders passed the TAAS reading test. Statewide, minorities and Limited English Proficient students have also increased their achievement. Black fourth-graders, for example, have seen their pass rates on the reading test rise from 56 to 88 percent. Seventh-grade Hispanic students saw their math pass rates go from 60 to 88 percent during this same period.[76] Typically, large urban school districts are notoriously resistant to change and often have the worst-performing schools. Yet, urban districts in Texas have also shown better results. In Houston, for example, pass rates on the TAAS reading and math exams have climbed. In 1994, less than 50 percent of students passed their mathematics exams. By 2000, 80 percent passed. San Antonio, El Paso, Fort Worth, Austin, and Dallas have seen similar leaps in achievement.[77]

Critics charge that the scores climbed because dropout rates ballooned during this same timeframe and that students unable to pass are driven out of school.[78] However, methodological questions have been raised about this critique, and another analysis has found that the overall dropout rate actually decreased from 45 percent in 1990 to 34 percent in 1999, with minority dropout rates holding firm.[79] Critics have also hypothesized that the climbing test scores are due to increased retention rates, especially of blacks and Hispanics. One researcher has gone so far as to denounce the gains as "an outright fraud" and estimates that "half the apparent increases" on state test scores are due to retention.[80] While scholars agree more students are being retained (especially at the ninth-grade level), it is unclear whether increased retention is weakening or improving the probability that students will graduate.[81]

A more serious charge has been made against the "Texas miracle": that gains on state tests were so large because the tests were so easy. The evidence indicates that this is true. Indeed, it is difficult to find anyone who is familiar with the content of the tests that can persuasively argue otherwise.[82] Thus, the disturbing example of Rosa Arevelo, a student who graduated from Houston's Jefferson Davis High School after a program of colle-

giate preparatory courses yet struggled to pass her freshman college courses.[83]

While more research is necessary to clarify the extent to which the
TAAS exams are "dumbed down," studies have shown that the achievement gains of Texas students are real (although less miraculous than they
seem). Most recently, the *New York Times* compared student scores on
TAAS exams and the widely used Stanford Achievement Test. *Times*
reporters familiar with the study have written that the study "raises serious
doubts about the magnitude" of the gains attributed to Houston students by
the Texas exams.[84] So while the size of the gains are in question, the gains
themselves are not.

This comports with previous examinations of Texas students' scores on
both the TAAS exams and other assessments. Two RAND studies of reading and mathematics data from 1990 to 1996 found that Texas pupils posted
large gains on the NAEP math exams, in spite of the fact that the state's
minority population (which tends to score lower, on average) had grown.[85]
In examining the rises in scores, Grissmer and Flanagan learned that
changes in per-pupil expenditures, student characteristics, pupil-teacher
ratio, and like resource variables were not the causes. Instead, Grissmer and
Flanagan suggested that the growth came from the state's "systemic
reform." In particular, gains may have been a result of Texas's creation of
"clear teaching objectives by grade through state-wide learning standards"
and implementation of "new, state-wide assessments closely linked to the
learning standards" and testing system.[86]

Further evidence supporting the standards and accountability hypothesis comes from a study of four school districts in Texas, three of which
have student populations that are mostly low income, black, and
Hispanic.[87] All four districts have shown high levels of student achievement. In Aldine district schools, 80 percent of black students passed their
mathematics exams.[88] Similarly, another district's Hispanic students on
average scored 105 points higher on their SAT exams than the state average.[89]

After interviewing over 200 teachers, administrators, and others
involved with school reform in these four districts, researchers concluded
that state-level emphasis on achievement and accountability played a major
role in raising student test scores. One district central office administrator
said, "I think state accountability has been a good thing. That it has gotten
everyone focused and showed people where we are or where we were and
where we need to be. . . . There is no doubt in my mind that this district
would not be where it is without it."[90] The authors, in terms that bring to
mind the dashed-lined diagram of systemic accountability shown in Figure
2.2, described these school districts as shifting from an "inputs-driven
accountability to an output-driven accountability. The change required

schools to get a specific percentage of students to pass a state assessment of reading, writing, and mathematics skills in order to maintain state accreditation."[91]

The Critics of Standards

Although standards-based reform has many advocates, there are some who think standards are bad for schools and students. The ideas of the most prominent of these critics, those whose books get wide media play, are considered herewith.

Deborah Meier: Institutionally Improper

In a recent symposium, Deborah Meier, an esteemed principal and school reformer, argued,

> Even in the hands of sincere allies of children, equity, and public education, the current push for [education standards] is fundamentally misguided. It will not help to develop young minds, contribute to a robust democratic life, or aid the most vulnerable of our fellow citizens. By shifting the locus of authority to outside bodies, it undermines the capacity of the schools to instruct by example in the qualities of mind that schools in a democracy should be fostering in kids—responsibility for one's own ideas, tolerance for the ideas of others, and a capacity to negotiate differences. Standardization instead turns teachers and parents into the local instruments of externally imposed expert judgement. It thus decreases the chances that young people will grow up in the midst of adults who are making hard decisions and exercising mature judgement in the face of disagreements.[92]

Clearly, Meier is unable to support these arguments with empirical data. Rather, this is a philosophical argument that holds that the education one receives will reflect the governance structure of the institution doing the educating. Schools with unitary, top-down management, presumably, will tend to turn out passive, obedient graduates, whereas schools with democratic governance will tend to create vigorous democrats.

It is an argument that is difficult to defend because there are so many examples that show the contrary. Most obviously, one may point to the system of schooling in France. In large part, it is centrally directed by a governmental agency (one far more imposing and powerful than any contemplated by standards advocates). It would require a considerable stretch of the imagination to view the French as suffering from inadequate democratic virtues due to schools' curricula being externally mandated.

Moreover, Meier's theory implicitly and explicitly holds that local control of schools, especially at the school level, is best for students. If pupils are to be in the presence of adults "making hard decisions," then teachers and administrators will have to have the power to decide what students study.[93] This school-level control, Meier thinks, will likely lead to better learning. Unfortunately, this approach has been tried in this country for over a century with less than impressive results. As the data in the previous portions of this chapter indicate, schools tend to lack academically rigorous curricula. They track students into vocational education and rudimentary coursework that does not appear to prepare them for vigorous civic life. The NAEP data in Chapter 1 showed that 77 percent of US high school seniors, who had or soon would have the right to vote, scored below the proficient level. Indeed, the entire point of externally mandating education standards came in response to the evidence that schools' freedom to set their own curricula has not resulted in academically proficient performance.

On the whole, Meier's argument ventures into perilous territory by extrapolating from her own successes as a school reformer at Central Park East in New York City and Mission Hills in Boston.[94] Through her stewardship, she created a couple of vibrant, high-achieving schools. This is commendable, but her model for reform is far-fetched insofar as it rests upon the assumption of an extraordinary person assuming the principalship of a school. What remains to be seen is whether Meier's successful schools will be successful after she passes from the scene. Do they have the institutional structures to continue to succeed? Or were their achievements mostly a function of Meier's talents? This most important question must be answered before policymakers ponder basing educational reform on Meier's philosophy.[95]

Alfie Kohn: Three Criticisms

Alfie Kohn has harshly criticized standards-based reform in myriad ways.[96] His criticisms, which are less theoretical than Meier's, can be boiled down to three main points.

First, "noninstructional factors explain most of the variance among test scores when schools or districts are compared."[97] Or, as Howard Gardner of the Harvard Graduate School of Education put it, "tell me the zip code of a child and I will predict her chances of college completion and probable income."[98] It is indisputable that demographic factors correlate strongly with educational success. It should be noted, though, that demography is not destiny and that research has shown that school qualities can alter academic achievement, either bettering student outcomes or worsening them.[99]

Though this point is worth remembering when pondering possible policies to raise educational achievement, it is largely irrelevant to the issue of establishing standards. The argument for raising education standards is an argument for using government power to improve government-funded schools. It is a question of improving the institutions for which government is directly responsible.[100] Government is obliged to see that they are operating as effectively as possible.

Kohn's second contention is that "standardized-test scores often measure superficial thinking."[101] This is not so much an objection to standards as it is about the means for assessing whether students are learning to the standards. This is a critical point, insofar as the entire operation of the system of feedback and self-correction described previously rests on accurate self-analysis. It is, though, a point decreasingly connected with the realities of testing. Recognizing the inadequacies of multiple-choice, rote memorization/recall standardized tests, test designers have designed increasingly sophisticated exams that demand critical thinking and conceptual understanding.

Kentucky, again, serves as an example of the possibilities for assessment. Kentucky uses multiple-choice exams, exams with constructed response questions, and student work portfolios to assess student learning, along with lab tests on subjects such as computer skills. Although states inevitably face a temptation to use only multiple-choice exams, which are less expensive and onerous to grade, better exams do exist, and there is no inherent reason why they cannot be utilized. In which case, Kohn's point serves more as a caution to policymakers than an objection to standards reform.

The third issue raised by Kohn concerns the effects that externally imposed testing can have upon curriculum. Specifically, he worries that classes and activities in the arts and electives might disappear because teachers will feel obliged to cut out those subjects that are not tested.[102] There is merit to this point. For example, researchers examining Kentucky's testing system (which tests students on different subjects at different grades, e.g., grades four and seven for writing, grade five for math, etc.), found that instructors tended to shift their classroom practices toward teaching the subjects that would be tested in the coming year.[103] Researchers found similar teacher behavior in Vermont after that state increased its testing and oversight of public-school results.[104]

However, again, this is more a caution against a possible side effect, one that might be seen as good or bad. And the solution to this problem would appear to lie within itself; namely, to prevent certain subjects from being deemphasized in the classroom (or emphasized evenly across grade levels), one could test all those subjects that are considered important on a yearly or nonstaggered bi-yearly basis.[105]

Susan Ohanian: One Size Fits Few

Susan Ohanian, a third-grade teacher and author of *One Size Fits Few*, is perhaps the most radical of all critics.[106] She argues, with little evidence, that "Standardistos" (those who favor creating education standards) are either part of the "military-industrial-infotainment complex" or are the useful idiots thereof. Standards are, at heart, an upper-class assault on the poor, whose children it hopes to drum out of the schools for failing to learn what a Mandarin class of standards setters say they should.[107] Setting aside these unsubstantiated ad hominem attacks, one does find that Ohanian has touched upon an important point: How does one reconcile the notion that all students should learn to the standards with the brute fact of student intellectual diversity? Ohanian prefers that teachers be given nearly total freedom to teach as they deem fit, to devise "oddball [schooling] plans . . . for oddball students."[108] She speaks with some pride that as a youngster, she did not have a curriculum so rigorous as those proposed by "Standardistos." Teachers taught her to knit, sing, and play the harmonica.[109]

Clearly, not all students can learn to the same high standards. Some suffer from severe mental, physical, or psychological problems. Obviously, exceptions ought to be made for these students, and doing so will no doubt involve some very complex decisions. However, where Ohanian errs is in underestimating the percentage of those students who are incapable of learning to high standards. Though she does not provide a number, the title of her book shows she thinks it is a minority (*One Size Fits Few*). Lacking data to support this claim, Ohanian's argument folds in the presence of the evidence cited earlier—James Coleman's Catholic schools study, the effective schools research, and the other studies of high-performing, impoverished schools. Furthermore, Chicago and a number of other cities exhibit possible options for handling students who are not disabled but are learning far less than their peers. Students who fail their competency exams due to disciplinary difficulties may be sent to special academies where they will receive extra assistance.

In short, then, as is often the case in public policy, the gulf between the position of Ohanian and those who favor standards ultimately is a matter of differing estimates of human capability.[110] Ohanian believes that only a few students are capable of learning to high standards and experiencing upward social mobility; the rest, she is confident, will become "chefs, plumbers, childcare workers," and so forth and should be educated for such.[111] Supporters of high standards believe otherwise, and the evidence favors them.

Linda Darling-Hammond: Teachers Know Best

Ensconcing education standards in an agency outside schools does amount, in some sense, to "telling teachers what to do."[112] Linda Darling-Hammond, who has criticized education standards on numerous grounds, takes particular issue with this.[113] Standards are belied by a "flawed assumption of hierarchical knowledge." By this Darling-Hammond appears to mean two things: that it is impossible to ever set down in print one set of knowledge that all students must possess, and that those who would create such standards are ipso facto removed from classrooms and in some way lacking the "street-level knowledge" of individual students required to teach children successfully.

Darling-Hammond's position on the subject of standards appears to be founded on a "constructivist" theory that children "construct knowledge in highly contextualized ways based on their diverse, culturally grounded experiences." Thus, "teaching must be highly adaptive, and curriculum must allow for many starting points and pathways." Moreover, knowledge is deeply intertwined with emotions, and so in some sense, individuals cannot be taught the truth but rather must construct it for themselves. Teachers, by virtue of being in the classroom and having the most knowledge (beyond parents) about individual children, then, are the best equipped to decide what students should learn, how, and how quickly. So good policy, according to Darling-Hammond, is not to set obligatory education standards but to provide teachers with more resources, training, and support. This will lead to better learning.

Darling-Hammond's position is a strange blend of the radical and the conservative in support of the status quo. Speaking to her second argument, which is conservative, in crafting education standards, policymakers are indeed making judgments as to what a child must learn and at what rate. It is only sensible that those who draft standards consult teachers and look to other nations' education standards, such as Japan's, for guidance. Teachers are aware of more of the nuances of the classroom than are policy analysts and politicians. However, Darling-Hammond provides no evidence to bolster the conservative, antistatist notion that government, be it state or national, is in some way inherently incompetent to craft standards. There is, of course, a possibility that once crafted, standards may become calcified and fail to evolve with the times. Rather than risk this possibility, though, Darling-Hammond seems to argue that it is best for government to not bother to try.[114]

Her second argument, that there "is no one curriculum Truth with a capital T that is waiting to be discovered and codified into a single set of guidelines superior to all others for all contexts and learning circumstances," is a canard.[115] Standards, while inherently embodying certain value claims as to what is important to learn, have not been pushed as a once-and-for-all answer to any questions about what children learn; nor are they hyper-prescriptive as Darling-Hammond makes them out to be. Standards do not describe how teachers can teach their children in "all contexts and learning circumstances." Standards explain what students should know and be able to do at the end of each grade level and then leave it to schools and teachers to devise the best techniques to get students there. But even this more restricted definition of standards appears offensive to Darling-Hammond's theory. Since there is "no one curriculum Truth," standards, by virtue of embodying certain values, are antidemocratic because they force values upon students instead of allowing them to construct their own knowledge. This is her radicalism, and it amounts to a claim that policymaking in education must be value neutral with respect to what students learn. This has educational implications that seem unlikely to be popular: neither states nor the federal government can specify what students should learn—not even schools. Only teachers, as leaders of small "democratic communities," would get to decide what parents' children are to be taught.

This policy prescription offends common sense insofar as it essentially asks the policymakers and the public to provide more funds for schools, and to simply trust teachers to do a better job. If, say, English teachers decide that grammar is not to be emphasized in the curriculum (as their professional group, the National Council of Teachers of English, did), their "expertise" is to be respected.[116] In short, Darling-Hammond essentially asks that the current unaccountable system be left as it is and for all of us to hope things get better.[117]

Peter Sacks: Standards Don't Work

In his 1999 polemic against standardized testing and the educational accountability movement, *Standardized Minds*, Peter Sacks attempts to demonstrate that the notion that standards and greater school accountability will mean high achievement is a "myth."[118] Utilizing an inventory of state assessment programs by the Council of Chief State School Officers (CCSSO) along with state scores on the NAEP state math and science exams for eighth-graders, Sacks teases out an interesting coincidence: states that test heavily tend to score lowest on the NAEP exams whereas states with low-stakes testing programs or no testing at all score better.[119]

It is an astonishing result, but it is not to be believed. There are a host of methodological problems. To begin, Sacks does not explain why he limited his test data to only science and math scores for eighth-graders. Much more data were available from NAEP, but it was not utilized. Moreover, the study Sacks cites only records how frequently states test their students. It does not inquire whether states have created the other components of the accountability system, that is, whether state tests and standards are aligned or if states have even created good standards. Sacks also fails to control for socioeconomic variables. An affluent state with less frequent testing (such as Delaware, where students score fairly well) is compared with poor states with more frequent testing (West Virginia and Louisiana). Only after presenting his analysis does Sacks note that "dozens of factors can influence any state's relative performance on the NAEP assessments, including population size, its relative income and education levels, [and] the number of residents living in poverty." He then dismisses this as irrelevant and writes:

> The larger point is the reductionist perspective of the reform crusaders in placing so much importance on testing and accountability, as the means to improve education, completely ignores this more complex and difficult reality. Indeed, as the evidence indicates, focusing exclusively on measurement and accountability may have precisely the opposite intended outcomes.

Setting aside the canards ("focusing exclusively . . .") and the sloppy social science, Sacks's argument is patently fallacious.[120] Sacks attempts to prove that standards-based reform does not raise achievement. To do this, one must at minimum determine which states or districts have undertaken standards reform, and then examine the changes in test scores since reform. This may show the policy effects. Sacks's analysis does not do this, and by design it cannot show the effects of standards reform. His effort is the analytical equivalent of measuring the temperatures in an igloo and a room in southern New Mexico in July that just had an air conditioner installed, finding that the igloo is cooler, and concluding that air conditioners do not cool rooms.

States' Failure to Establish High Standards

Upon reading the preceding, one might agree that standards are wise policy but ask, "What about federalism? Why does the federal government have to get involved? Why not let states raise standards themselves?" The answer is that states have had decades if not centuries to raise standards, and they have, for the most part, not done well.

The Tradition of No or Low Standards

Historically, federal and state policymakers have

> delegated authority over public education to local school districts, particularly in matters of curriculum and instruction. Districts have further entrusted the curriculum to teachers or text book publishers, and have done little to provide or develop instructional guidelines. . . . What little direction states or districts have provided has often been limited to listings of course requirements or behavioral objectives. Few states have prescribed the content of courses or curricula, and even fewer have provided instructional guidance.[121]

This allowed individual schools great freedom in determining the rigor of the education students must master to progress through the grades toward a high school diploma. Unfortunately, the result was a curriculum that during the twentieth century decreasingly emphasized academics.[122] Students, especially at the high school level, were given greater and greater sway in selecting their courses. For example, at the beginning of the 1980s, the only specific course-taking requirements that California students had to meet to receive their diploma were two years of physical education. The rest were electives.[123] "No state required foreign language study for high school graduation, and most states required only one year each of science and mathematics," and "learning to cook or drive often garnered as much credit toward graduation as chemistry or history."[124] Even now, more states have physical education courses (29) than algebra (13) or biology (8) as a graduation requirement.[125] Moreover, surveys to this day indicate that teachers' expectations as to what students should know and their competence differs markedly from the opinions of employers and college professors. Teachers generally expect less.[126]

Then there is the long-existent problem of tracking students. Through both the judgments of teachers and scores on standardized tests, students have been divided into groups: the few who are talented and pushed toward college preparatory courses, and the rest, who are steered into less academically rigorous classes and vocational education.[127] Researchers have found that all too often teachers' "estimates of [students'] native ability . . . have closely matched the income and educational background of their parents," the effect being a "vast sorting system" based on race and class.[128] Thus, black, Hispanic, and low-income children are more intensely affected by low education standards, being placed in non-college preparatory and vocational coursework much more frequently than other students even when capable of taking more rigorous courses.[129] For example,

> Hispanic students are more often than not tracked into general courses that satisfy only the basic requirements and not those that provide access to four-year colleges or to rigorous technical schools. More Hispanic students (50%) are enrolled in general programs of study than either whites (39%) or blacks (40%). Only 35% of Latino students are enrolled in college preparatory or academic programs, compared to 50% of whites and 43% of blacks.[130]

In the late 1970s and early 1980s, legislatures acted to raise educational achievement in public high schools. As part of this "back to basics" movement, as it is often called, elected officials pressured state departments of education to raise the number of academic courses students had to take to graduate and instituted "minimum competency testing," which required students to pass norm-referenced exams to proceed to higher grade levels and graduate.[131] The results of this policy were mixed. Florida, for example, saw positive results. As more and more of its minority students were required to enroll in and pass academic courses, the rate at which they passed their graduation exams on the first attempt soared. In 1977, 23 percent of blacks passed on the first try. By 1984, over 60 percent did.[132]

Unfortunately, evidence began to mount that the emphasis on the basics helped those pupils who were doing the worst in schools, but did little for the majority who already knew the basics but weren't being taught more advanced materials.[133] Thus far, state-level development and implementation of standards has been slow and problematic.[134] States first endeavored to establish curricular frameworks, which would more generally clarify the subject matters to be studied and the levels of mastery students were to gain to progress through grade levels, and which would lay the foundation for creating more explicit education standards. By 1995, a study of twenty-eight states found only fifteen had created framework documents that either "present[ed] higher standards or assist[ed] local districts and schools to meet national standards" in math and science as Goals 2000 urged and the 1994 reauthorization of Title I required. Moreover, these framework documents varied greatly in length, with math frameworks ranging from thirteen pages (Wyoming) to 339 (Wisconsin), indicating that states were having difficulty discerning what a framework is and how descriptive and prescriptive it should be.[135]

The standards themselves were lenient. In 1996, Mark Musick, president of the Southern Regional Education Board (SREB), compared the percentages of seventh- and eighth-grade students scoring at the proficient level on state tests (e.g., meeting state standards) in the 1994–1995 school year to the percentages of those scoring at the proficient level on NAEP in 1992.[136] From a social scientific perspective, it was a crude comparison. But it illuminated the disparity in performance standards between states (see Table 2.2).

Georgia claimed that 83 percent of its seventh- and eighth-graders were performing adequately in math, but only 16 percent were found to be at or above proficiency on the NAEP exam. Louisiana and Oklahoma also claimed vast majorities of students meeting state standards, yet only 10 percent of Louisiana's eighth-graders and 21 percent of Oklahoma's scored at the proficient level or better. Musick found similar disparities when he compared reading scores for third- and fourth-graders (e.g., the percentage of students meeting Tennessee's reading standards was 62 percent whereas 27 percent met the standard of NAEP).

Subsequent studies of state education standards have supported Musick's findings. In 1998 the American Federation of Teachers, the Council for Basic Education, and the Thomas B. Fordham Foundation all published analyses of state education standards. There was some disagree-

Table 2.2   Students Meeting State Standards vs. NAEP Standards

State	Percent of Students Meeting State Proficiency Standards, 1994–1995	Percent of Eighth-Grade Students Meeting NAEP Standards, 1992
Connecticut	47	30
Delaware	13	18
Georgia	83	16
Illinois	83	N/A
Kentucky	29	26
Louisiana	80 (7th grade)	10
Maryland	48	24
Michigan	55 (7th grade)	23
New Jersey	39	28
North Carolina	68	15
Oklahoma	70	21
Oregon	84	N/A
South Carolina	68	18

Source: Mark Musick, *Setting Standards High Enough,* 1996.

ment among them as to what constituted a clear and challenging academic standard.[137] However, all three studies concluded that most states lacked clear, rigorous academic standards and assessments that: (1) provided guidance to teachers; and (2) could be used to create aligned examinations for measuring how well students are learning to standards. In summation:

- The American Federation of Teachers found that only nineteen states had standards that are "generally clear and specific and grounded in particular content."[138]
- The Council for Basic Education counted seven states with very rigorous standards in English-language arts and sixteen states with very rigorous standards in mathematics.[139]
- The Thomas B. Fordham Foundation study cumulatively rated state standards a D (on an A to F grading scale).[140]

In reviewing the data of the three studies, Achieve Inc., a nonprofit corporation created to benchmark standards, concluded that "when one looks at both the curriculum standards and the tests states are using to measure those standards, the states presently do not share a rigorous common core of expectations for their students."[141]

Despite the struggles, states have made progress in the past few years. In 2001, *Education Week* reported that forty-seven states had adopted standards for English, math, social studies, and science.[142] All fifty states now test their students in one or more subject areas. The American Federation of Teachers' most recent rating of state standards (2001) also finds improvement. Twenty-nine states have "clear and specific standards" in English, mathematics, social studies, and science.[143] In terms of the rigor of state standards, though, the picture is less rosy. The Thomas B. Fordham Foundation's rating of state standards showed that states have improved their standards. Nineteen states earned A's for their English standards, and eighteen did for their mathematics standards, up from six and twelve, respectively, in 1998. Still, state standards across the nation collectively earned a C–.[144] The American Federation of Teachers notes that social studies standards "remain weak across the states" and that "these standards tend to lack specific reference to United States and/or world history."[145]

In view of the absence of clearly articulated high education standards, it is not surprising that US public school curricula are unfocused, repetitious, and more rudimentary than those of many other nations.[146] A study of US school math curricula compared to nineteen other nations, titled *The Underachieving Curriculum*, declared, "In school mathematics the United States is an underachieving nation, and our curriculum is helping to create a nation of underachievers. We are not what we ought to be; we are not even close to what we can be."[147] In looking for the causes for American 12-year-olds' low math scores relative to other nations, this study's researchers noted that neither the backgrounds of the children, student attitudes, class size, nor teacher preparation or training were to blame. Instead,

> the culprit that seems to be central to the problems of school mathematics is the curriculum. . . . Content is spread throughout the curriculum in a way that leads to very few topics being intensely pursued. Goals and expectations for learning are diffuse and unfocused. Content and goals linger from year to year so that curricula are driven and shaped by still unmastered mathematics content begun years before.[148]

Almost a decade later, a review of the 1996 TIMSS math and science curriculum studies echoed *The Underachieving Curriculum*'s conclusion:

> Geometry is almost never taught at Grade 8. In fact, the content covered in eighth-grade mathematics classes in the U.S. is generally covered in the seventh-grade in other countries. Accordingly, U.S. mathematics textbooks cover less demanding content than German and Japanese textbooks, which devote more space to algebra and geometry. In addition to being less challenging, the U.S. curriculum sacrifices depth for breadth . . . [and this] weakness is reflected in classroom practice.[149]

Furthermore, a recent study found that one reason there has been so much remediation among first-year college students (as noted in Chapter 1) is that high school coursework in English and other major subject areas is not as demanding as it ought be, leaving students unprepared for the work they face in college.[150] When in 1994 the federal government examined the course transcripts of 25,575 high school graduates, it found that only three out of fifty states required graduates to study more than two years of math.[151] This review also found that more than a third of graduates did not take a full course in basic algebra, and only about one in eight took trigonometry. On the whole, just ten states required students to master tenth-grade material in order to graduate from high school.[152]

Even students, it appears, realize that public schools typically are not particularly demanding of them. Almost three-quarters of high school students confessed that they would pay more attention in class were there higher graduation requirements and graduation examinations. More than 60 percent said that they could do better in school if they tried harder, and nearly 80 percent declared that they would learn more were they required to show up to class on time and turn in their homework more often.[153]

With standards, an accountable system of feedback and self-analysis and correction is possible; without them, all parties involved—students, teachers, administrators, parents, and policymakers—are in the dark. Discerning whether grades are honest assessments of exhibited student achievement is difficult, as is assessing the efficacy of teachers. In short, there is an information shortage that inhibits efforts to improve schooling and achievement.[154]

This is, for the most part, the case at present. State school systems, as presently constituted, do not have clear feedback and resource allocation systems like the one described earlier. Some have argued that this lack of accountability is a conspiracy carried out by unionized teachers.[155] Others have argued that it is the result of a lack of competition and organizational disorganization or that it was a mix of the cultural and conspiratorial: the teachers, dominated by anti-intellectuals, resist having their work assessed because they fear they will be exposed.[156] Other research would suggest that pubic schools' lack of accountability might be the legacy of the early idea that educators are above politics, that they should not be held accountable by the public or politicians lest they be improperly influenced.[157] Thus, each teacher, to a great degree, has been permitted to teach what he or she pleases.[158]

Regardless of the root causes, the reality is clear: most states do not have clear, high standards that establish what students ought to know and be able to do. This leaves states without a coherent system of self-analysis and self-correction. "[D]espite the prominence of standards-based reform in the policy debate, there are few examples of districts or states that have put the entire standards-based puzzle together, much less achieved success through it."[159] Thus, states' assessments tend to be unaligned with what is being taught in classrooms. One study of teaching and state exams in ten states reports that coincidence between the two varied from 5 to 46 percent.[160] Another study of four states' assessments and standards found that alignment between assessments and standards "varied across grade levels, content areas, and states without any discernible pattern." It further revealed that "generally, assessment items required a lower level of knowledge and did not span the full spectrum of knowledge as expressed in the standards."[161] No state reported relying entirely or even mostly on criterion-referenced exams that were aligned with state standards.[162] Worse, only twenty-two states have accountability systems that hold poor and minority students (who are in Title I schools) to the same standards as all other pupils.[163]

Logically, without standards and assessments aligned thereto, states have struggled to create linkages between student learning and governmental policy and self-correction. Thus:

- In a 1995 survey of the assessment divisions of state education departments, just two reported that low student test scores had any consequences for school staffs. A 1999–2000 study found that only seventeen states hold school districts accountable for student performance on examinations. Nineteen states have policies to intervene and reconstitute persistently failing schools.[164]
- Only twenty states have the authority to impose penalties on schools for repeatedly posting low test scores; fewer exercise it.[165]
- High standards have not reached most classrooms. A survey of fourth- and eighth-grade teachers indicates that most do not have high expectations for students. Surveys of student estimates of teacher academic demands find similarly.[166]

A recent examination of state standards and accountability found that few states have high-quality standards and that states' standards-based accountability systems remain underdeveloped and of unimpressive quality.[167]

Conclusion

In the 1980s, research began to show that some schools were able to reform themselves. Research by Ronald Edmonds and others showed that schools with strong leadership and rigorous academic standards were able to educate all pupils at high levels.[168] Typically, these great reform stories centered on great men and women assuming principalships and enacting these reforms. Though inspiring, this is not a formula for widespread reform. Great principals and miracle workers are inevitably in short supply.

To get around this problem, policymakers must refashion the school systems through legislation. Through systemic reform, founded upon high academic standards and accompanying accountability tools, policymakers can encourage and coerce students, teachers, principals, and administrators to do better. The underperforming, unaccountable school can be replaced by schools that have to answer to state officials and the public about their record in educating children.

The evidence indicates that this approach is working. The coincidence between creating high academic standards and subsequently rising test scores is striking. There are examples of this happening at the school, district, and state levels. Intuitively, establishing clear academic standards that explain what students should know makes sense, and where this has been done the results on student achievement have been positive.

Public opinion stands strongly in favor of standards reform generally, and the American public are largely in favor of federal action to do so. In light of this, then, one can envision what the United States ought to have: high-quality national education standards and aligned examinations for all grade levels. States that wanted to partake of federal school aid would be obliged to implement the national standards and assessments. The federal government would monitor state compliance by periodically reviewing state examinations in order to see if they embody the national standards.

How would the national standards be created? Perhaps, legislation could be passed that would provide for the following: a caucus of teachers, university scholars, parents, and other stakeholders would be gathered to sketch out national standards for all grade levels. Once this framework is devised, educators and scholars could draft the actual standards. Both the caucus and a joint congressional committee could review the standards to ensure that they are appropriate and then vote them up or down. If approved, the standards become the national standards. All this seems so logical.[169] So, why has this not happened?

Chapters 3 through 5 explain why, despite the attractiveness of education standards, the federal government has made ineffective rather than effective standards policy and has only done so recently. The politics surrounding the efforts to make standards policy are situated within the context of previous political debates on federal education policy, revealing a troubling paradox: despite the likely efficacy of standards reform, politics has kept congressmen and presidents from making good standards policy.

Notes

1. Kearns and Harvey, *A Legacy of Learning*, pp. 9–17; Goldberg, "Education and the Economy," pp. 9–16.

2. Molnar writes, "The surging economy of the 1990s suggests either that American public education improved dramatically during the 1990s or that the link between schooling and the economy described in *A Nation at Risk* is spurious." Molnar, "Comment," p. 102.

3. Hanushek, "The Seeds of Growth," *Education Next*, p. 11.

4. Schultz, "Capital Formation by Education," pp. 571–583; Denison, "The Sources of Economic Growth in the United States and the Alternatives Before Us"; and Jorgenson and Griliches, "The Explanation of Productivity Change," pp. 249–283.

5. Nye Jr., "Limits of American Power," p. 555; and Kindleberger, *Economic Response*, pp. 185–236.

6. Barton, *What Jobs Require*.

7. Public Agenda and Education Week, *Reality Check 2002*. See also *Reality Check 2001*.

8. National Commission on the High School Senior Year, *Raising Our Sights*; and Olson, "K–12 and College Expectations Often Fail to Mesh."

9. As quoted in Mollison, "US Falling Behind in Educating Workers." Hanushek comes to a similar conclusion; see Hanushek, "The Seeds of Growth," pp. 10–17.

10. Goldin, "The Human Capital Century," pp. 73–78.

11. Almond and Verba, *The Civic Culture*; and Gutmann, *Democratic Education*.

12. Thus, the American Council of Trustees and Alumni's recent report, *Losing America's Memory, Historical Illiteracy in the 21st Century*. They discovered that graduates from elite US colleges tend to be ignorant of much of early US history, especially history that centered on the founding of the United States and the nature of republican government.

13. Ravitch, "Dumbing Down the Public: Why It Matters," *Hoover Institution Online*.

14. Delli Carpini and Keeter, *What American Know About Politics and Why It Matters*, p. 8.

15. On the relationship between political knowledge and participation, see Milner, *Civic Literacy*, pp. 38–50.

16. Viteritti, *Choosing Equality*, p. 180.

17. Greenwood, "New Developments in the Intergenerational Impact of Education," pp. 503–511.

18. The literature is voluminous; for an introduction see Jencks and Phillips, eds., *The Black-White Test Score Gap*.

19. Wolfe and Zuvekas, "Nonmarket Outcomes of Schooling," pp. 491–501.

20. Day and Curry, *Educational Attainment in the United States: March 1998 Update*, p. 1. See also Hall, *Investment in Education: Private and Public Returns*.

21. There has also been debate as to the degree to which schooling acts as a sorting mechanism, channeling the most able students into further learning and economic success and the less able into remedial classes and ultimately lower economic classes. For an antisorting position, see Nie et al., *Education and Democratic Citizenship in America*; for the schooling as sorting position, Verba et al., *Voice and Equality: Civic Voluntarism in American Politics*.

22. For a review, see Ashenfelter and Rouse, "Schooling, Intelligence, and Income in America: Cracks in the Bell Curve." In the late 1970s, Jencks and a team of researchers found that four years of high school likely had the effect of raising a future adult's income 15 to 25 percent, and four years of college could be expected

to raise income 30 to 40 percent. As "past research has generally concluded," when "an individual first enters the labor market, the highest grade of school or college he has completed is the best single predictor of his eventual occupational status." Jencks et al., *Who Gets Ahead? The Determinates of Economic Success in America*, pp. 188–189, 223–224. Twenty years later, further research has reached similar conclusions. Jencks and Phillips, "Aptitude or Achievement: Why Do Test Scores Predict Educational Attainment and Earnings?" and Winship and Korenman, "Economic Success and the Evolution of Schooling and Mental Ability."

23. *NAEP 1996 Trends in Academic Progress*, pp. xiv–xv, 13–15, 62–64, 112–114, 160–162; and Thernstrom and Thernstrom, *America in Black and White: One Nation Indivisible*, p. 19.

24. Viteritti, *Choosing Equality*; and Grubb, "Reducing Inequality Through Education: Millennial Resolutions."

25. Immerwahr and Johnson, *Americans' Views on Standards*, p. 8.

26. Phi Kappa Delta, *The 29th Annual Phi Delta Kappa/Gallup Poll of the Public's Attitudes Toward Public Schools*.

27. Elam, *How America Views Its Schools: The PDK/Gallup Polls, 1969–1994*, p. 13.

28. Lake Snell Perry with Deardourff, "Report on Findings from Seven Focus Groups," p. 42.

29. "Schools Rank First as Spending Priority,"*New York Times*, editorial, p. B8.

30. NEA/Greenberg Quinlan Research, *Education Poll*, February 2000.

31. Polling data provided by Gallup.

32. E.g., Free and Cantril, *The Political Beliefs of Americans*.

33. Elam, *How America Views Its Schools: The PDK/Gallup Polls, 1969–1994*, p. 21.

34. Public Education Network, Education Week, *Accountability for All: What Voters Want from Education Candidates*.

35. Diagnostic, as opposed to punitive (using test scores to punish students, teachers, etc.). Traub, "The Class War over School Testing"; Public Agenda and Education Week, *Reality Check 2002*; Hoff, "Polls Dispute a 'Backlash' to Standards," pp. 1, 16.

36. Immerwahr and Johnson, *Americans' Views on Standards*, pp. 3–4.

37. A Public Agenda poll in 1996 found 61 percent of Americans agreeing that "academic standards are too low and kids are not expected to learn enough." Ibid., p. 8. In a January 2000 poll by the National Education Association, some 65 percent of citizens polled said that a "lack of academic standards for promotion and graduation" posed a "very big" or "serious" problem. NEA/Greenburg Quinlan Research, February 2000. Since 1970, no less than 69 percent of those polled favored requiring the public schools in their community to use national standardized tests to measure student achievement. Hochschild and Scott, "The Polls' Trends: Governance and Reform of Public Education in the United States," p. 79. When asked if they would support "having students pass an academic examination in order to graduate from high school," since April 1976, 65 percent or more of those polled responded "yes." In 1996, 67 percent favored a national graduation examination. Ibid., p. 79. See also *The 29th Annual Phi Delta Kappa/Gallup Poll of the Public's Attitudes Toward the Public Schools*. Public Agenda's study of citizens' attitudes toward national education standards and assessments found that 65 percent of those polled felt the children in their community should be required to pass standardized tests to be promoted from grade to grade. Immerwahr and Johnson,

Americans' Views on Standards, p. 9. When told that any policy change may require higher taxes and then asked if they favored "instituting national standardized testing" in their community to improve schools, 71 percent of those polled favored the idea. Gallup Poll for *Life* magazine. All Gallup polling data provided to author by Gallup.

38. "Opportunity-to-learn" standards will be addressed in Chapter 7.

39. See, for example, Linn, "Assessments and Accountability," pp. 8–10; and Smith and O'Day, "Systemic School Reform."

40. Public Agenda, *Survey Finds Little Sign of Backlash Against Academic Standards or Standardized Tests.*

41. These "opportunity-to-learn standards" are addressed in Chapter 7.

42. Tucker and Codding, *Standards for Our Schools*, pp. 76–77; see also the literature review in Lee and Smith, "Social Support and Achievement for Young Adolescents in Chicago: The Role of School Academic Press."

43. Porter, "External Standards and Good Teaching: The Pros and Cons of Telling Teachers What to Do," p. 343.

44. Controlled for demographics, studies have found that students taking more challenging courses than their peers later see higher scores on tests. See Porter, "The Effects of Upgrading Policies on High School Mathematics and Science"; Girotto and Peterson, "Do Hard Courses and Good Grades Enhance Cognitive Skills?"

45. Public Agenda and Education Week, *Reality Check 2002*, p. S2.

46. Wixson and Dutro, "Standards for Primary-Grade Reading: An Analysis of State Frameworks," p. 3.

47. Accountability is the relationship between two parties where one party is expected by the other to perform a task, and said task performer's work can be assessed for adequacy.

48. On systemic reform, see Smith and O'Day, "Systemic School Reform."

49. Assessments also provide information to the public, which can serve to encourage improved results through embarrassment for low scores or accolades for good scores.

50. Consortium for Policy Research in Education, "Putting the Pieces Together"; Newmann, "Beyond Common Sense in Educational Restructuring," pp. 4–13, 22; and Spillane, "State Policy and the Non-Monolithoic Nature of the Local School District: Organizational and Professional Considerations," pp. 35–63. Clarity of mission, not surprisingly, "has been identified as an important factor in defining effective schools"; see Lee and Smith, "Social Support and Achievement for Young Adolescents in Chicago," p. 912. Industrial psychologist Mason Ahire noted, "What gets measured gets done. If you are looking for quick ways to change how an organization behaves, change the measurement system." Quoted in Lynch and Cross, *Measure Up!* p. 144.

51. E.g., Izumi, *They Have Overcome*; Reid, "From Worst to First"; and Viadero, "Against Odds, School Propels Its Students to College."

52. Tucker and Codding, *Standards for Our Schools*, p. 71.

53. Carter, *No Excuses: Lessons from 21 High-Performing, High-Poverty Schools*, pp. 7–9.

54. Barte et al., eds., *Dispelling the Myth: High Poverty Schools Exceeding Expectations*, p. 2.

55. As cited in Elmore and Rothman, eds., *Testing, Teaching, and Learning*, p. 19. See also Calwelti and Protheroe, *High Student Achievement: How Six School Districts Changed into High-Performance Systems.*

56. Zernicke, "In Two Years, Mt. Vernon Test Scores Turn Around."

57. Schmidt et al., *Why Schools Matter*.

58. The effect was mostly indirect; government-prescribed standards affected the content of school textbooks, which in turn greatly influence what teachers teach. Ibid., pp. 353–357, quotes at 355 and 357. On textbooks' influence on teaching, see National Science Foundation, *Decade of Achievement*.

59. See, for example, Achieve, Inc., *Three Paths, One Destination*.

60. For an early descriptive study of Kentucky's reforms, see Lusi, *The Role of State Departments of Education in Complex School Reform*, chapter 3.

61. *Rose v. the Council for Better Education, Inc.*, KY, 790 SW 2d 186 (1989).

62. KERA, it must also be noted, included other important reforms, such as the equalization of per-pupil funding and the rooting out of corruption and misuse of funds. See Kentucky Department of Education, *Results Matter: A Decade of Difference in Kentucky's Public Schools 1990–2000*, pp. vii–viii.

63. Koretz et al., *The Perceived Effects of the Kentucky Instructional Results Information System (KIRIS)*.

64. Tucker and Codding, *Standards for Our Schools*, p. 137.

65. Stecher et al., *The Effects of Standards-Based Assessment on Classroom Practices*; see also McDonnell and Choisser, *Testing and Teaching*.

66. Stecher and Barron, *Quadrennial Milepost Accountability Testing in Kentucky*.

67. Although 1999 scores are available, due to the switch to CATS and alterations to the exams, the scores are not strictly comparable to those from the earlier KIRIS years. Though devised in 1998, CATS did not replace KIRIS until 1999. Kentucky Department of Education, *Results Matter*, pp. 14–15.

68. Viadero, "Schooled Out of Poverty," pp. 35–41.

69. Kentucky Department of Education, *Results Matter*, p. 83; Wise, *Impact of Exclusion Rates on NAEP 1994 to 1988 Grade Four Reading Gains in Kentucky*; see also NAEP data at http://nces.ed.gov/nationsreportcard/states.

70. Blackford, "Kentucky Test Scores Improve to US Average."

71. Kentucky Department of Education, *Results Matter*, pp. 83–84.

72. Haney, "The Texas Miracle in Education." Though tougher than the previous exams, the TEKS exams are not especially challenging. See Clopton, "Texas Mathematics Education in Transition," pp. 49–66. In 2002–2003, a new assessment system was rolled out: TAKS (Texas Assessment of Knowledge and Skills). "As mandated by the 76th Texas Legislature in 1999 . . . TAKS measures the statewide curriculum in reading at Grades 3–9; in writing at Grades 4 and 7; in English Language Arts at Grades 10 and 11; in mathematics at Grades 3–11; in science at Grades 5, 10, and 11; and social studies at Grades 8, 10, and 11. The Spanish TAKS is administered at Grades 3 through 6. Satisfactory performance on the TAKS at Grade 11 is prerequisite to a high school diploma." As quoted on the Texas Education Agency website at http://www.tea.state.tx.us/student.assessment/.

73. American Federation of Teachers, *Making Standards Matter, 1998*, p. 91; Joftus and Berman, *Great Expectations?* p. 35; Finn and Petrilli, eds., *The State of State Standards 2000*, p. 3.

74. Texas Education Agency, http://www.tea.state.tx.us/teks/.

75. All data drawn from Texas Education Agency webpage at http://www.tea.state.tx.us/student.assessment/reporting/.

76. Johnson, "In Texas District, Test Scores for Minority Students Have Soared," pp. 14–15. See also Just for Kids, *Promising Practices*, pp. 7–8.

77. Hannaway and McKay, "Taking Measures," pp. 9–12.

78. Haney, "The Texas Miracle in Education."

79. Greene, "The Texas Reform Miracle Is for Real," p. 78.

80. Viadero, "Testing System in Texas Yet to Get the Final Grade," pp. 1, 20–21. For Haney's views, see Haney, "The Texas Miracle in Education."

81. Viadero, "Testing System in Texas Yet to Get the Final Grade," pp. 20–21.

82. On the softness of the Texas state assessments, see http://www. educationnews.org.

83. Schemo and Fessenden, "Gains in Houston: How Real Are They?"

84. Ibid.

85. Grissmer and Flanagan, *Exploring Rapid Achievement Gains in North Carolina and Texas*; and Grissmer et al., *Improving Student Achievement*.

86. Grissmer and Flanagan, *Exporing Rapid Achievement*, pp. 14–16, 19–21. Texas eighth-graders recorded large gains on the 2000 NAEP mathematics assessment and showed the most progress in shrinking the black-white test score gap. On the 1998 NAEP writing assessment, "Black eighth-graders outscored White students in seven states—a first"; see Achieve, Inc., *Aiming Higher: Meeting the Challenges of Education Reform in Texas*, p. 37.

87. Skrla et al., *Equity-Driven, Achievement-Focused School Districts: A Report on Systemic School Successes in Four Texas School Districts Serving Diverse Student Populations*.

88. Ibid., p. 1.

89. Ibid.

90. Ibid., p. 7.

91. Ibid., p. 6.

92. Meier, "Educating a Democracy: Standards and the Future of Public Education."

93. Ibid., pp. 8–9.

94. Meier explicitly cites her work at these schools on page 7 of her essay as an example of the right sort of school reform.

95. The question of how to structure an institution so that it may outlive its great leader is an old one, and the wise answer to this question has been: create good structures that uphold the critical qualities of the institution. See, for example, Niccolo Machiavelli, *The Prince*, chapter xxv; and Macchiavelli, *The Discourses*, book III, 9.

96. Kohn, *The Case Against Standardized Testing*.

97. Kohn, "Standardized Testing and Its Victims."

98. Gardner, "Paroxsyms of Choice," p. 49.

99. See the effective schools and the studies on standards cited earlier. On the successes of Catholic schools to educate the poor and minorities of this country, see Coleman et al., *High School Achievement*.

100. In simple terms, there are institutional and noninstitutional factors that affect student learning. Institutional factors include the quality of curriculum, teachers, and pedagogical equipment. Noninstitutional factors are those outside the school (e.g., sociological, economic, cultural, parental, etc.). For an introduction to this subject, see Barton, *Parsing the Achievement Gap*.

101. Kohn, "Standardized Testing and Its Victims."

102. Ibid.

103. Stecher, "Consequences of Large-Scale, High-Stakes Testing on School and Classroom Practice," pp. 79–100; Stecher and Barron, *Quadrennial Milepost Accountability Testing in Kentucky*.

104. Stecher and Mitchell, *Portfolio-Driven Reform*. McNeil's case study of three magnet high schools in Houston, Texas, reports that teachers in these schools began focusing their class time on test preparation. McNeil, *Contradictions of School Reform: Educational Costs of Standardized Testing*.

105. Stecher and Barron, *Quadrennial Milepost Accountability Testing in Kentucky*, p. 34.

106. Ohanian, *One Size Fits Few*.

107. Ibid., pp. 3, 6, 12.

108. Ibid., p. 2.

109. Ibid., p. 25.

110. On estimates of human capacity and public policy prescriptions, see Mead, *The New Politics of Poverty*.

111. She repeatedly scoffs at the quadratic equation and the notion that all students should understand the quadratic equation and utilize it in order to graduate, e.g., p. 3.

112. Porter, "External Standards and Good Teaching," pp. 343–356.

113. Including that standards and tests cannot drive schools to reform, a critical assertion that Texas and Kentucky have shown to be untrue. For the quotations in this paragraph and those following, see Darling-Hammond, "National Standards and Assessments: Will They Improve Education?" pp. 478–510.

114. Interestingly, Darling-Hammond does say that it might be acceptable if standards were crafted by government, but only if they are not made mandatory (p. 480). This would seem to conflict with her distrust of government competence and indicate that what is most important to her is that teachers not be told what to do—ever.

115. Darling-Hammond, "National Standards and Assessments: Will They Improve Education?" p. 480.

116. On the NCTE and grammar, see Mulroy, "Reflections on Grammar's Demise."

117. For contrasting findings on resources and student achievement, see Hanushek, "The Impact of Differential Expenditures on School Performance," pp. 45–51, 62; Grissmer et al., *Improving Student Achievement*.

118. For quotations in this section, see Sacks, *Standardized Minds*, pp. 87–93.

119. Council of Chief State School Officers, *Trends in State Student Assessment Programs*.

120. Grissmer and Flanagan, *Exploring Rapid Achievement Gains in North Carolina and Texas*.

121. Wixson and Dutro, *Standards for Primary-Grade Reading*, p. 2.

122. Ravitch, *Left Back*; Angus and Mirel, *The Failed Promise of the American High School*, pp. 160–170; see also Hofstadter, *Anti-Intellectualism in American Life*, chapter 12.

123. Ravitch, *Left Back*, p. 408.

124. Ibid., p. 413, citing National Commission on Academic Excellence, *A Nation at Risk*, pp. 18–23. More recently, see Perkins, *The High School Transcript Study*, on student freedom to avoid academic coursework.

125. Zernicke, "Why Johnny Can't Read, Write, Multiply, or Divide," p. WK5. See also The Education Trust, *Thinking K–16*, pp. 14–15.

126. For example, see Public Agenda, *Survey Finds Little Sign of Backlash*; and Metropolitan Life Company, *Metropolitan Life Survey of the American Teacher 2000*.

127. Linn, "Assessments and Accountability," p. 5.

128. Tucker and Codding, *Standards for Our Schools*, p. 34. On the history of sorting and the curriculum, see Ravitch, *Left Back: A Century of Failed School Reforms*, especially chapters 4–5.

129. Feldman, "Passing on Failure," pp. 4–10; Gamoran et al., "Upgrading High School Mathematics Instruction: Improving Learning Opportunities for Low-Achieving, Low Income Youth," pp. 325–338; and Bloom et al., *Evaluating the Accelerated Schools Approach*.

130. National Center for Educational Statistics, *Trends Among High School Seniors, 1972–1992, 1995*, p. 4.

131. Blank and Pechman, *State Curriculum Frameworks in Mathematics and Science*, p. 3.

132. Linn, "Assessments and Accountability," p. 6.

133. Ibid., pp. 6–7; Clune et al., *The Implementation and Effects of High School Graduation Requirements*. Also, Educational Testing Service, *The Education Reform Decade*; Porter, "National Standards and School Improvement in the 1990s."

134. It has also been found that districts in high-poverty areas are having the greatest difficulty implementing standards-based reform. See Hannaway with Kimball, *Reports from the Field*.

135. Blank and Pechman, *State Curriculum Frameworks in Mathematics and Science*, chapter 2.

136. Musick, *Setting Standards High Enough*. SREB is a group of reform-minded Southern governors and policymakers. Musick is also president of the National Assessment Governing Board (NAGB), which oversees the NAEP assessments.

137. Archibold, *The Reviews of State Content Standards in English Language Arts and Mathematics*.

138. American Federation of Teachers, *Making Standards Matter, 1998*.

139. Joftus and Berman, *Great Expectations?*

140. Finn and Petrilli, eds., *The State of State Standards 1998*. See also Massel et al., *Persistence and Change*. On state standards for primary school reading, see Wixson and Dutro, "Standards for Primary-Grade Reading: An Analysis of State Frameworks."

141. Achieve, Inc., "Benchmarking to the Best," p. 2. Disturbingly, only twenty-one of fifty states asked to provide Achieve with their math and science standards and assessments did so.

142. Education Week, Pew Charitable Trust, *Quality Counts 2000: A Better Balance*, p. 87.

143. American Federation of Teachers, *Making Standards Matter 2001*. CBE did not repeat its rating of standards before shuttering its doors in 2004.

144. Finn and Kanstoroom, "State Academic Standards," pp. 141–143.

145. American Federation of Teachers, *Making Standards Matter 2001*, p. 25. See also Stern, *Effective State Standards for US History*.

146. See, for example, Porter, "A Curriculum Out of Balance: The Case of Elementary School Mathematics," pp. 9–15.

147. McKnight et al., *The Underachieving Curriculum*, p. 4.

148. Ibid., pp. 9, 50–83.

149. National Education Goals Panel, *The National Education Goals Report*, pp. 13–15.

150. Education Trust, *Ticket to Nowhere*.

151. *The 1994 High School Transcript Study Tabulations*, as cited in Gross, *The Conspiracy of Ignorance: The Failure of American Public Schools*, p. 107.

152. Education Week, Pew Charitable Trust, *Quality Counts 2000: Who Should Teach?*

153. As quoted in Wahlberg, "Uncompetitive American Schools: Causes and Cures," in Diane Ravitch, ed., *Brookings Papers on Education Policy 1998,* p. 192.

154. Editorial, "High Schools Inflate Grades and Parents Are Fooled"; Hoxby, "Testing Is About Openness and Openness Works," p. 9; and Evers, "What Do Tests Tell Us?" p. 9.

155. Moo, *Power Grab.*

156. Chubb and Moe, *Politics, Markets, and America's Schools*; Wahlberg, *Spending More While Earning Less*; and Gross, *The Conspiracy of Ignorance.*

157. Tyack, *The One Best System.*

158. Thus, the all-too-frequent end of the school year episode: students eagerly await to learn how tough their classes will be next autumn. Small hands tear open envelopes, and pupils groan or cheer upon learning they will be in the class of a "hard" teacher (read: a teacher with high standards and assigned homework) or an "easy" one.

159. Elmore and Rothman, eds., *Testing, Teaching, and Learning,* p. 16.

160. Council of Chief State School Officers, *Using Data on Enacted Curriculum on Mathematics and Science*, pp. 24–26. Specific figures cited in Boser, "Study Finds State Exams Don't Test What Teachers Teach." See also Council of Chief State School Officers, *New Tools for Analyzing Teaching, Curriculum, and Science.*

161. Webb, *Research Monograph No. 18*, p. vii.

162. National Education Goals Panel, *Profile of 1994–95 State Assessment Systems and Reported Results*, p. ii.

163. Goertz and Duffy, *Assessment and Accountability Systems in the 50 States*, p. 29.

164. National Education Goals Panel, *Profile of 1994–95 State Assessment Systems and Reported Results,* p. ii; Goertz and Duffy, *Assessment and Accountability in the 50 States*, pp. 25–28.

165. Education Week and Pew Charitable Trust, *Quality Counts 2002*, p. 69. The Thomas B. Fordham Foundation's 2000 survey found that only five of eighteen states claimed they had used this power. Finn and Petrilli, eds., *The State of State Standards 2000*, p. ix.

166. Barnes and Finn, *What Do Teachers Teach?*; and Education Week and Public Agenda, *Reality Check 2002.*

167. Cross et al., eds., *Grading the Systems.*

168. Edmonds, "Effective Schools for the Urban Poor," pp. 15–18, 20–24; "Programs of School Improvement," pp. 4–11; and "Characteristics of Effective Schools," pp. 93–104.

169. This is not to say that other means for adopting national education standards might not be tried. No doubt a number of approaches for creating good standards and getting them implemented in US schools might be devised.

3

Education Policy
and Politics Before 1993

*There's too much federal involvement in education. . . . We set out and
promised that we would eliminate the federal department. I think we
should remove federal influence from education.*
—Ronald Reagan, June 6, 1983[1]

Since the earliest days of the US republic, presidents, members of
Congress, and leading lights have extolled the virtues of education. In
1775, preacher Moses Mather declared, "The strength and spring of every
free government is the virtue of the people; virtue grows on knowledge,
and knowledge on education."[2] More than one hundred and fifty years later,
President Franklin Delano Roosevelt said, "Democracy cannot succeed
unless those who express their choices are prepared to choose wisely. Upon
our educational system must largely depend the perpetuity of those institutions upon which our freedom and our security rests."[3]

Yet, for all the talk about the importance of schooling, the federal government did precious little until the middle of the twentieth century. A number of factors impeded the nation's elected officials from making policy:
partisanship, disagreements over the practicality and efficacy of proposed
policies, and environmental factors like budget constraints were among
them. From 1789 until the mid-nineteenth century, the federal government
had its hands full: there were wars (the War of 1812, the Civil War) and
financial crises (panics, a national banking system to erect, and currency to
establish). There was also the problem of administration: how to make federal school policy when one has little sense of the boundaries of the nation
and who lived where. During those years, then, Congress and presidents
were limited in what they could achieve. Their education policymaking
was, excepting the occasional small project such as founding the Industrial
School for Girls in Alabama, limited to passing land ordinances.[4] The fed-

eral government offered settlers a deal of sorts: you settle the unknown lands, and we will recognize the legitimacy of your settlements. These bargains frequently included provisions for public schools. The Northwest Ordinance of 1785, which predated the creation of the US federal government by four years, required, "There shall be reserved the lot N. 16, of every township, for the maintenance of public schools within the said township." These ordinances, it must be noted, did not oblige the federal government to see to it that schools actually were established or to contribute anything to their establishment. Effectively, then, the federal government encouraged schools but left their creation and operation to localities, states, and private individuals. This was the federal schooling policy for the better part of a century.[5]

Yet, beyond the practical difficulties, the federal government faced a further impediment to making school policy: philosophical disagreement. At times, congressmen and presidents heatedly debated the propriety of federal involvement in education. The US Constitution gave the federal government no power to create or run schools. Moreover, schools had, since at least the late 1600s, been erected by private individuals, localities, and states. This was the policy tradition. Thus, early proposals for a federal university and a federal school system went nowhere. Even the debate over whether to have an education committee made for impassioned debate. In 1829, the House of Representatives killed the idea by tabling it indefinitely (the vote was 156 to 52).[6]

At the close of the Civil War, Congress confronted the question of what to do with the freed slaves.[7] In 1870, Representative George Hoar (R-MA) introduced a bill that provided that should the president find any state with insufficient numbers of schools, the federal government had the authority to establish schools as needed.[8] It also empowered the federal government to lay a tax on any offending states to pay for the expenses involved and gave it supervisory powers over the production of school textbooks.[9] Hoar and other proponents argued in favor of the bill on the grounds that citizens—and newly freed blacks, in particular—needed to be educated before they could take up the duties of citizenship.[10] Because the South lacked the will and finances to educate the newly freed blacks, the federal government was obliged to step in.

Hoar's bill marked the birth of liberalism in federal education politics, and it invited a full-throated antistatist response from congressmen from western and southern states.[11] They derided Hoar's bill as unconstitutional, inappropriate, and a plot to impose northeastern ideals on southern and western states. Hoar's bill went nowhere. In the 1880s, history repeated itself. Antistatists blocked the passage of more moderate education bills that sought to provide federal funds to help build schools for children in poor parts of the nation.[12]

In the twentieth century, liberals made headway. They often were aided in their press for federal policy by crises. One study of the period 1776 to 1976 found that 81 percent of all major education legislation was made during a time of national crisis.[13] For example, concern over immigration and dropouts helped fuel support for the Smith-Hughes Vocational Education Act, which provided federal funding for industrial and domestic arts classes in the public schools. Those who thought that US schools curricula were too lax and that college was too expensive for too many students construed the launch of the Sputnik satellite by the Soviet Union in 1957 as a national education catastrophe. They pushed Congress and President Dwight D. Eisenhower to pass the National Defense Education Act, which provided federal funds for advanced high school coursework and financial aid.[14]

This, though, did not mean that antistatism went away. In fact, politically it was almost as if Newton's third law of motion was at work: for every liberal action to increase the federal role in schooling there was an equal and opposite antistatist reaction to defend state and local prerogatives. Supreme Court orders to desegregate met "massive resistance" in the South, and attempts to increase the federal role in schooling faced incredible political challenges. And astonishingly, for all the decades of rhetoric about the importance of a good education for all children, not once did the federal government pass *general* education legislation (that is, policy aimed at improving the schooling of all children). One after another, general schools bills—to build more schools, to increase teacher pay, and so forth—were attacked as unconstitutional power grabs by the federal government and defeated by antistatists.[15] Indeed, for a time, Congress was unable to handle the issue of desegregating the public schools: the antistatists, especially in the South, controlled key committees in Congress and squelched any talk of desegregating the schools. Desegregation only occurred when liberal and civil-rights interest groups circumvented Congress and took their pleas to the federal courts. In a series of nation-rattling decisions, the courts ordered an end to "separate but equal" schooling and mandated that black children be bused to white schools and white children to black schools, a policy that provoked howls from the far right to impeach Supreme Court Chief Justice Earl Warren and other federal magistrates who judged segregation unconstitutional.

Nevertheless, liberals slowly but surely expanded the federal role in schooling. The watershed moment in education policy came in 1965, when President Lyndon Johnson signed the Elementary and Secondary Education Act (ESEA). As initially crafted, ESEA called for $1.4 billion in funding. The vast majority of the funds ($1.06 billion) were allocated to the Title I program, which funded compensatory education programs for low-income children. The remaining funds were for instructional materials, supplementary educational services provided by institutions other than schools, educa-

tional research and training, and improvement of state education departments. From 1965 through the 1990s, Title I provided approximately $125
billion to state school systems. Beyond the financial support for schools,
ESEA was significant because it expanded and fortified the Supreme Court
decision in *Brown v. Board of Education* (1954) that all children deserve a
good education and that the federal government may rightfully take action
to achieve this goal. Almost a century after George Hoar began the fight in
Congress for good schooling for marginalized children, the federal government was, at last, deeply involved in making that happen.

After the passage of ESEA, Congress made policies to help other
underserved children. It provided aid to schools so they might better educate children with limited English-language proficiency (PL 91-230, 1968)
and handicapped children (PL 90-247, 1973). Then, in a move that particularly outraged antistatists, Congress established the Department of
Education in 1979 (PL 96-88). Federal education spending was at an all-
time high: nearly 10 percent of school funding came from the federal government, and, it seemed, more was sure to come.

But then another education crisis arose, one to which liberals had no
convincing answer. With this, the politics of education shifted dramatically.

The Making of an Education Crisis

In the 1980s, the education achievement crisis erupted. Large numbers of
researchers, policymakers, and members of the public became convinced
that US schools were failing to provide children with a rigorous education.
This perspective was fueled by a number of factors. For one, there was the
economy. Congressman John Brademas noted, "since 1970, the United
States ha[d] suffered three major recessions, each more severe than the one
before. More Americans were out of work during the recession of 1981–82
than at any time since the Great Depression."[16] While the American economy flagged, the stock market sagged, and the prime interest rate soared to
20 percent. Overseas, the West German and Southeast Asian high-tech
economies boomed while the United States faced an expanding "rust belt"
and inflation.[17]

Public discontent with the schools was fueled, in part, by the media. It
was not until the 1970s that the major media outlets began to carry stories
on test scores.[18] Prior to 1974, no television network news program reported test score trends. Even though scores had begun sliding a decade earlier,
the *New York Times* began to report Scholastic Aptitude Test scores only in
1976.[19] The state of education, though, soon became newsworthy. Between
October 1975 and September 1977, the major networks aired seven stories
on test score trends. During the period of 1982 to 1987, major network

news programs broadcast stories on falling test scores six times.[20] Angus and Mirel note that in

> November 1977, for example, Time magazine ran a cover story that declared, "the health of U.S. education in the mid-1970s—particularly that of the high schools—is in deepening trouble." The article mentioned rising levels of violence, truancy, and falling SAT scores. In April of 1981 Newsweek ran a similar piece. It declared that "public schools are flunking."[21]

The *Newsweek* article also presented a Gallup poll that revealed that almost half of those polled rated the work done by the schools as poor or fair. It was a "verdict that would have been unthinkable just seven years ago, when two-thirds in a similar poll rated schools excellent or good."[22] The poll further revealed that nearly 70 percent of the public wanted schools to place more stress on academic basics.

Among researchers, meanwhile, there was a revolution in the making.[23] In the late 1960s, James Coleman's research began recalibrating the field of educational research.[24] His studies on schooling highlighted a number of provocative issues.[25] Critically, Coleman's work raised the question of what factors were related to educational achievement and raised doubts about any neat, causal relationship between school inputs and achievement.

Researchers also had begun the task of looking at successful schools. The media often reported examples of schools in high-poverty areas that produced high-achieving students.[26] And the "effective schools" research by Ronald Edmonds added scholarly weight to the media anecdotes by identifying the characteristics of schools that educated their students to high levels.[27] As the 1980s progressed, more and more researchers began to focus on the academic curriculum of schools as a key causal factor in underachievement. The logic was irresistible: children are not achieving at high levels because they are not being taught at high levels. Children's socioeconomic backgrounds and resource-starved schools were not the real public policy problem; schools with lax curricula were. Mortimer Adler of the University of Chicago wrote *The Paideia Program: An Educational Syllabus*, which criticized differential tracking in the schools and called for all students to receive a rigorous education. Theodore Sizer, Ernest Boyer, and other eminent scholars and researchers weighed in similarly.[28]

Furthermore, the federal Title I program began to come under criticism.[29] The trouble that was to come had appeared in 1966, just a year after ESEA was signed into law. During the first day of the hearings of the House General Subcommittee on Education, John Brademas (D-IN), a supporter of increased aid to education, asked Secretary of Education Francis Keppel,

> How can we be sure that if we spend more money on education for low-income children we will in fact improve the quality of their education? To put it another way, do you plan to undertake any cost-quality analysis to make sure that we will in fact improve the educational level of these children under this proposal, or will they still wind up at the bottom of the educational heap?[30]

Keppel could provide no solid response, offering only that the bill was up for reauthorization in three years and that there were state reporting requirements. Brademas continued:

> What are these kinds of data? There are obviously simple but extremely important ones. At the end of three years will the holding power [i.e., graduation and completion rates] of these schools that have these low-income children go up? Can we make it go up higher? In these areas what is the delinquency rate? Almost every district has a testing system of its own.

Keppel fumbled on but could name no benchmarks by which the work of states and localities could be measured.[31]

According to Phyllis McClure, who researched and followed the politics of Title I for the NAACP Legal Defense and Educational Fund, Inc., from 1969 to 1993, the program faced an array of criticisms.[32] It was derided as a form of tracking that promoted lower levels of education for poor and minority kids. It was said to inadequately serve poor children whose native language was not English. Most damning was the accusation that Title I was not getting children up to grade level or closing the achievement gap between Title I students and other children.[33] A number of causes for Title I's shortcomings were hypothesized by advocates for reform. It was argued that the congressional "who gets what" bargaining that created Title I spread its funding too thinly for it to be effective (thus, as noted previously, some 90 percent of all congressional districts received monies). Congress had also seen to it that the federal government would have little oversight of the use of the Title I funds.[34] Thus, stories about funds being spent on new carpeting for teachers' lounges, new sod for athletic fields, and the like were swapped by persons in the education policy network.[35] Title I's shortcoming were also associated with its pedagogical emptiness. Title I programs pulled students out of classes and put them into brief "compensatory" education programs that operated under no federal standards for what students were to be taught.[36]

All of these factors helped feed a widespread sense that the public schools were failing. In 1983, this sense metastasized into an official crisis with the publication of the governmental report *A Nation at Risk*.

A Nation at Risk

In early January 1981, president-elect Ronald Reagan's staff vetted possible candidates for secretary of education. Terrel H. Bell's name came up, possibly at the suggestion of the incoming secretary of defense, Caspar Weinberger.[37] Bell had previously served in the Office of Education, and, in short order, he was nominated and appointed to the position. Reagan had made a campaign promise to abolish the Department of Education, which many of his closest advisers considered a "great, bureaucratic joke."[38] Though a Republican, Bell did not agree with the "movement Republicans," who saw little or no role for the federal government in education. Bell thought the nation's educational institutions were in desperate condition and that someone needed to both preserve a federal role in education and "rally the American people around their schools and colleges."[39] He concluded that he might achieve at least the latter goal by having the federal government craft a report pointing out the condition of US education.[40] Bell's proposal to create a commission to study this topic was rebuffed by the White House. So, Bell used his secretarial authority to create the National Commission on Excellence in Education, which he charged with this task.

In April 1983 the commission, headed by David Pierpont Gardner, president of the University of Utah, presented its draft, *A Nation at Risk. The Imperative for Educational Reform*, to Bell. Written in terms as alarmist as its title, the report described an education system that was rudderless and sinking. The nation had twenty-three million illiterates, and test scores had been falling steadily for almost two decades. It declared that the very livelihood of the United States was threatened by the poor state of the educational system, the foundations of which were being "eroded by a rising tide of mediocrity."[41] Bell forwarded the report to President Reagan, who read it and kept to his promise to hold a press conference on it.

On April 26, 1983, President Reagan spoke before a heavily attended conference in the state dining room of the White House. He agreed with David Gardner, who spoke before him, that the state of the schools and colleges was poor. Reagan quoted Jefferson's dictum that "If a nation expects to be ignorant and free, it expects what never was and never will be." He noted,

> We spent more on education at all levels than any other country in the world. But what have we bought with all that spending? I was interested to see . . . the almost uninterrupted decline in student achievement scores during the past two decades, decades in which the Federal presence in education grew and grew.[42]

The president then claimed that the best federal policy response was a program of educational vouchers, school prayer, educational savings accounts, and tuition tax cuts for parents who send their children to private schools. The crisis was to be handled by parents and localities, and the federal government was to reduce its detrimental meddling in the public schools.

That night, United Press International's newswire carried a piece on the report, "Panel Backs More—and Harder—School Work."[43] Within the next few weeks, hundreds of newspapers reported *A Nation at Risk*'s grim findings on American education. David Gergen, presidential assistant for communications, recalled, "The report just took off in the media."[44] In the next five weeks, over 100,000 copies of *A Nation at Risk* were distributed.[45]

A Nation at Risk was followed immediately by reports and studies by the Education Commission of the States, the Business–Higher Education Forum, the Twentieth Century Fund, the National Science Board, and others.[46] All concluded that schools were not educating children as well as they should and that the federal government could make policy to contend with it.

The National Education Association responded to *A Nation at Risk* by launching a multimillion-dollar advertising campaign, warning that raising standards in the schools would increase the number of school dropouts.[47] It was to no avail. *A Nation at Risk* received so much attention from the media that Reagan made education reform a major topic in his campaign against the Democratic nominee, Walter F. Mondale.[48] At an April 26 press conference, Reagan had pointed out that a 1982 Gallup poll found that the majority of those surveyed thought "Washington should exert less influence in determining the educational program of the public schools."[49] But after the release of *A Nation at Risk*, polls began showing widespread public concern for the state of education.[50] In December 1980, 52 percent of those asked about education spending said the United States was spending too little. By 1984 that number had increased to 64 percent, and it stayed between 60 and 64 percent through the end of Reagan's term in 1988.[51] National Opinion Research Studies (NORC) show there was a shift in public opinion on education spending in the 1980s. In 1973, 49 percent of the public wanted to spend more for education and 47 percent wanted it to stay the same or reduce it. As of 1988, 64 percent favored increased spending on education and 33 percent thought otherwise.[52]

By early June 1983, some in the White House saw that the proposal to abolish the Department of Education did not square with the declaration of an education emergency. When a reporter asked White House spokesman Larry Speakes whether the president still intended to abolish the department, he responded, "Obviously it could be very difficult legislatively. It hasn't come up."[53] The crisis was swallowing Reagan's policy proposals to roll back federal involvement in the schools. Reagan responded by touring the country with Bell and delivering speeches that decried the condition of education, further fueling the public's sense that there was a crisis in education. He emphasized a "back to the basics" message and insisted that more federal involvement and spending were not the answers to the problem.[54]

Reagan's message of less spending and less federal involvement did not take with the press or public. There was a basic dissonance in the logic. A federal governmental report and the president of the United States had declared that the country faced a national crisis in schooling. Yet, the US federal government, which is supposed to "promote the general welfare" and contend with "great and national interests," was planning to decrease its role in the schools.[55] Worse, for Reagan, was that *A Nation at Risk* did not endorse any of the devolutionary and privatizing policies he was pushing. Although the federal role was limited, the report's authors wrote that "we believe the Federal Government's role includes several functions of national consequence that states and localities are unlikely to be able to meet." Among the tasks listed were "supporting curriculum improvement and research on teaching, learning, and the management of schools." It further declared that the "Federal Government has the primary responsibility to identify the national interest in education" and that "educational excellence costs, but in the long run, mediocrity costs far more."[56]

In late December 1983, the *New York Times* reported that at the recent National Forum on Excellence in Education, President Reagan made no mention of abolishing the Department of Education to the governors and policymakers assembled.[57] The following year, Reagan gave up hope of abolishing the Department of Education.[58] As education policy analyst Denis P. Doyle quipped, "The whole situation [was] replete with irony." Reagan sought to reduce the federal role in schooling; ultimately, though, he fueled the public's demand for more federal involvement in education.[59]

The Education Crisis and the New Politics of Education

Dissatisfaction among the public and researchers and the publication of *A Nation at Risk* combined to transform the politics of education. The debate had shifted. First, school curricula became a topic of national discourse. Gary L. Jones, undersecretary of education in the Reagan administration, said that the conception of the federal role had broadened "to include not only access and equity but standards and quality."[60] The publication of *A Nation at Risk* and Reagan's subsequent stumping spread the message that American schools were failing to adequately educate pupils. Both firmly affixed the blame on the schools. They had abandoned an academic curriculum in favor of nonacademic coursework. Reagan called for schools to get back to the basics. *A Nation at Risk* proposed that schools should require every student to complete four years of English; three years of math, science, and social studies; and a half-year of computer science in order to earn a diploma.

Second, both Reagan and *A Nation at Risk* stated that student underachievement was not localized to any particular group or population of students. The Smith-Hughes Act, the National Defense Education Act, and the ESEA sought to improve the schooling received by a small slice of the student population: the children of immigrants, students who showed superior aptitude, and the children of the poor and nonwhite. According to Reagan and *A Nation at Risk*, though, all of the nation's educational institutions, from elementary schools to universities, were failing. Student underachievement was a national issue affecting the schools generally, and the result was that the economy was faltering. And mounting research showed that the poor and the nonwhite were still doing worst of all, in spite of Title I.

These revelations turned almost every American into a stakeholder in the issue, thereby altering the politics surrounding federal education policy. In Elmer Schattschneider's terms, the debate about the schools had been transformed by a "widening of the loop" of persons who were party to the discussion.[61] Previously, the debates about education policy had been dominated by members of the education policy network, which included committee chairmen in Congress, leaders of interest groups such as the National Education Association, and representatives of slivers of the student population that benefited from federal programs. Now, the number of interested parties had expanded dramatically. Academics, researchers, feminists, and civil rights leaders dissatisfied with the education provided to women and minorities clamored with parents for reform. As the decade wore on, major leaders from various parts of society joined in the call for more rigorous schooling. They included Albert Shanker of the American Federation of Teachers, secretaries of education such as Terrel Bell and William Bennett, and reform-minded governors including Roy Romer (CO), Carroll A. Campbell Jr. (SC), Richard W. Riley (SC), and William J. Clinton (AR). They were joined by the heads of major businesses, including David Kearns, chief executive officer of Xerox, and Lou Gersterner, chief executive officer of IBM. Fifty years earlier, business groups such as the Chamber of Commerce and the National Association of Manufacturers had aggressively fought federal aid to education, arguing that it was unconstitutional and threatening to liberty.[62] In the 1980s, the business community argued that the health of American businesses and the economy was in part dependent on the skills and knowledge of workers. Schools had to teach students more.

Finally, the old politics of education had many splits, but most enduring was the row between liberals, who thought the federal government had a legitimate role in seeing that adequate public schooling was available to children, and antistatists, who believed that the Constitution and tradition afforded little if any federal role in schooling. The shift of big business to a pro–federal education policy position gave both parties—especially Republicans, who traditionally have been the party of business—a strong incentive to rethink their old liberal and antistatist positions. Moreover, Reagan and *A Nation at Risk* had further weakened the rhetorical appeal of the antistatist position by making educational underachievement a national crisis. The nation's continued economic health, and perhaps its continued existence, depended on making schools more rigorous. In the face of a national calamity, then, principled arguments calling for federal restraint in the name of localism and constitutionalism lost much of their power to persuade. To the pragmatic public, the logic of the situation was simple: a national crisis demands a national response, and that is to be done through federal policy. Principled opposition to action, then, seemed like an anachronism or the abrogation of duty to many.[63]

The upshot was a new politics of education. The old politics of education featured liberals and antistatists. Now the debate on federal education policy included a new coalition, whom we will term *quality schools advocates*. The old politics had many debates, but central among them was the question of federalism, which focused on the proper scale of government. Liberals believed the federal government could and should make policy to increase resources for schools serving the poor and nonwhite. Antistatists did not. With the entry of the quality schools advocates, the debate now included more persons who were favorable toward federal involvement in education. Moreover, with them came a new question to the debate, a policy question that ignored the federalism question: *Why are the children not learning as much as they should?* Just as the academic community had to confront the issue of educational results, so now did the education policy network in Washington, DC.

It was this new politics that the America 2000 initiative both represented and confronted. Though much in the politics was new, as will be seen, much of the politics from years past remained, bedeviling America 2000.

The New Federal Politics of Education and America 2000

National education standards were, to a degree, implicit in the ideas of *A Nation at Risk*. The report focused on how much students were learning, used test scores as proxies, and determined that students were not learning as much as they should (which implies a standard of some sort). As noted earlier, *A Nation at Risk* declared that the federal government had a role in improving the schools and "supporting curriculum improvement." It also declared that curricular standards should be raised and that students should be required to complete a slate of academic coursework in order to receive a high school diploma.

National standards began to emerge as an idea and move on to the federal systemic agenda at the Education Summit in Charlottesville, Virginia, in September 1989.[64] President George H. W. Bush, who likely saw an opportunity to capture the education issue from Democrats and earn votes in the next election, attended, as did the governors of the states. By the gathering's close, President Bush and the governors had committed themselves toward establishing national education goals and reporting annually on the state of US education. On January 31, 1990, Bush announced the national goals to the American public in his State of the Union Address. They were:

1. All children in America will start school ready to learn;
2. The high school graduation rate will increase to at least 90 percent;
3. *American students will leave grades four, eight, and twelve having demonstrated competency in challenging subject matter, including English, mathematics, science, history, and geography* [emphasis added];
4. US students will be first in the world in science and mathematics;
5. Every adult American will be literate and possess the knowledge and skills necessary to compete in a global economy and exercise the rights and responsibilities of citizenship;
6. Every school in America will be free of drugs and violence and will offer a safe, disciplined environment conducive to learning.[65]

The National Governors Association (NGA) met on February 25 and added twenty-one objectives to the six national goals. Many of these objectives focused on the resources that the governors thought would be necessary to reach the six goals.[66] The governors also agreed to create an annual national report card that would measure the progress toward these goals, which were to be achieved by the year 2000. They founded the National Education Goals Panel (NEGP) to carry out these tasks.

Though neither the Bush administration nor the governors were calling for national standards and assessments at that time, they had laid the groundwork for them to emerge. The leaders had agreed that school curricula were not challenging enough and that students nationwide needed to learn to higher levels. Again, it was not the case that certain portions of the American public school student population were doing poorly and in need of assistance. Rather, the achievement of most students was lacking—in which case, all schools across the nation needed to adopt more rigorous curricula and assessments. Goal three, therefore, insisted that all children demonstrate "competency" in five subject areas of challenging subject material.

Moreover, because the nation had goals, it needed, logically, to measure progress toward those goals. Thus, NEGP had said it would create a national report card to measure the nation's progress toward the goals. These reports were supposed to rally the public around the national goals. The higher achievement that *A Nation at Risk* called for would be met by raising the public's expectations of the quality of education provided by the public schools, which, in turn, would raise their academic expectations for students.[67] And if these reports were to measure the progress of children's learning to high levels in five content areas, then it would seem that some standards for what constituted challenging subject material (content standards) and student knowledge thereof (performance standards) would need to be drawn up. And measuring student knowledge and performance standards would imply formulating assessments that were aligned to the standards. All of this strongly hinted at the need for national standards and examinations.

Early Signs of Resistance

President Bush's relationship with the Democratic-controlled Congress began poorly and grew worse with time. By the end of the first year, he and Congress had crossed swords twice.

In April 1989, the Bush administration offered its Educational Excellence Act of 1989 (HR 1675, S 695). The act was significant on two counts. First, here was a Republican president seeking to expand the federal role, albeit modestly. The Educational Equity Act was to provide over $400 million in funding beyond that authorized by the revised Title I.[68] Moreover, the act was based upon the thinking that the public schools were failing to educate children as well as they should. It sought to spur schools to innovate by creating magnet schools, rewarding schools with extra funds where children showed large achievement gains (e.g., merit schools), and bringing new blood into the profession by creating alternative principal and teacher certification.[69] The Senate responded favorably and actually passed the bill. House Democrats, though, rejected it out of hand. Chairman Augustus Hawkins (D-CA) refused to act on the bill, and the Democrats brought out their own legislation. Whereas the Bush bill represented some of the quality schools advocacy thinking on reform, the Democrats' proposal was thoroughly liberal. It conceptualized the problem of the public schools as a matter of money. Like advocates from Representative Hoar in the 1870s onward, the House Democrats believed that insufficient state spending was the cause for the malaise of the public schools. The name of their bill indicated the differing emphasis: the *Equity* and Excellence in Education Implementation Act (EEEIA). This bill was breathtaking in its scope. It asked for $5.7 billion in additional funding, most of which would go to Head Start and Title I. EEEIA offered very little that was designed to spur school change.[70]

Late that summer, on hearing that the president was to meet with the governors, the Democrats again tried to reassert their ownership of the education issue. Senate majority leader George Mitchell (D-ME) and House majority leader Richard Gephardt (D-MO) publicly issued their own national education goals just days before the Charlottesville meeting.[71] This was the second major action by congressional Democrats in what became a lengthy campaign to thwart the administration's education reform efforts.[72]

The administration tried to work with Congress on EEEIA and to get a bill that was both fiscally practical and fostered innovation in the schools. Congress, though, was stacked against the president. Democrats outnumbered Republicans 56 to 44 in the Senate and 267 to 167 in the House.[73] Bush's first year in office ended with him deadlocked with Congress over education.

The Bush administration's relationship with Congress grew more contentious in 1990. Democrats responded to the president's January announcement of the national education goals by launching their own proposal to create a national goals panel. Senator Jeff Bingaman (D-NM) introduced the National Report Card Act of 1990. Bingaman had held hearings the previous autumn in response to the president's gathering with the governors in Charlottesville. The act would create a ten-person panel of "highly respected, bipartisan experts" who would issue an annual report card detailing the nation's progress toward meeting the goals.[74] Bingaman's bill didn't become law, but it did create grief for the administration.[75]

Beyond politics, evidence mounted indicating that the Bush administration and Democrats in Congress were philosophically far apart. In March 1990, the House Subcommittee on Elementary, Secondary, and Vocational Education held hearings to discuss the capabilities of the National Assessment of Educational Progress (NAEP) and the subject of national testing. In general, those who testified expressed apprehension toward the use of federal examinations to raise educational achievement. During the course of the two-day hearings, only three of the seventeen witnesses spoke strongly in favor of creating national examinations.[76] Another two of the witnesses were sanguine toward expanding the number of pupils taking the NAEP exams, though they did not argue in favor of using tests as a tool for raising educational achievement. Herbert Walberg, on behalf of the National Assessment Governing Board, for example, testified in favor of an annual national report card of educational progress.[77] To this end, the federal government would have to clarify national education standards and expand the use of the NAEP exams, testing more students at the fourth, eighth, and twelfth grades.[78]

Eleven persons before the subcommittee adamantly opposed expanding national tests and using them as a tool for raising achievement.

Representative William Goodling (PA), the ranking Republican on the sub-committee, was particularly critical.[79] Before the hearings had scarcely gotten under way, Goodling took strong positions against national testing and read an excerpt from an article that reflected his position:

> Everyone is concerned about the quality of our schools, and yes, everyone wants more accountability from our schools. . . . Here are seven reasons why national tests won't improve our schools. One, they do nothing to help students learn. Two, they are poor indicators of student performance. Three, they provide no in-depth assessment of the curriculum in a particular school district. Four, they encourage teaching to the test. Five, they categorize and label students. Six, they are racially, culturally, and socially biased. Seven, they measure trivial information easily tested by multiple choice.[80]

The following day Goodling belittled an article that contended "a well-schooled youngster in Alabama should possess the same knowledge and skills as one in Minnesota."[81]

Representative Major Owens (D-NY) joined Goodling in criticizing the expanded testing. Like Goodling, he thought testing was bad policy. Owens also argued that the root causes of educational underachievement were the socioeconomic background of the children and underfunded schools. Testing, therefore, was a rigged game that would punish and stigmatize poor and minority children who would likely fail the assessments.[82] Three other witnesses concurred with Owens. Dr. Edward D. Roeberer, supervisor of assessment and accreditation for the Michigan Department of Education, did not take a firm stand on expanding the use of the NAEP, but he discouraged federal authorities from doing so without consulting states and localities.[83] Roy Romer, governor of Colorado and chairman of the NEGP, urged the federal government to respect states' rights. He voiced approval for expanded assessment but cautioned that it must be voluntary. Education politics, he said, were too ideological for a national mandatory testing program.[84]

Some at the hearing decried national testing as a conspiracy. Representative Charles A. Hayes (D-IL) declared that national testing was part of an "effort to almost privatize the public educational system, which will diminish the opportunities for the economically disadvantaged."[85] Trevor Sewell, acting dean at Temple University's College of Education, also saw a nefarious plot in the making:

> I believe that the proposed national test, rooted in the assumption of higher national standards, might be a thinly veiled effort to use a scientific rationale to advance an elitist social structure in the United States. If not so, why then, given the rich American tradition of local control over the educational enterprise, should a national high school test dictate employment, a high school diploma, or college admission?[86]

Based upon this hearing, then, any federal education policy proposal coming from the Bush administration would likely face a number of objections, four of which were formidable. There was the policy objection (that they would not work); there was the philosophical question of the extent of federal power and local control; there was an equity concern (testing is unfair to those children who were poor, minority, and/or attended underfunded schools); and there were conspiratorial objections.

President Bush's second year closed without an education policy victory. The Democrats had tried to force Bush to sign a compromise version of the Equity and Excellence in Education Implementation Act. But in late October 1990, conservative Republicans killed the bill on a parliamentary maneuver. They were philosophically opposed to the bill's effort to greatly increase federal spending on schools. House education committee members were enraged.[87] Not surprisingly, measurements of congressional partisanship for the years 1989 and 1990 were very high.[88]

America 2000 Arrives

The goals adopted at Charlottesville in 1989 became the basis for America 2000, which was unveiled on April 18, 1991. The plan, or more properly, the strategy, was crafted largely by the secretary of education, Lamar Alexander, and by the deputy secretary of education, David Kearns.[89] In recognition of the historically limited federal role in education and keeping in line with the Bush administration's general conservatism, America 2000 "was designed to promote ground-level, populist education reforms, not an enlargement of the federal role."[90] It was a complex collection of initiatives, but its main policies were:

- Codifying the six education goals agreed upon in January 1990;
- Developing "world-class standards" in education;
- Creating voluntary American Achievement Tests aligned to the standards (to be done in conjunction with the National Education Goals Panel);
- Continued collaboration between the president and the NEGP to craft an annual report card on the progress toward the goals;
- Creating 535 New American Schools that would serve as models for school reform;[91] and
- Permitting children in failing schools to use their Title I federal education funds at the school of their choice, be it public, private, or parochial, but in accordance with state and local laws.[92]

Education standards and examinations were to be national, not federal. The difference was this: Federal standards would be drawn up by a federal agency and imposed on states, much as the standards for vocational educa-tion had been.[93] National standards and assessments, as envisioned by the Bush administration, would be created by someone other than the federal government and would serve as a model for state or locally fashioned stan-dards.[94] In addition, any national assessments would be voluntary.[95] Who would draw up the standards was unclear. Diane Ravitch, who later led the effort to create national standards as the assistant secretary for educational research and improvement, recalls that the matter was not decided at the launching of America 2000.[96] Bush said that governors would be involved in some fashion. "Working closely with the governors, we will define new World Class Standards."[97]

Albert Shanker, leader of the American Federation of Teachers, lauded America 2000 publicly. He called America 2000

> broad and comprehensive, more so than any President has come with. In the past federal initiatives were targeted toward minorities, the poor, the handicapped . . . but this is the first time the federal government really puts out a package . . . to improve American education over all.[98]

America 2000 was remarkable because it was not general education aid (i.e., a proposal to send federal funds to states and localities to spend on all schools) yet it was to have the effect of general aid. America 2000 aimed at improving the schooling of all children. Moreover, it was, as Secretary Alexander said, "more 'revolution' than 'program.'"[99] Rather than increase the federal government's influence over the public schools by adding more rules to the conditions of aid in federal acts, America 2000 would respect state and local control of education. It would not alter the federal-state bal-ance of power. Rather, it would foster innovation in schooling by encourag-ing private and local initiatives. A private corporation would fund and direct the New American Schools (NAS) initiative. NAS schools, it was hoped, would serve as models for reform and catalysts for other schools to change their ways. States would receive more funding to foster their own reforms. America 2000 would encourage school improvement by granting school choice to Title I recipients. Federal dollars would be, in what came to be the parlance, "strapped to the back of the child." If parents chose to send their child to a private or religious school, that child's allotment of Title I funds would go to the coffers of the school he or she attended. (The ESEA, it must be noted, had always permitted a small amount of public funds to pay for textbooks and instructional tools in public and private and religious schools. This policy change, if enacted, would have dramatic effects, diverting huge numbers of children and public funds to nonpublic schools.) The federal government would both guide and support state and local reforms and market forces turned loose through the Title I school choice provision. America 2000 enunciated national goals, and the NEGP would measure the nation's progress toward them. National standards would be created along with voluntary national exams. These would serve as models for the states to make their own standards and assessments. America 2000 would authorize the NAGB to expand the NAEP to collect state-level data, which states could use to track their students' educational achievement.

America 2000 Meets Political Resistance

By the time that America 2000 was made public, it was in trouble. Those who helped craft and launch the initiative note that it was little supported by the political right. Conservatives were more interested in a strong school choice bill than a national strategy and were uncomfortable with the idea of national standards and tests.[100] As for the left, they found little to like in America 2000.[101] Stung by the defeat of the Equity and Excellence in Education Implementation Act the previous autumn and hoping to keep ownership of the education issue, the Democrats again pushed their own legislation. The Democratic leadership cobbled together its own education bill. Drawing on the EEEIA, they had revised a minor literacy bill (S 2), expanding the programs it would offer and increasing its proposed authorization from $160 million to nearly $500 million.[102] S 2, like America 2000, also would codify the national education goals adopted by the Bush administration and the National Governors Association. On April 17, one day before Bush unveiled America 2000, the Senate Labor and Human Resources Committee passed S 2 by voice vote. And in September the House would birth its own omnibus education reform bill, the $700 million HR 3320.[103] Neither S 2 nor HR 3320 included education standards and a number of other provisions that America 2000 possessed.

Before April's end, it was obvious that America 2000 would face major obstacles.[104] Not a week after it was announced, Senator Ted Kennedy (D-MA) criticized America 2000 on both liberal and strict-separationist grounds. He complained that "the administration's proposals involve no new resources for education." He also warned that "offering public dollars to private schools, including religious schools," threatened to "reopen the bitter and divisive policy and constitutional debates of the past."[105]

On April 23 the House Subcommittee on Select Education held a hearing on the value of educational testing. The hearing was an ambush of America 2000. Liberal Democratic chairman Major Owens had stacked the witness list with liberal academics and others whom he could count on to savage the bill.[106] All of them vigorously objected to more testing, raised questions as to the validity of national assessments, and testified that they were unfair to minorities and those students whose first language was not

English.[107] Just one witness testified in favor of America 2000. Eight of the eleven were strongly opposed to federal testing as a means for raising student achievement.

A second formidable objection to America 2000 appeared at the hearing. Though America 2000's school choice component was not the subject of the hearing, Representative William J. Jefferson (D-LA) made it one:

> That's what's wrong with the whole choice idea. There's no market, there's no free market in education. That's ridiculous. There's not a store on this corner and one on that corner, that can advertise better, and lower their prices, attract more people. That's not how it works. The legislature appropriates money. The school board appropriates money. Teachers get assigned. Students get assigned. Even if you take out that last fact and say students aren't assigned, the rest of it is the same.[108]

In terms of appropriate federal policy to raise education standards, the majority present reiterated the liberal position that the House Subcommittee on Elementary, Secondary, and Vocational Education expressed in the March hearing. Underachievement was largely a function of insufficient school resources and students' socioeconomic circumstances. Thus, to improve achievement the federal government must provide more funding for resources and compensatory education.[109]

Things became more difficult for President Bush in May. Recognizing that Congress was dominated by Democrats who were unlikely to brook "quality schools" reforms, the administration had sought to actuate the ideas within America 2000 with as little legislation as possible. Businesses were asked to pledge $150 to $200 million to create the New American Schools Development Corporation (NASDC). The NASDC would help the Department of Education choose which plans for New American Schools would be approved and given $1 million each in federal seed money.[110] The Bush administration also sought to allocate discretionary funds and reassign funds in a pending appropriations bill to cover the cost of developing standards, national exams, and other minor portions of the America 2000 strategy. This strategy elicited a sharp response from Congress. Members of the House Education and Labor Committee testified before an appropriations panel that congressional approval would be needed for virtually all of America 2000's programs.[111] Four months later, Congress took further action to thwart America 2000. Democrats earmarked funds in a pending education bill so that the money could not be used by Secretary Alexander for America 2000 initiatives.[112]

The same month, the administration ran into further difficulties. Secretary Alexander, as part of the America 2000 strategy, was working with the NEGP to create an advisory committee to investigate the feasibility of national standards and assessments. The advisory committee would be staffed by twenty-five to twenty-seven persons appointed by the NEGP's chairman and vice chairman, Governor Roy Romer of Colorado (Democrat) and Governor Carroll A. Campbell Jr. of South Carolina (Republican). Representative William Goodling (PA), a Republican and minority leader of the House's education committee, would sit on the committee, as would Senate Republican Orrin Hatch (R-UT). Again, House Democrats tried to co-opt the administration. Dale E. Kildee (D-MI), chairman of the Subcommittee on Elementary, Secondary, and Vocational Education, immediately pushed legislation to establish a similar advisory council, which would be staffed by those sympathetic to the Democrats' perspective.[113] Not only would it investigate the feasibility of standards and tests but, reflecting Democrats' reticence toward standards and tests, it would also research their desirability. Secretary Alexander and Representative Goodling opposed the idea, but not wanting to see two advisory groups formed, they chose to bargain.

On June 10, the House Committee on Education and Labor issued a conference report that urged the creation of a bipartisan council. It would study a number of complex questions, including the feasibility of creating national standards and examinations "while respecting State and local control of education . . . [for] this reflects a major concern voiced by witnesses at the hearing on national testing."[114] The council was also to research the "fairness" of any tests, "i.e., the absence of bias for or against any racial, ethnic, economic, linguistic, or gender group."[115] Congress passed the Education Council Act of 1991 on June 27. The act authorized "appropriations to establish . . . a National Council on Education Standards and Testing."[116] Title IV of the act charged the council, NCEST, with studying "the desirability and feasibility of establishing national standards and testing in education" and to provide a report thereon by December 31, 1991.[117] At best, NCEST was a mixed blessing for President Bush. On the one hand, if NCEST offered a report that strongly favored national education standards and assessments, the administration might see some growth in congressional support for America 2000. But on the other, if the report was not staunch in support of national standards and examinations, America 2000 would remain mired. Whatever the final report might say, though, the commissioning of NCEST was a blow to the administration because it gave Congress justification to hold off on voting on standards and assessments until early 1992, an election year.

The House Subcommittee on Elementary, Secondary, and Vocational Education held hearings on America 2000 during three days in June and July. Twenty persons present spoke to the bill. Of the twenty, eight were from outside Congress (one of whom was Secretary Alexander), and the other twelve were members of the committee.[118] Eleven of the twelve congressmen who testified were Democrats. Three Republicans—Representatives Goodling, Steve Gunderson (WI), and Susan Molinari (NY)—were present, but only Molinari spoke clearly on the subject of education. Secretary Alexander and Sister Lourdes Sheehan, the secretary of education for the US Catholic Conference, were the only persons who testified in favor of America 2000.[119]

Fourteen individuals, though, came out strongly against America 2000. Their chief target of criticism was America 2000's school choice provision. Representative Jack Reed (D-RI) derided school choice as "passing out parachutes," and Representative Charles Hayes, perhaps seeing choice as a tool to reverse desegregation, claimed that something diabolical was afoot. "I'm afraid of the rise in racism that's going to occur with the voucher system and choice. And I don't think it's an accident; I think it's by design."[120] Hayes's complaint was misguided. It is true that school choice had in the 1960s been promoted by bigots (often on the right) who wanted to help white parents get their children out of schools that were forced to accept black children by the courts. However, voucherizing Title I was very different. It would not be the case that only white children would get the funds to enable them to transfer schools. Rather, all poor children, white and nonwhite, who participated in Title I programs would be empowered to escape failing schools.

Nine of the witnesses framed the policy problem as a matter of inadequate funding, in particular, of compensatory services such as Title I and Head Start. Just two of the witnesses spoke to the subject of standards and the correlative subject of the proper extent of federal power in education. Only Gordon Ambach, executive director of the Council of Chief State School Officers, said anything that could be remotely construed as antistatist. He expressed disappointment that he could find nothing in America 2000 that referred to the use of state or local educational agencies.[121] Edward Kealy, then director of the National School Board Association (NSBA), explains that the big issue for state and local education groups was not standards per se, but who would have influence over governing the schools. "National standards, we were favorable towards. . . . We thought they were doable and reasonable." America 2000, though, was in large part designed to work around local education agencies. This was troubling. America 2000 "was essentially disrespectful of local school boards. . . . If school reform is needed, there's an institution, locally elected, right there to do it. So why would you invest some other body [e.g., America 2000 community committees] to be the engine of school reform?"[122]

Meanwhile, the National Education Goals Panel was beginning to become embroiled in a dispute that impinged on the Bush administration's plan. At the June meeting, panel chair Governor Romer asked what the federal government should do to help students reach higher standards. While "everyone agreed on the need for setting high academic standards," members of the NEGP were divided whether the federal government should "develop and report indicators of services provided by the states and the federal government."[123] These measures of services were thought desirable by the Democratic governors and some members of the panel because they measured what would come to be known as students' "opportunity-to-learn." In short, this was a new variant of the liberal versus quality school advocacy debate as to what is the primary cause for student underachievement. As noted earlier, liberals emphasized the amount of resources available to children. Quality schools advocates emphasized the behavior of the schools as an organization. Thus, when it came to higher standards, though there was agreement among the NEGP members that higher standards were critical to raising student achievement, this did not mean that resources were wholly irrelevant to student achievement. Students are unlikely to meet the challenging levels if, say, they lack books that cover the subject material or do not have teachers who are trained in the standards. This raises three obvious questions:

- Who should decide what constitutes adequate delivery standards; localities, the states, or the federal government?
- Who should provide the funding to see that schools have the means to teach children to the standards?
- Which should be implemented first, the delivery standards or the content and performance standards?

As will be seen, these questions loomed large in the standards debates to come.

By summer's end, it was clear that no portions of America 2000 were going to be passed by Congress. The House education committee, including the ranking Republican, Representative Goodling, was overwhelmingly against it. While this was happening, the NEGP released its first report, which presented a "sober and accurate diagnosis of our educational performance." It showed that student achievement was still less than desirable and argued that for Americans to "prosper as individuals and as a nation, we must have world-class standards."[124] It failed to stir Congress to offer any support to national standards. No more hearings were held on America 2000.[125] For the remainder of the year, Congress worked on its own bills, negotiating with the administration to see what they had to do to get President Bush to sign S 2/HR 3320.

In the meantime, NCEST was working to complete its study on the advisability of national standards and assessments. At the September meeting, the matter of school delivery standards (later called opportunity-to-learn standards) came up. The chair of NCEST's standards task force, Marshall Smith, presented a short paper that said that there should be standards for what students should know (content standards), how much of the content they should know (performance standards), and what resources schools should have to teach to the standards (delivery standards). At the next meeting in October, Smith's standards task force distributed a longer paper that said school delivery standards should only include the qualities and resources that enabled the schools to instruct students in the subject areas.[126]

On January 24, 1992, NCEST issued its report on the advisability and feasibility of national standards and assessments.[127] *Raising Standards for American Education* was important because it was produced by a bipartisan group of federal and state officials as well as diverse stakeholders from the academic, educational, and business communities. The report was also significant because it was the first official study charged with taking the question of standards head on, asking if they were desirable, feasible, and how they might be developed and implemented.

Raising Standards for American Education noted that "high national standards tied to assessments are desirable." The report stated that standards were not only justified as an obvious means to measure progress; standards and assessments were an essential vehicle for educational progress. "The Council initially discussed standards and assessments as a way to help measure progress toward the National Education Goals but came to see the movement toward high standards as a means to help [in] achieving the goals."[128] NCEST justified the value of standards as policy by stating that due to the "absence of well-defined and demanding standards, education in the United States has gravitated toward de facto national minimum expectations."[129] These de facto standards hurt all pupils, but particularly the poor and nonwhite, because the standards helped keep them from working their way into the American middle class.[130] Thus, national standards were

> critical to the nation in three primary ways: to promote educational equity, to preserve democracy and enhance the civic culture, and to improve economic competitiveness. Further, national education standards would help to provide an increasingly diverse and mobile population with shared values and knowledge.[131]

The report endorsed national standards and tried to extinguish any fears that national standards would result in federal control. Standards were to be voluntary and national; they were not to be imposed by the federal government and were not to be a national curriculum. Assessments should consist of multiple measures of individual student abilities in the five curricular areas listed in the third national education goal (English, mathematics, science, history, and geography). In order to measure student achievement toward the national education goals over time, NCEST recommended creating "large-scale sample assessments" similar to those used by the NAEP.[132] The NEGP and a new national board, the National Education Standards and Assessment Council (NESAC), would certify state standards and assessments as being in line with the federal standards.[133]

The report was not without ambiguities. It did not say who should create the educational standards. Nor did it name who would fashion the assessments, beyond "a wide array of developers."[134] States and localities were free to adopt the standards and assessments, but they were, as the report repeatedly noted, not required to do so. The report also spoke to the question of school delivery standards. It declared that there had been a "fundamental shift of perspective among educators, policymakers, and the public from examining inputs and elements of the educational process to examining outcomes and results."[135]

Raising Standards for American Education also said that to "ensure that students do not bear the sole burden of attaining the standards and to encourage assurances that the tools for success will be available to all schools, the Council also recommends that states establish school delivery standards."[136] Though this excused the federal government from the contentious matter of who should define delivery standards, it did not answer the two other questions: *Who should provide the funding to see that schools have the means to teach children to the standards?* and *Which should be implemented first, the delivery standards or the content and performance standards?*

Despite its cautious tone and clear refusal to call for national tests, NCEST's report provoked an outcry. The same day of its release, a group of educators, academics, and activists released to the press a denunciation of national testing. Those "opposing national tests said . . . that such examinations would end up penalizing students who attend bad schools and depriving local communities of control over what their students learn."[137] Five days later, *Education Week*, a prominent newspaper among educators and education policy people, ran a commentary piece asserting that

> The simplistic logic underlying the proposal for a national examination system . . . is that such a system will reform schools and improve student learning. By testing students on what they have learned, schools and teachers will be held accountable, will modify what they are doing in the classroom, and, therefore, students will learn more. This logic essentially ignores the gross inequities in instructional conditions—classroom and supplemental instruction, high-school curriculum track, quality of teaching and counseling, and availability of social-support services—that can affect the learning outcomes of students from non-European backgrounds.
>
> These conditions often mirror the caste-like status of non-European groups in American society and reflect not only financial inequities between school districts but also inequities in the opportunity to learn the appropriate content, skills, and knowledge that may be embodied in a test.

> . . . Without considering these instructional conditions, the proposed exams would unfairly penalize students of color in financially strapped urban districts and result in "blaming the victims" for their shortcomings.[138]

And, surprisingly, just before the report was to be released, NCEST member Marshall Smith joined a few dozen scholars and researchers in publicly denouncing any immediate moves to create a single national examination, though none had been contemplated by *Raising Standards for American Education*.[139]

Two months later, the House Subcommittee on Elementary, Secondary, and Vocational Education considered NCEST's report. Its members quickly became embroiled in a debate about the wisdom of national tests. Liberals on the subcommittee criticized NCEST for failing to define school delivery standards more broadly. They were displeased that the report said the federal government should let states, which had so often failed to ensure schools had the equipment and people they needed, define delivery standards.[140]

By not calling for a clear federal hand in creating education standards and assessments and by sidestepping the question of school delivery standards, *Raising Standards for American Education* offered little boost to the stymied America 2000 initiative. Worse, with the presidential election coming in November, congressional Democrats had no incentive to work with President Bush on these matters. They had a clear electoral incentive to not help Bush fulfill his promise to be the "education president." Indeed, in this final year of his single term in office, Bush's rate of getting any policy proposals, education or otherwise, enacted by Congress fell to its lowest level.[141] The administration spent much of the year bargaining with Congress, hoping it would include some of the components of America 2000 in S 2 and HR 3320. Congressional Democrats, particularly blacks and liberals, faulted the NCEST proposal's failure to guarantee equal resources and questioned whether tests would stigmatize the poor and racial minorities.[142] And the already difficult negotiations were further tripped up on the question of school choice.[143] Chairman Ford had previously agreed to support a small experimental voucher program ($30 million) for poor families that included private schools. When the Senate stripped that language from S 2, Ford reneged and removed the choice program, enraging the administration and conservatives.[144]

By summer Congress and the Bush administration were hopelessly deadlocked. Congress was willing to fund education standards but insisted on the development of "delivery standards," which would detail what constitutes an adequate amount of school spending per capita, physical resources, teacher education, and so forth. HR 4323 offered no funding for national assessments, "break the mold" schools, or school choice. This utter rejection of both America 2000 and the NCEST proposal prompted a veto threat from the White House.[145] HR 4323 passed the House on September 30, 1992, on near party lines, 279 votes to 124. The Senate attempted to pass a similar bill, placing President Bush in the position to either accept a bill nothing like his America 2000 or risk voters' wrath by vetoing an education bill just before the election. He was rescued from this dreadful choice when Republicans in the Senate filibustered S 2 and the Senate failed to invoke cloture by one vote on October 2.

Conclusion

The movement for national education standards and assessments that began in 1983 with *A Nation at Risk* ran aground in 1992. A complex mix of politics old and new had thwarted America 2000. In part, America 2000 was the victim of election-year partisan politics. Republicans wanted to capitalize on the perception of an educational crisis while Democrats fought to maintain their historic control of the issue.

But the disputes went beyond mere partisan politics. As Chapters 4 and 5 will indicate, previously advocates for more federal aid to education came from the left and justified it on the basis of need—states simply had not provided enough resources, physical or financial. Opponents, typically on the right, argued in constitutional and philosophical terms: education was a state and local function.

America 2000 faced little opposition from antistatists. For one, conservatives in Congress were mostly silent on the question of federal control. Few raised objections because America 2000 was a bottom-up blueprint for policy reform and included a school choice program. They raised no objections to the administration's contention that students were underachieving and that the federal government could do something about it. That said, though, conservatives did not offer much help to the Bush administration's push for national standards and assessments.

America 2000 did run head-first into liberalism. Issues of federal education policy and race and religion reappeared, sometimes evoking shrill battles of earlier decades.[146] The left in Congress, with rare exception, intensely opposed the idea of any additional federal dollars being used to support school choice. They stridently opposed national standards and testing because they believed that it was unfair to expect poor and minority students to meet standards until their schools had equal resources and most, if not all, of their socioeconomic handicaps were ameliorated.

In short, representatives and senators on the left held to the traditional liberal school reform position: American public schools were underfunded and inequitably funded. The role of the federal government was, first and foremost, to alleviate the inequities by providing additional funding and resources to schools in poor neighborhoods and then all other schools.

Though the movement to raise education standards through federal policy had stalled, it had not dissipated. There were factors in its favor. The widespread sense that the nation's public schools were failing had not abated. Even those most hostile to America 2000 did not deny that schools could do better and that all children could be expected to achieve higher. Importantly, a new president and quality schools advocate was soon to assume office. He had in mind a proposal bearing substantial similarity to America 2000. He favored national standards and assessments. During his presidency, the subject of the next two chapters, he would push three major standards-raising initiatives: Goals 2000, the Improving America's Schools Act (IASA), and voluntary national tests (VNTs). By reviewing his presidency, we can see just how new yet old the new federal politics of education was.

Notes

1. As quoted in Thomas Ferraro, "Senate Proposal for National Education Conference."

2. As quoted in Wood, *The Creation of the American Republic*, p. 120.

3. As quoted in Brademas, *Washington DC to Washington Square*, p. 23.

4. Lee, *The Struggle for Federal Aid*, p. 12; and Mitchell, *Federal Aid for Primary and Secondary Education*, p. 3.

5. Swift, *A History of Public Permanent Common School Funds in the United States*; Treat, *The National Land System*; and Rakove, "Ambiguous Achievement: The Northwest Ordinance."

6. Tyack et al., *Law and the Shaping of Public Education, 1785–1954*, p. 35.

7. Butchart, *Northern Schools, Southern Blacks, and Reconstruction*, pp. 99–110.

8. Lee, *The Struggle for Federal Aid*, pp. 50–55; and Hoar, *Autobiography of Seventy Years*, pp. 254–257.

9. Lee, *The Struggle for Federal Aid*, pp. 42–43.

10. Hoar, *Autobiography of Seventy Years*, pp. 254–257.

11. Lee, *The Struggle for Federal Aid*, pp. 51–53.

12. On the Perce bill, see Lee, *The Struggle for Federal Aid,*, pp. 57–58; on the Blair bills, see Mitchell, *Federal Aid for Primary and Secondary Education*, pp. 48–121. Similarly, when the representatives from the Confederate states returned to Congress, they wasted no time in attacking the Department of Education (created in 1865). Congress slashed the department's budget, moved its offices repeatedly, and downgraded the department to an office and then a bureau. Warren, *To Enforce Education*, pp. 86–150.

13. Robinson, *An Analysis of the Relationship Between Federal Education Legislation and Identifiable Economic, Political, or Social Crises in the United States*.

14. For a fuller examination of the history of the federal role in schooling and the politics thereof, see Kosar, *National Education Standards and Federal Politics*, chapters 4–5.

15. For a particularly vivid account of antistatist education politics, see Bendiner, *Obstacle Course on Capitol Hill*.

16. Brademas, *Washington DC to Washington Square,* p. 41.

17. On the US "obsession with Japanese economic dominance," see Kelman, "The Japanization of America," pp. 70–83; quote at p. 78. This time saw a number of books to this effect, for example, Vogel, *Japan as Number One: Lessons for America*; and Woronoff, *World Trade War.*

18. Dorn notes that though test scores had existed since the turn of the twentieth century, they had previously been for "internal consumption," that is, for the bureaucracy, not the public. Dorn, "The Political Legacy of School Accountability Systems."

19. See SAT trends in Chapter 2.

20. Ibid.

21. Angus and Mirel, *The Failed Promise of the American High School 1890–1995,* p. 165.

22. Ibid.

23. Finn writes that a "body of research dating back to James Coleman's pathbreaking studies has found that there is no direct relationship between the amount of resources a school receives and its level of academic performance. This realization has led reforms to emphasize results rather than inputs." Finn, "Making School Reform Work," p. 86.

24. Coleman et al., *Equality of Educational Opportunity*; Coleman, *Trends in School Desegregation 1968–1973*; Coleman et al., *High School Achievement*; Coleman et al., "Public and Private Schools"; Coleman and Hoffer, *Public, Catholic, and Private Schools.*

25. Ravitch, "The Coleman Reports and Education."

26. Finn, "Making School Reform Work," p. 86.

27. Edmonds, "Effective Schools for the Urban Poor." On Edmonds's research, see Viteritti, "Agenda Setting: When Politics and Pedagogy Meet."

28. Sizer, *Horace's Compromise*; Boyer, *High School*; Goodlad, *A Place Called School*; Powell et al., *The Shopping Mall High School*; and Doyle and Kearns, *Winning the Brain Race.*

29. As early as 1975, liberals felt obliged to defend Title I from critics. For example, see the statement of Representative Carl D. Perkins, *Congressional Record,* April 24, 1975, pp. 11823–11825.

30. Brademas's remarks are from House of Representatives, General Subcommittee on Education, *Aid to Elementary and Secondary Education, Part 1,* 89th Cong., 1st sess., p. 141.

31. Ibid.

32. Author interview: Phyllis McClure, December 6, 2002.

33. See Carter, *A Study of Compensatory and Elementary Education.* For a later study that confirmed these disappointing results, see Puma et al., *Prospects: Final Report on Student Outcomes.*

34. Cohen and Moffitt, *Title I: Politics, Poverty, and Knowledge.*

35. Author interview: Gerald Sroufe, December 12, 2002; and author interview: Phyllis McClure, December 6, 2002. See also Murphy, "The Education Bureaucracies Implement Novel Policy," pp. 160–199.

36. Cohen and Moffitt, *Title I: Politics, Poverty, and Knowledge,* pp. 79–81.

37. Bell, *The Thirteenth Man,* p. 2.

38. Bell attributes that phrase to Chief of Staff Edward Meese. See ibid., p. 2.

39. Ibid., p. 115.

40. Ibid., p. 116.

41. National Commission on Excellence in Education, *A Nation at Risk,* p. 5.

42. Public Papers of the Presidents, http://www.nexis.com.

43. Ferraro, "Panel Backs More—and Harder—School Work."

44. Kirschten, "The Politics of Education," p. 1448.

45. Ferraro, "The Sorry State of US Schools."

46. Reports include the Task Force on Education for Economic Growth of the Education Commission of the States, *Action for Excellence*; Business–Higher Education Forum, *America's Competitive Challenge*; Twentieth-Century Fund Task Force on Elementary and Secondary Education Policy, *Making the Grade*; and National Science Board Commission on Precollege Education in Mathematics, Science, and Technology, *Educating Americans for the 21st Century*. As quoted in Brademas, *The Politics of Education*, pp. 63–65.

47. Angus and Mirel, *The Failed Promise of the American High School*, p. 182.

48. One White House aide said that education had become a "dynamite issue that has sent an early surge of adrenaline into the nascent 1984 campaign." Kirschten, "The Politics of Education."

49. Public Papers of the Presidents, http://www.nexis.com.

50. Kirschten, "The Politics of Education," p. 1447.

51. Niemi et al., *Trends in Public Opinion: A Compendium of Survey Data*, p. 84.

52. Mayer, *The Changing American Mind*, p. 86.

53. Ferraro, *Untitled Newswire, United Press International*. Bell reports that David Stockman, director of the Office of Management and Budget and a strong advocate for major reduction of government spending, backed off further cutting the Department of Education's budget. Politically, education had become a "sensitive issue." Bell, *The Thirteenth Man*, p. 131. Just a day earlier, though, Reagan reaffirmed his desire to abolish the Department of Education. Ferraro, "Senate Proposal for National Education Conference."

54. Kirschten, "The Politics of Education," p. 1448.

55. Preamble, *The Constitution of the United States of America;* and Federalist No. 10, p. 47.

56. National Commission on Excellence in Education, *A Nation at Risk,* p. 33.

57. Fiske, "Top Objectives Elude Reagan as Education Policy Evolves," p. A1.

58. Horiuchi, *The United States Department of Education, 1981–1985, Agenda for Abolishment*.

59. Quoted in Fiske, "Top Objectives Elude Reagan as Education Policy Evolves," p. A1. The public reacted to the Reagan cutbacks similarly, though not as strongly, in other areas of social policy. Mayer, *The Changing American Mind*, p. 86.

60. Fiske, "Top Objectives Elude Reagan as Education Policy Evolves," p. A1.

61. Schattschneider, *The Semi-Sovereign People: A Realist's View of Democracy*.

62. Farnand, *A Study of the Social Philosophies of Three Major Interest Groups Opposed to Federal Aid to Education*.

63. In the wake of the September 11, 2001, attacks, we are seeing something similar: conservatives who once stood against more federal intrusion in public affairs are backing numerous measures that increase federal police and surveillance powers.

64. The systemic agenda is "essentially a discussion agenda" among those in a policy network. Anderson, *Public Policymaking*, p. 94. On state standards reforms that preceded Charlottesville, see Schwartz and Robinson, "Goals 2000 and the Standards Movement," pp. 173–206.

65. Looking back, Roy Romer, then governor of Colorado and later chair of

the NEGP, said that the point of having national goals and an accompanying report card was to "capture the attention and resolve of Americans to restructure our schools and radically increase our expectations for student performance." National Education Goals Panel, *The National Education Goals Report, Building a Nation of Learners 1991*, p. iii.

66. Vinovksis, *The Development and Demise of the National Education Goals*, p. 60.

67. National Education Goals Panel, *The National Education Goals Report: Building a Nation of Learners 1991*, p. iii.

68. Before Bush took office, Congress and President Reagan had enacted the 1988 Hawkins–Stafford amendments to Title I. PL 100-97 (1988), Augustus F. Hawkins–Robert Stafford Elementary and Secondary School Improvement Amendments.

69. Vinovskis, *The Development and Demise of the National Education Goals*, pp. 91–92.

70. Ibid., pp. 99–101.

71. Miller, "Democrats Stress Party's Historic Role With Set of Six Key Goals for Schools."

72. Charles Kolb, who served in the Bush administration, notes that the Bush administration intended to send the message to Congress that "You're a non-player." Kolb, *White House Daze*, p. 134.

73. At the time there was one independent in the House.

74. Bradley, "Bingaman Would Require Annual Report Card on Goals."

76. To reiterate a point made in Chapter 1 on methodology, this research traces the policy dialogue surrounding major pieces of education legislation. Accordingly, *witness* in this chapter and succeeding ones means both those persons who were invited to speak and any members of the committee who took a clear stand on the issue. Those who remain silent or spoke ambiguously are not counted.

77. The NAGB "is an independent, bipartisan group whose members include governors, state legislators, local and state school officials, educators, business representatives, and members of the general public. Congress created the twenty-six-member Governing Board in 1988 to set policy for the National Assessment of Educational Progress." Quote at http://www.nagb.org.

78. Walberg also urged that the NAEP be expanded, more data should be collected from states, and Congress should repeal the prohibition against collecting data below the state level (which would enable researchers to discern the performance of districts and localities but not individual students). US Congress, House of Representatives, Subcommittee on Elementary, Secondary, and Vocational Education of the Committee on Education and Labor, *Hearings,* 102nd Cong., 1st sess., March 12, 14, 1991, pp. 3–35.

79. Goodling also was the top Republican on the Committee on Education and Labor.

80. US Congress, House of Representatives, Subcommittee on Elementary, Secondary, and Vocational Education of the Committee on Education and Labor, *Hearings,* 102nd Cong., 1st sess., March 12, 14, 1991, p. 2.

81. Ibid., p. 136.

82. Ibid., pp. 137–138.

83. Ibid., pp. 61–72.

84. Ibid., pp. 139–148.

85. Ibid., p. 138.

86. Ibid., pp. 174–183, quote at p. 176.

87. Olson and Miller, "Congress Set to Fight over Panel Overseeing Goals"; Miller, "Conservatives Succeed in Killing Omnibus Education Bill"; Congressional Quarterly, *Congressional Quarterly Almanac 1990*, pp. 610–615; and Charles Kolb, *White House Daze*, pp. 134, 138.

88. On partisanship, see Congressional Quarterly, *Congressional Quarterly Almanac 1990*, pp. 8–12, 32, 39.

89. Miller, "Bush's School Plan Is 'Lamar's Baby', Participants Agree." See also Kolb, *White House Daze,* p. 142. Chester E. Finn Jr. was also involved. His book, which advocated standards and national tests, came out in 1991. See Finn, *We Must Take Charge*, especially pp. 247–256 and 263–266.

90. Ravitch, ed., *Debating the Future of American Education*, p. 5.

91. On the fate on the New American Schools, see Mirel, *The Evolution of the New American Schools*.

92. For a full description of the numerous America 2000 initiatives, see *America 2000: An Education Strategy*.

93. The Smith-Hughes Act (1918) created the Federal Board for Vocational Education, which had the power to specify curricula and teacher qualifications.

94. Who would draw up the standards was unclear. Ravitch notes that the matter was not decided at the launching of America 2000. Alexander hinted that governors would be involved in some fashion.

95. No state would be required as a condition of aid to use them.

96. Author correspondence, December 20, 2001.

97. George H. W. Bush, "Remarks by the President at Presentation of National Education Strategy," p. 2.

98. Rothman, "Educators, Analysts Hail Strategy as Bold Departure."

99. Alexander, *Proposed Education Strategy*, as cited in Vinovskis, *The Development and Demise of the National Education Goals*, p. 108.

100. Author interview: Scott Hamilton, special assistant to Secretary of Education Lamar Alexander, December 6, 2002.

101. Author interview: Chester E. Finn Jr., April 17, 2002; and author interview: Bruno V. Manno, May 22, 2002.

102. Zuckman, "Elbowing Democrats Aside, Bush Unveils School Plan," p. 983.

103. HR 3323, the Comprehensive Neighborhood Schools Revitalization Act, would later be renamed HR 4323.

104. US Congress, House of Representatives, Subcommittee on Select Education and Labor, *Hearing,* April 23, 1991.

105. US Congress, Senate, Committee on Labor and Human Resources, *Hearing on the Administration's Education Reform Proposal*, April 23, 1991, pp. 1–2.

106. That Representative Owens knew what to expect from the witnesses is clear. When it was Dr. Edward DeAvila's turn to speak, Owens stated, "Dr. DeAvila, the reason you're here is to get on the record your outrage, your disagreement with the national test proposal."

107. US Congress, House of Representatives, Subcommittee on Select Education and Labor, *Hearing,* April 23, 1991, pp. 59–125.

108. Ibid., p. 93.

109. Ibid., pp. 59–125.

110. Weisman, "Businesses Sign on to Bush Plan, but Many also Raising Concerns."

111. Representative William D. Ford (D-MI), the second-ranking Democrat on the House's major education committee and subcommittee, admitted to a reporter

that he was guarding his committee's turf. See Miller, "Most of Bush Plan Would Need Congressional Nod, Lawmakers Say."

112. Miller, "Administration Says It Lacks Funds to Support Goals Panel."

113. HR 2435 would create the thirty-member council, which would likely have no more than twelve Republicans; the rest would likely be Democrats or those sympathetic to them. Specifically, the council would have five members appointed by the speaker of the House (who was a Democrat); five by the majority leader of the Senate (also a Democrat); three by the minority leader of each body; and eight members appointed by the secretary of education, of whom not more than six could be Republicans. Zuckman, "House Panel Moves on National Test," p. 1449.

114. US Congress, House of Representatives, *National Council on Education Standards and Testing Act, Report 102–104*, p. 7.

115. Ibid.

116. PL 102-62 (1991).

117. PL 102-62, Title IV, sec. 402, 405 (1991). This was not the only partisan jockeying over panels. Congressional Democrats felt that the National Education Goals Panel did not represent Democrats or Congress adequately and sought to create their own education goals panel through S 2. Zuckman, "Small Panel, Big Goals," p. 1062.

118. US Congress, House of Representatives, *Hearings Before the Subcommittee on Elementary, Secondary, and Vocational Education of the Committee of Education and Labor,* June 18, 27, and July 11.

119. Four others testifying expressed technical policy concerns, for example, regarding the feasibility of allowing Title I funds to follow children who participated in choice programs.

120. US Congress, House of Representatives, *Hearings Before the Subcommittee on Elementary, Secondary, and Vocational Education of the Committee of Education and Labor,* June 18, 27, and July 11, p. 67.

121. Ibid., p. 147. This was correct: state reform efforts were to be driven by governors. Representative Gunderson, perhaps trying to squelch the federal control issue, replied to Ambach, "Cheer up, there isn't one reference to Congress either." Gunderson quote at p. 147.

122. Author interview: Dr. Edward Kealy, June 12, 2002. The NSBA later fought to empower school boards to alter district committee reform plans. Miller, "Buoyed by Senate Vote, Ford Backs Off Deal on School Choice."

123. Vinovskis, *The Development and Demise of the National Goals Panel*, pp. 150–151.

124. National Education Goals Panel, *The National Education Goals Report: Building a Nation of Learners*, p. iii.

125. In late July 1991 the National Education Association (NEA) at its annual convention voted to "oppose development or implementation of new federally mandated national tests and a national testing program as being contrary to the diverse interests and needs of children." Rothman, "Efforts to Create National Testing System Move into High Gear."

126. Vinovskis, *The Development and Demise of the National Goals Panel*, pp. 157–158.

127. National Council on Education Standards and Testing, *Raising Standards for American Education*.

128. Ibid., p. 8.

129. Ibid., p. 2.

130. In words that foreshadowed the second Bush administration's proposal, standards and assessment would help to raise expectations, especially for young-

sters from groups that have historically experienced less academic success," thereby "leaving no one behind." Ibid., p. 10.

131. Ibid., p. 3. NCEST further argued that a national effort to create standards and assessments was also desirable because it was more cost effective than having each state do the same. Ibid., p. 18.

132. Ibid., pp. 2–4.

133. Ibid., p. 7.

134. Ibid., p. 5. See also pp. 13–16. This ambiguity was intended. NCEST did not want to enter the fray over who should raise standards; it kept itself to the advisability of standards. Author interview: Francie Alexander (executive director, NCEST), March 26, 2003.

135. Ibid., p. 8.

136. Ibid., p. 3.

137. Chira, "Prominent Educators Oppose National Tests," p. B9.

138. Winfield and Woodard, "Where Are Equity and Diversity in America 2000?"

139. Geiger, president of the NEA and an NCEST panel member, also signed the protest. Rothman, "Group Urges 'Hitting the Brakes' on National Test."

140. Miller, "Legislation to Create National System of Standards, Assessments Comes Under Fire."

141. During his first year in office, Bush had succeeded in getting over 60 percent of his bills passed. In his last year, he got slightly over 40 percent enacted. On the whole, his legislative win rate was dramatically lower than his predecessor, Ronald Reagan (72.4 percent), and his successor, William J. Clinton (86.4 percent in his first two years). See Congressional Quarterly, *Congressional Quarterly Annual Almanac, 1994*, p. 4c. On the ideological divide between Bush and the House, see Cameron, "Studying the Polarized Presidency," *Presidential Studies Quarterly*.

142. Miller, "Legislation to Create National System of Standards, Assessments Under Fire."

143. Miller, "Buoyed by Senate Vote, Ford Backs Off Deal on School Choice."

144. Ford did this by replacing HR 3320 (which included choice) with HR 4323 (which did not).

145. Miller, "Bush Administration Is Seeking to Block Congressional Alternative to America 2000."

146. To take but one of many examples, in a June 1991 Senate hearing on another education bill, Senator Howard Metzenbaum (D-OH) broke the chamber's genteel protocol and berated Secretary Alexander over the America 2000 proposal to allow Title I dollars to follow poor children to the schools of their choosing: "Mr. Secretary, you're going to ruin the lives of millions of kids." As quoted in Pitsch, "School-Choice Plan Could Endanger Entire Bush Proposal."

4

The Politics of Goals 2000

*It is my sense that at this time in this country there is a certain zeitgeist,
there is a certain spirit of the times that is upon us that makes it possible
to do something very significant.*
　　　　—House Representative Ted Strickland (D-OH), April 22, 1993[1]

The First 100 Days

In mid-January 1993, the Democratic Party occupied the presidency and
held majorities in both houses of Congress for the first time since the Carter
administration. William Ford (D-MI), chairman of the House Education
and Labor Committee, described the psychic shift that he and other congressional Democrats had to make. It was like "trying to take a football
team that's only ever played defense and asking them to play offense. I'm
telling them, "Let's don't launch any great offensive and start running our
own plays until the coach tells us what he wants to do."[2] President William
Jefferson ("Bill") Clinton, of course, was that coach. The partisan balance
had shifted only slightly. Democrats grabbed another seat in the Senate in
the November elections, increasing their control of the chamber to 57 to 43.
Democrats lost nine seats in the House, yet still dominated it, holding 258
seats to the Republicans' 176.[3]

　　The Clinton administration characterized itself as "new Democrats."
Whereas the old left believed in more government and the old right favored
less government, the new Democrats struck a third way: smarter government. This philosophy comported nicely with the quality schools advocacy
position, and the Clinton administration advocated raising education standards through federal policy.

　　Although America 2000's proposal for national standards attracted little congressional support, education standards were fast gaining near hege-monic status among members of the federal education network.[4] Indicative of this was the 1992 presidential election. All three of the front-runners in the election—President George H. W. Bush, Bill Clinton, and H. Ross Perot—had endorsed education standards.[5] Clinton had been particularly clear on this point, writing that

> By the year 2000, we should have national standards for what our children should know at the fourth, eighth, and twelfth grades in math and science, language, geography, history, and other subjects, and we should have a meaningful set of national exams to measure whether they know what they're supposed to know.[6]

Furthermore, in spite of congressional antipathy, quietly the federal govern-ment already had moved to have national standards created. In 1992, the US Department of Education (in conjunction with the National Endowment for the Humanities and other agencies) made grants to the National Academy of Sciences, scholars, researchers, and others for the purpose of developing national standards in civics, history, geography, science, English, the arts, and foreign languages.[7]

Five weeks after President Clinton's inauguration, the Senate Committee on Labor and Human Resources held a hearing on "Examining the Need to Improve Education Standards and Job Training Opportunities."[8] Secretary of Education Richard W. Riley and Secretary of Labor Robert Reich were the only witnesses invited. Each of them spoke on the proposed standards in the soon-to-emerge Goals 2000 legislation.

Robert Reich described a transforming US economy, one that was becoming both more interlaced with other nations' economies and increas-ingly based on technology and information.[9] These qualitative changes pre-sented three problems for American businesses and workers: increased competition with workers in other nations, workers losing their jobs due to the disappearance of certain industries (called outsourcing), and a widening gulf between the skills workers possessed and the new skills American businesses sought.[10] To contend with these problems, workers needed more training and retraining. Reich and the administration thought the federal government could assist in this effort by partnering with US industries to create national occupational skills standards. Occupational standards would be useful in two ways. First, they would make clear to workers the training they needed for various jobs. Second, occupational standards would "create the possibility" that "the noncollege graduate could gain a credential" from a technical school in a skill area to show "potential employers a degree of mastery."[11]

Secretary Riley spoke in favor of the creation of education standards and assessments for US public schools.[12] Like Secretary Reich, Riley justified the need for federal action primarily on the basis of economics: "Building a world class American work force starts with building a world class educational system."[13] The schools were failing students because they did not have rigorous curricula based on "challenging content standards." Though the "task of developing content standards has begun . . . we must continue to build on these ongoing efforts to establish standards in math, science, English, language arts, geography, history, the arts, and foreign languages that will be the envy of the world."[14]

Riley sketched out legislation for a federal program that would be wholly voluntary. Participating states would receive funds to develop their own education standards and assessments, which they could submit to a national council that would give them a "Good Housekeeping Seal of Approval." It was unclear on what basis the council would certify the standards and assessments. Would the council have its own set of national standards drawn up that would serve as an educational gold standard for certification? If so, who would create these standards? Riley was ambiguous on this point. "This board of prestigious Americans will provide an essential service to this country. It will consider the fundamental issues about what our children should learn as they go through our Nation's schools."[15] The legislation to come also would create the Opportunity-to-Learn Commission that would develop

> voluntary standards to address such issues as: the capability of teachers to provide quality instruction to their areas; the extent to which teachers and administrators have continuing and ready access to the best knowledge about teaching and learning and how to make needed school changes, and the quality and availability of challenging curricula geared to meet world class standards.[16]

In light of the fate of America 2000, it might have been expected that the nebulous powers of the national standards council and the creation of a commission to craft opportunity-to-learn (OTL) standards would provoke an outcry from conservative members of the committee. This did not occur, in part due to the absence of three conservatives, Dan Coats (R-IN), Judd Gregg (R-NH), and David Durenberger (R-MN). Strom Thurmond (R-SC) and Orrin Hatch (R-UT) were present and said little during the hearing. Liberal James M. Jeffords (R-VT), who left the GOP eight years later, and a moderate, Nancy L. Kassebaum (R-KS), did not oppose national standards in principle. Kassebaum, though, did profess concern about the creation of OTL standards, wondering whether they and the forthcoming legislation might result in federal "micromanagement" of the schools.[17] This, remarkably, was the lone criticism Riley and Reich faced that day. Nobody objected to national standards and assessments as such, and Senator Jeffords agreed federal action was sensible because the public school systems suffered from "inertia" and were resistant to reform.[18]

The Democrats, who outnumbered Republicans nine to seven and had seven members present, were generally enthusiastic about the bill. Committee chairman Edward Kennedy (D-MA) agreed that international economic competition was a compelling reason for national standards, as did Senator Tom Harken (D-IA).[19] Democrats raised a few technical questions regarding the standards, but they were exploratory, not critical.

However, there were signs of trouble to come, rooted primarily in the divergent views on the causes of educational underachievement. Secretary Riley had emphasized the need for high standards and assessments. The aim of the new federal policy was to goad the schools into improving the quality of education they offered. The logic was sound: children could not possibly learn to high levels if they were not taught to high levels. Yet, Riley also testified that states needed to better ensure that all schools had adequate resources. Here, Riley was drawing on the idea of systemic school reform as advocated by scholars Marshall Smith and Jennifer O'Day. Smith had served on the NCEST standards task force and had joined the Clinton team. He and O'Day persuasively argued that the fundamental problem of student achievement was a matter of teaching. School curricula contained "little depth or coherence" and emphasized "isolated facts and basic skills."[20] In order to spur reforms in all schools, rigorous standards and aligned assessments were needed and schools had to be refashioned to focus on teaching to the standards. Smith and O'Day's argument tread between hard-line standards advocacy and liberalism. Like the quality school advocates who favored standards, Smith and O'Day wanted a school system that taught students to higher levels and held teachers and administrators accountable. However, like the liberals, Smith and O'Day argued that more spending on opportunity-to-learn standards (narrowly defined as teacher retraining, books, and other items clearly connected with teaching to the standards) might be needed.

Committee Democrats agreed with Riley that raising standards was important; however, they insisted that policy should not primarily target curricula. School curricula were inadequate, but the real sources of underachievement were inadequate school resources and the socioeconomic environments of children. Both Christopher Dodd (D-CT) and Senator Harken pointed to the financial inequities built into the school funding system. They argued that policy should be made to reform states' reliance on property taxes, which create gross disparities in per-pupil funding between localities. Senator Paul Simon (D-IL) asked the secretary whether the legislation should address the problem of adult illiteracy, since parental illiteracy can have negative effects on the educational achievement of the young.

In light of the role of resources and family characteristics in producing educational achievement, Democrats such as Howard Metzenbaum (D-OH) wondered whether it was fair to expect children in resource-poor schools and broken families to be held to high standards.[21]

The Clinton administration had a tougher time with the House. The administration intended to unveil the Goals 2000: Educate America Act at March's end. It was delayed and forced back to the drawing board after a heated meeting with members of the House Education and Labor Committee. In part, the matter seemed territorial; House members appeared to have felt the administration did not consult with them enough.[22] Thomas Wolanin, who served as an assistant to Representative Ford, suggests his boss did not really understand Goals 2000 or standards reform. Having served in Congress for over thirty-five years, Ford was focused on the reauthorization of Title I, which would involve ten times as much money as Goals 2000. So Ford was taken aback; Goals 2000 seemed like a pointless and time-consuming diversion.[23]

Most problematic, though, was the subject of opportunity-to-learn standards. Ford, also the Education and Labor Subcommittee chair, told the administration through the media, "the legislation will not come out of my committee unless service-delivery standards are equal to or slightly ahead of any testing or standards."[24] Ford was a pro-union liberal who had joined the House in 1965 and helped pass the ESEA. To him and liberals like Major Owens (D-NY), federal education policy was first and foremost about money. Too many schools had too little of it, and the job of the federal government was to ameliorate this problem. Confronted with a White House pushing standards, Ford and other liberals did not attack standards. Instead, they attempted to get what they always wanted (more resources) by defining delivery or OTL standards much more broadly than did the administration (and Smith and O'Day, for that matter).

Other issues also loomed: the control and composition of the council that was to certify state standards and assessments, the use of state assessments to retain pupils or deny them graduation, and apportioning responsibility and power over standards in relation to schooling at the various levels of government.[25]

Navigating Politics Left and Right

The administration altered the bill in an attempt to accommodate the concerns of Democrats and public school interest groups, who stressed the importance of resources in educational achievement, and Republicans, who were more than happy to blast the new president for encroaching on local control. Clinton backed away from the idea of fashioning a set of national

.exams and dropped the idea of creating an opportunity-to-learn commission since both would likely provoke an antistatist backlash.[26] On April 21 the administration rereleased its proposal. The major provisions of the bill provided for:

1. Codifying six education goals that bore substantial similarity to those agreed upon by governors in 1989 and contained in America 2000 (see Figure 4.1).[27]
2. Creating the National Education Standards and Improvement Council (NESIC), which would certify voluntary national content and student performance assessments, and voluntary opportunity-to-learn standards.[28]
3. Codifying the National Education Goals Panel (NEGP), which, among other things, would prepare a "national report card" that would report on the progress toward the education goals, nominate members of NESIC, and review the decisions of NESIC.
4. Empowering the secretary of education to provide grants for the development of assessments and opportunity-to-learn standards.
5. Establishing an application process through which states could receive Goals 2000 funds to support efforts at "fundamental restructuring and improvement of elementary and secondary education" through the "establishment or adoption of challenging content and student performance standards."[29]

The administration requested $400 million for 1994 and "such sums as may be necessary for each of the fiscal years 1995 through 1998."[30]

On the question of opportunity-to-learn standards, the administration had attempted to steer a middle course between the conflicting interests. As Riley later described it, "The Clinton administration inherited a major political dilemma pitting civil rights and education groups, on the one hand, against conservative members of the House and Senate, business groups, and governors and legislators on the other."[31] Clinton's proposal required a participating state to submit a reform plan as a condition of aid. Among the required components of a reform plan were "a strategy and timetable for . . . adopting or establishing opportunity-to-learn standards [and] ensuring every school in the State achieves the State's opportunity-to-learn standards."[32] Liberal Democrats wanted to see the word "timetables" used to ensure that states, one day, could be held accountable for improving resource distribution among schools. Liberals also wanted to assure that the new standards and tests would not decrease the grade advancement and graduation of minority and poor students. Thus, they saw to it that Goals 2000 prevented NESIC from certifying any exam states or localities used for graduation, grade promotion, or retention decisions.[33] In the name of

Figure 4.1   Goals 2000 Educational Goals

1. By the year 2000, all students in America will start school ready to learn.

2. By the year 2000, the high school graduation rate will increase to at least 90 percent.

3. By the year 2000, American students will leave grades 4, 8, and 12 having demonstrated competency over challenging subject matter including English, mathematics, science, foreign languages, arts, history, and geography.

4. By the year 2000, America will be first in the world in mathematics and science achievement.

5. By the year 2000, every adult American will be literate and will possess the knowledge and skills necessary to compete in a global economy.

6. By the year 2000, every school in America will be free of drugs and violence and will offer a disciplined environment conducive to learning.

Source: William J. Clinton, *Proposed Legislation—"Goals 2000: Educate America Act,"* Title I.

fairness to poor and nonwhite children, whom they believed would fail to reach standards, liberals sought to prevent states and localities from transforming their present tests into high-stakes exams before OTL standards were developed.

Governors, in contrast, were adamantly against being coerced by the federal government to adopt OTL standards. Both Clinton and Riley appreciated the liberals' contention that students in resource-poor schools might not perform as well as students who attended schools rich in the latest computer technology, science equipment, and educational facilities. However, as former governors, they recognized that opportunity-to-learn standards had the potential to create numerous policy and political problems for governors. Some of the more obvious problems were:

- Any official measure of an OTL would set up states to be sued for the failure to meet these standards.
- Taking funds away from wealthier schools and giving them to poorer ones was politically impractical. Therefore, OTL standards would force states to raise taxes in order to bring underresourced schools up to standard.
- Measuring an opportunity to learn is difficult. There are an enormous number of factors that may be reasonably construed as affect-

ing the opportunity to learn (e.g., adequacy of teacher subject knowledge, age of textbooks, child access to health care, social factors such as the income of parents, etc.).[34]

Furthermore, if states were forced to move quickly to create and implement opportunity-to-learn standards, poorer states would be unlikely to participate in Goals 2000. Perversely, those states most in need of the extra funds from Goals 2000 would not apply because bringing their schools up to standard would cost them more than the Goals 2000 funds would benefit them. Thus, the Clinton administration included the phrase "strategy and timetable for adopting or establishing opportunity-to-learn standards" to give poor states the right to long delay the expenses associated with meeting OTL standards.

To defuse the potential antistatist charge that Goals 2000 would create a national school board that would dictate school curricula, the Clinton administration made Goals 2000 a voluntary, stand-alone grant program.[35] No state would be obliged to participate in it, and none could have funds from other education programs withheld for nonparticipation in Goals 2000. Moreover, the per annum funding for Goals 2000 was less than one-tenth that of Title I of the ESEA, and the bill's oversight features were very modest. Two federal entities would be created. One of them was the already existent and uncodified NEGP. Its eighteen members would include eight governors and four members of Congress, a group that would be unlikely to create a federal school board or slap unfunded mandates upon states. Goals 2000 would also birth NESIC, which had two enumerated powers. It would:

1. Certify national education standards and assessments, which would be created by someone other than NESIC (e.g., educational consortia or university researchers); and
2. Assist the secretary of education in certifying state-submitted education standards, performance assessments, and opportunity-to-learn standards.

In both these duties, the NEGP could override NESIC's decisions. NESIC would not be a hulking federal bureaucracy like the Internal Revenue Service. It would have twenty members: five professional educators, five representatives of business and industry, five members of the public, and five education experts. They would be nominated by the NEGP, appointed by the president for a three-year term, and could serve for no more than two consecutive terms each.[36]

States, again, were under no compulsion to participate. A state that did so was required, in the first year, to submit an application describing "the process by which [it] will develop a school improvement plan" to bring about statewide standards-based reform.[37] In subsequent years, a state need only submit reports detailing progress on its plan, how it spent the previous year's funds, and how it plans to spend additional funds. There were no expressed limits on how long a state could take to create, let alone implement, standards.[38]

Congress Responds

Both houses of Congress held hearings in short order. The House took up Goals 2000 on April 22, May 4, and May 18; the Senate, on May 4 and May 14. Intriguingly, of those five days of hearings, just two were devoted to the topic of education standards for the public schools (April 22 in the House, and May 4 in the Senate). The remaining hearings focused on Title IV, the national jobs skills standards portion of the bill. Considering the dramatic alteration to the federal role that the bill posed, more time spent deliberating the policy sense of using federal power to raise education standards might have been expected. Again, according to Wolanin, Ford, who had the power to investigate the matter of standards at length, did not do so because he was more concerned with the upcoming renewal of Title I of the ESEA.[39] Instead, the only witness called by the House Subcommittee on Elementary, Secondary, and Vocational Education and the Senate Committee on Labor and Human Resources was Secretary Riley. No scholars, school principals, state education department administrators, teacher or union representatives, or parents were invited to speak on the bill. In the Senate, there were just five witnesses: Secretary Riley, two teachers, a local administrator, and a businessman.[40] Generally, Congress consciously chose not to debate the wisdom of standards policy.

Before the House, Secretary Riley once again characterized the cause of underachievement as a "watered down curriculum" and low expectations "for far too many of our students."[41] Riley also reiterated Secretary of Labor Reich's observations: the American economy was increasingly based on high technology and information utilization, and its health was increasingly a function of its workers' education vis-à-vis the rest of the world.[42] Of the forty-three members of the subcommittee (28 Democrats, 15 Republicans), only nineteen members were present (14 Democrats, 5 Republicans), fourteen of which had anything to say during the hearing. Marge Roukema (NJ) was the sole Republican to express opposition to the idea of national education standards on antistatist grounds:

> Mr. Secretary, I don't think you are going to win me over on this. . . . I am absolutely convinced . . . that the so-called voluntary national system of

skills standards combined with opportunity-to-learn standards will inevitably, like night follows day, lead to a national curricula [sic], to which I am unalterably opposed.[43]

Two Republicans, Thomas Petri and Steve Gunderson of Wisconsin, spoke but did not express opposition to using federal power to raise standards. Petri wondered if Goals 2000 was overly bureaucratic in structure, whereas Gunderson questioned the secretary over the language concerning OTL standards, the composition of NESIC, the power for the secretary of education to waive certain regulations on the states, and the difference between national education standards and a national curriculum.[44]

Democrats raised more difficult questions, but, again, did not question the notion of using federal power to raise education standards. As before, the majority of their queries were rooted in the belief that increasing educational resources and social services in schools serving children of the poor and nonwhite should come before or concurrently with raising standards. To this end, George Miller (D-CA) and Major Owens sought to define opportunity-to-learn standards broadly. Representatives Tim Roemer (IN), Jolene Unsoeld (WA), Carlos A. Romero-Barcelo (PR), Karan English (AZ), and Lynn Woolsey (CA) stressed the importance of funding for drug-free schools, more teacher training, and the importance of early childhood education.[45]

In the Senate, Goals 2000 and Secretary Riley faced even fewer difficult questions. Riley again identified the cause of underachievement as a "watered down curriculum" and spoke of the changing American economy.[46] Four of the five other witnesses—a school teacher, a deputy city school superintendent, a state school superintendent, and a vice-president for human resources of a hospital—agreed that the education problem was the result of low expectations in public schools and that national policy to raise standards was required.[47] The other witness, a teacher, was skeptical of using federal power to improve academic standards. He questioned whether it would adversely affect ongoing state reforms. Said schools needed "adequate resources," better pay to attract better teachers, and smaller class sizes. He also wondered "about a national curriculum being around the corner," which he opposed.[48]

As for the committee itself, all seven Republicans were present for the May 4 hearing, but only three of the ten Democrats appeared. Despite the preponderance of Republicans, there was little direct criticism of raising standards through federal policy. Six of the ten members present expressed outright support for Goals 2000, including committee chairman Ted Kennedy, who noted that a decade had passed since *A Nation at Risk* and the United States still had not responded.[49] Senator Judd Gregg (R-NH) fretted over more federal dictates being placed on the states and wondered if noncompliance by nonparticipating states would bring a reduction in funding in other programs, such as the ESEA. He was told unequivocally that it would not. Senator Dan Coats (R-IN) thought Goals 2000 was overly bureaucratic and asked why private school choice was not part of the bill. Senator Dave Durenberger (R-MN) seconded Coats on the latter point.[50] Three of the Republican senators (Kassebaum, Hatch, and Thurmond) raised sharp questions over opportunity-to-learn standards and whether Goals 2000 would force states to adopt them. Thurmond stated that he "firmly" agreed with the ends of the bill but thought that OTL standards should be left to localities.[51] Senator Paul Wellstone (D-MN) took the opposite position, hinting that he wanted to see the OTL provisions strengthened, a point on which Vermont's state school superintendent and witness, Richard Mills, agreed.[52]

In May, both chambers of Congress began marking up Goals 2000. The House's Elementary, Secondary, and Vocational Education Subcommittee met on May 6. A number of minor amendments were proposed and adopted without much debate, including adding another goal to Goals 2000 that would provide more teacher training. Representative John Boehner (R-OH) offered a school choice amendment, but it failed on a voice vote. Then trouble erupted. Jack Reed (D-RI) moved to amend the bill so that a state as a condition of aid would be required to list specific corrective actions if a school or school system did not meet its opportunity-to-learn standards. The response from Republicans was swift and sharp: Gunderson called it a "deal buster," and Representative William Goodling (R-PA) said such an amendment would turn "this side of the aisle" against the bill.[53] Democrats backed the amendment, and it passed on an 18 to 7 party line vote. Goodling, referring to the possibility that the OTL standards would make states the targets of lawsuits, groused, "If, five years from now, all the money goes to the courts rather than children, I want to be able to say 'I told you so.'"[54] The subcommittee passed HR 1804 as amended by a vote of 17 to 9.

When Goals 2000 had been announced in April, business had shown its support again. The Chamber of Commerce of the United States, the Business Roundtable, and the National Association of Manufacturers all agreed Goals 2000 might better prepare the young for work. Governors, however, withheld their support. Goals 2000 raised profound and complex issues for them. Three questions were paramount:

- Would it mandate opportunity-to-learn standards?
- What would be the extent of federal oversight?
- How much gubernatorial discretion would there be over the use of Goals 2000 funds?

After the Reed Amendment passed, though, the governors entered the fray. Governors Romer and Campbell, on behalf of the National Governors Association (NGA), wrote Secretary Riley and voiced their opposition to opportunity-to-learn standards and the powers to be given to NESIC.[55] They stated, in part, "Even on a voluntary basis, some of the Governors believe that this is an example of federal intrusion into an area that has historically been the responsibility of the states."[56] Governor Campbell wrote an additional letter to the secretary that complained the legislative process already had begun transforming the administration's proposal from "performance based accountability to accountability based on inputs [i.e., resources]." Campbell also thought that NESIC was far too powerful and that the United States was being led "inevitably toward a federalization of what has been, until now, a pact that recognized and respected the preeminent role of states in education reform."[57]

The president and secretary both recognized that the Reed Amendment could make passage, to say nothing of implementation, of Goals 2000 difficult. Governors were against it, and the Reed Amendment invited the anti-statist charge that the Clinton administration was usurping local control over schools. In May, the National Education Association, a major donor to the Democratic Party and Clinton's campaigns for president, added to the administration's difficulties.[58] The association released a public statement calling for OTL standards in Goals 2000. It defined OTL very broadly, far beyond what the administration desired. OTL should include quality measures of a school's teaching staff, opportunities for staff development, class size, course diversity, library and research resources, staff and facilities for disabled students, counselors and healthcare professionals, education support employees, and the condition of school buildings.[59] Clinton and Riley hit the stump and privately began trying to sway lawmakers to more narrowly define opportunity-to-learn standards.

The House continued its work. The full Committee on Education and Labor met on June 23. Nineteen amendments were offered during the turbulent gathering.[60] Representative Richard Armey (R-TX) attempted to scrap the whole bill and replace it with a school choice program. His proposal was voted down 35 to 7. Representative Goodling moved to delete the Reed Amendment. Reed responded by arguing that it was not fair for the government to raise education standards without guaranteeing that all students have an opportunity to learn in the form of adequate resources. Reed did, though, offer to word the amendment so that a state would not be required to stipulate specific redresses of resource reform. Instead, a state would have to draw up a process for contending with resource inadequacy. Goodling and Gunderson both argued against this weaker amendment, reasoning that it would discourage states from applying for needed school aid.[61] By a 28 to 15 vote along party lines, the Reed Amendment, in weakened form, was accepted. Thus, the OTL provisions of the bill required each participating state "to establish a plan and timetable" for:

1. Adopting or establishing opportunity-to-learn standards prior to or simultaneous with the establishment or adoption of challenging content and student performance standards.
2. Ensuring that every school in the state is making demonstrable progress toward meeting the state's opportunity-to-learn standards.
3. Ensuring that the state's OTL standards address the needs of all students.
4. Providing for periodic independent assessments of the extent to which OTL standards are being met throughout the state.
5. Periodically reporting to the public on the extent of the state's improvement in achieving such standards and providing all students with a fair opportunity to achieve the knowledge and skill levels that meet the state's content and student performance standards.[62]

That same day the Education and Labor Committee approved HR 1804 by another partisan vote of 28 to 15.

Little has been written about what took place in the Senate's Labor and Human Resources Committee meetings on May 19, 1993. It is certain, though, that Goals 2000 had an easier time there than in the House. Senator Kassebaum negotiated with Democrats to reduce the requirements placed on states for participation in Goals 2000 from twelve to four pages of regulations. Liberals did raise the issue of opportunity-to-learn standards, but, likely at the urging of Chairman Kennedy, they did not press the matter. The only real divide was over the composition of the board that would develop job skills standards.[63] The committee voted 14 to 3 in favor of the bill, with conservative senators Gregg, Hatch, and Coats in dissent. Significantly, S 846 lacked an OTL provision.

In the meantime, there had been rumblings outside Congress. Interest groups weighed in on opportunity-to-learn standards and the proper extent of federal power. In mid-July, the right-wing Concerned Women for America along with Phyllis Schlafly of the ultraconservative Eagle Forum mailed letters to Congress and asked members to take up the Armey school choice bill instead of Goals 2000. Armey's bill, unlike Goals 2000, they claimed, would not funnel federal dollars to controversial programs such as outcomes-based education, sex education, and clinics in the schools, and it avoided taking a step down the road to federally imposed education standards and tests.[64] The conservative Heritage Foundation and the Free Congress Foundation published critical circulars on Goals 2000 that conjured the specter of federal control.[65] Armey and the Family Research Council circulated a number of inflammatory letters warning that Goals

2000 was a gross power grab by the federal government that spelled the end for "three and a half centuries" of local control and educational liberty in the United States.[66]

In August, the NGA released a thick booklet on the subject of opportunity-to-learn standards and a statement that declared:

> The Governors strongly affirm that states, not the federal government, should assume the responsibility for creating an educational delivery system that enables all students to achieve to high standards. Each state has the constitutional responsibility to determine its own education delivery system. The federal role is important, but limited.[67]

Governors Campbell and Romer also penned a letter to Senator Kennedy, saying they strongly preferred the Senate bill over the House one due, in great part, to the House's inclusion of OTL standards.[68] And in a speech before the NGA late that summer, Senator Robert Dole (R-KS) stoked the antistatist fire:

> The House version [of Goals 2000] seeks to reverse local control of our schools and impose what are now called national delivery standards. . . . Rather than concerning ourselves with whether our students are actually learning, the federal government could dictate class size, the number of computers per student, possibly even the text books used.[69]

The House debated HR 1804 in October 1993. Members worked swiftly and mostly in concert. To stave off poison pill amendments, the Rules Committee required any proposed amendments be submitted ahead of the debate itself and printed in the *Congressional Record*. Thus, only ten amendments made it to the floor. The Rules Committee allowed Goodling's amendment forbidding any unfunded federal mandates in the form of opportunity-to-learn standards. This passed easily, 424 to 0, and likely helped mollify some concerned conservatives.[70]

Though the Rules Committee did thwart all amendments raising explosive social issues—such as sexual education and school prayer—Representative Armey's amendment to scrap the bill and replace it with a school choice bill was allowed. It was defeated 300 to 130. The House left intact the modified Reed Amendment, which had been rendered weaker by Goodling's amendment, and voted 307 to 118 in favor of HR 1804. There was a clear partisan divide in the vote: 249 Democrats were in favor, and only 2 against; 57 Republicans were in favor, and 119 were against. The Senate put off consideration until after the winter recess.

In his State of the Union Speech on January 25, 1994, President Clinton stumped for Goals 2000. He insisted the nation needed "tough, world-class academic and occupational standards for all our children." He further declared that the nation should "measure every one of our children by one high standard: Are our children learning what they need to know to compete and win in the global economy?"[71] The president appeared to have the public's support on this. A December poll had found that 82 percent of Americans supported the idea of national standards, and 81 percent wanted schooling to be more rigorous.[72]

The Senate debated Goals 2000 in February, and in March both the Senate and House debated and voted on the conference bill.[73] The debates and negotiations were sometimes fierce. Once again, the differences between liberals and conservatives were not over the wisdom of raising standards to improve educational achievement. Almost without fail, members of Congress, in accordance with the administration, insisted educational achievement was lacking and that the federal government was obliged to improve the educational achievement of all public school students so that the United States could better compete in the international economic arena. Senator Jeffords, who was instrumental in shepherding the bill through Congress, declared,

> In 1983, the landmark report, "A Nation at Risk," brought to the public's attention what many already knew—that we faced a rising tide of mediocrity in our schools which threatened our very future as a nation and a people. In no uncertain terms, this report described the problems that were plaguing American schools—low expectations for students, a watered down curriculum. . . . This issue is critical for our future economic security. . . . It is so critical to remind ourselves that we are entering a very, very competitive world market system . . . and improving our standard of living depends entirely on our ability to compete in those world markets.[74]

Senator Bingaman (D-NM), agreed: "More than 85 percent of Americans believe that the nation needs higher education standards in order to be economically competitive. I think we all agree with that."[75]

The points of dispute centered upon opportunity-to-learn standards and the amount of power Goals 2000 would give the federal government over school curricula.[76] In order to blunt antistatist critiques, both the House and Senate versions of Goals 2000 mentioned the word *voluntary* some seventy times. The lead sponsors of the bills, Senators Kennedy, Kassebaum, and Jeffords in particular, took to the floor early to give speeches describing the things Goals 2000 would not do. Kennedy repeatedly emphasized that Goals 2000 was not a federal imposition but a plan for "bottoms [sic] up reform."[77] Kassebaum told colleagues, "This bill does not: federalize education, establish a national curriculum or school board, require that States adopt national standards . . . dictate to schools how much they must spend per pupil, how to license their teachers [or tell them] which textbooks to use."[78]

Some senators remained skeptical. The more strident critics, such as Senators Gregg, Hatch, and Bob Smith (R-NH), characterized opportunity-to-learn standards in almost sinister terms. "'Opportunity-to-learn,' that is a nice euphemism," scoffed Senator Gregg. "What it really means is a federal methodology for teaching. . . . It is the methodology of how people teach and what they are taught and the atmosphere in which they are taught."[79] Gregg also promised to stand against the bill and "guard the Constitution."[80] Hatch was equally suspicious, seeing Goals 2000 as the bedrock of a "system of stealth standards" that would lead to "the national homogenization of education policy." Hatch also cited an article that claimed NESIC would inevitably be dominated by activists for whichever party controlled Congress and the White House. NESIC would become a propaganda organ that would slant school curricula against the other party. Hatch further claimed that Goals 2000 was an effort at "educational programming through national standards."[81] A few other senators referred to NESIC as an incipient national school board.

Oddly, the antistatist right occasionally was joined by the far left in its suspicions of national standards and testing. Senator Carol Moseley-Braun (D-IL) associated standards and testing with eugenics and racism:

> There are possible dangers in assessing the achievement of students—especially economically and socially disadvantaged students. As Stephen J. Gould highlights in his book, "The Mismeasure of Man," intelligence and achievement tests have been misused throughout history to "rank people in a single series of worthiness, to find that oppressed people and disadvantaged groups—races, classes, or sexes—are invariably inferior and deserve their status."[82]

Meanwhile, liberals such as Senators Wellstone and Simon fought to add OTL language in Goals 2000 and spending for early childhood intervention programs. A number of senators referred to Jonathan Kozol's *Savage Inequalities*, a book that details, among other things, the often gross disparities between the physical resources of schools and the social environments of the children who attend them.[83] Without providing more resource aid to poor schools, Senator Wellstone declared, Goals 2000 would "set up goals that many young people cannot reach, and . . . fail them again."[84]

Yet, policy differences were not the sole impediment to passage of Goals 2000. Social issues among members of Congress loomed equally large and threatened to trip up passage of the bill. Amendments were offered to prevent the federal government from promoting or distributing contraceptives in public schools and to ban the use of tobacco on school grounds.[85] There was also debate over the use of pupil surveys by schools. Senator Charles Grassley (R-IA) put forth evidence that some schools were querying students about their sexual behavior and other private matters without parental consent.[86] Senators also spent a great deal of time delivering colloquies in favor of a Sense of the Senate amendment to Goals 2000 that would condemn Nation of Islam minister Khalid Abdul Muhammad.[87]

Most explosive, though, was the debate over school prayer, which provoked intense arguments over the law, the Constitution, the free exercise of religion, and the extent of the federal government's powers. Senator Jesse Helms moved to amend the bill to withhold all federal education funds to any state or local education agency "which has a policy of denying, or which effectively prevents participation in, prayer in public schools by individuals on a voluntary basis."[88] Prima facie, Helms's amendment seemed inoffensive. He was only asking that any states allowing its schools to violate student civil liberties be punished by the loss of federal funds. Moreover, said Helms, this amendment was reasonable because similar language was often included in federal education bills. The education appropriations bill of 1993 stipulated: "No funds appropriated under this Act may be used to prevent the implementation of programs of voluntary prayer and meditation in the public schools." And it was true. Students' freedom to express their religious beliefs in the public schools had decreased over the past half century.[89]

That said, the Helms amendment was problematic because it was overly broad. It is one thing to forbid a state to use federal funds to "prevent the implementation of programs of voluntary prayer" (1993 language cited above), and quite another to cut off all aid to a state or school district if it did anything that inhibited student prayer (Helms amendment). The 1993 language sought to keep federal money from being used to stop any programs of prayer; the Helms amendment aimed at action by any school officials that inhibited a student's free exercise. The latter would, then, allow the federal government to cut off the funding of an entire state if, say, one of its principals did something inappropriate. Setting aside the harshness of the penalty, this amendment is problematic because federal courts have not neatly drawn the boundaries of constitutionally permitted prayer in public schools. States and local education agencies cannot be entirely sure what rules are constitutionally permissible and which lurch into the realm of denying the right of free exercise. Worse, states and school districts had long faced legal action by the American Civil Liberties Union and strict-separationist groups for allowing too much religion on school grounds. If Helms's amendment passed, they would likely face more suits for brooking too little religious activity.

The Helms amendment made for dramatic political theater. Helms attempted to amend the Goals 2000 bill in February and was rebuffed. He asked House members to attach an identical amendment and failed. On March 23, the House voted overwhelmingly, 306 to 121, in favor of the conference report. But the partisan divide was sharp. Among Democrats,

246 voted yea, only 6 voted nay. Of the 121 votes against, 115 were cast by Republicans. Two-thirds of the Republicans who voted (115 of 174) cast their lots against Goals 2000. Particularly telling was the Americans for Democratic Action (ADA) ideological liberalism measure of the advocates and opponents.[90] The mean ADA score of those who voted for Goals 2000 was a fairly liberal 65.9; opponents scored a very conservative 9.6.[91]

Senator Helms exacted his revenge on Friday, March 25. He began a filibuster of the Senate vote on the conference report. A number of his colleagues were outraged. Senators had assumed they would vote on the report and then leave Washington for their home states for the weekend. The Senate's observant Jews were faced with the choice of staying for the vote and failing to return home before sundown (a violation of their faith) or letting Helms scuttle Goals 2000. Other senators had to alter or cancel their travel plans. Helms, much to the displeasure of his colleagues, held the floor for part of the day, turned it over to a few junior conservative allies who continued the filibuster, and exited the Capitol to catch a flight home.

In the early hours of Saturday, March 26, the Senate invoked cloture and approved the conference report. The partisan split on the conference report vote was very similar to the vote in the House. Yeas outnumbered nays 63 to 22. Among Democrats, 53 Democrats were for Goals 2000 and only one was against it. Ten Republicans supported Goals 2000, and 21 (two-thirds) voted nay. The mean ADA score of Senate proponents of Goals 2000 was 75.8, of opponents 16.0. Five days later, President Clinton signed Goals 2000 into law.

The Effect of Politics on Goals 2000

Politics Hobbles Goals 2000, Part I:
Liberal and Antistatist Compromises

Federal legislation is inevitably the result of compromise. Seldom does any group or interest get everything it wants to the exclusion of others. Goals 2000 was a compromise, but an extreme one. It was, in great measure, the legislative output of a collision of three political-policy ideations: *antistatism*, *liberalism*, and *quality schools advocacy*, which we began to consider earlier.[92]

Antistatists are reflexively distrustful of increased federal involvement in public schooling.[93] They tend to stand against education bills (especially general ones) on principled grounds. Some antistatists are strict constructionists, who argue that the Constitution does not empower the federal government to make education policy. They emphasize the long tradition and "genius" of local control over education. Other antistatists see the federal government as naturally inefficient, heavy-handed, blind to local differences, and tending to accrete power. Some take a benign view of the inadequacies of the federal government, reasoning that inefficient federal education policy is caused by bureaucratism and the government's distance from localities. Others, however, attributed to the federal government an insatiable hunger for power and, in the case of federal education policy, a desire to indoctrinate children in ideology.[94] All variants of the antistatist critique were aired during the debates on Goals 2000, including that Goals 2000 would create a national school board[95]; that it was a plot to teach children liberal, atheistic social values; and that it was a crude, likely hapless intrusion on a matter properly and best handled by states.[96]

Liberals, meanwhile, tend to trust the federal government more than state and local governments. They often note that it was the federal government that coerced states to recognize and uphold civil liberties; it was the federal government that endeavored to desegregate the schools, aid the poor, and deliver badly needed funds to impoverished school districts. In this view, the history of local and state schooling is replete with unequal treatment of the poor and nonwhite. Accordingly, in the debates on Goals 2000, liberals often decried the "widespread and systemic" underfunding that starved schools attended by children of the poor and nonwhite. Senators and representatives alike cited Kozol's *Savage Inequalities* as proof that many children are discriminated against.[97] To liberals, Goals 2000 was a small but welcome increase in federal involvement.[98] Yet Goals 2000's emphasis on raising standards and creating assessments without guaranteeing equal or at least adequate educational resources in schools for the poor and nonwhite struck liberals as unfair. Behind low test scores, liberals perceived a system that was, perhaps intentionally, stacked against poor and nonwhite children. Their low test scores were products of their inadequate social environment (broken families, violent neighborhoods) and enrollment in resource-poor schools with old books, leaky ceilings, and ill-trained teachers. Thus, raising standards and toughening assessments—without providing more resources and programs to compensate for injuries done to children by their environment—would result in increased numbers of demoralized dropouts.

The quality schools advocates, roughly speaking, come in two types: those who think educational achievement can be improved through the interjection of market forces (choice advocates), and those who think it can be improved through governmental action to raise standards (standards advocates).[99] Goals 2000 was standards legislation primarily.[100] Standards advocates concede that an inadequate social environment and resource-strapped schools can have adverse effects on student educational achievement. However, they differ from the liberals in their assessment of the primary cause of educational underachievement and its remediability. Standards advocates locate the source of underachievement in school curricula. They take an optimistic view of student achievement: all children can learn at high levels if schools teach them at high levels. Because schools have shown themselves frequently unable or unwilling to set high standards, government must therefore compel or induce them to do so.

These philosophical divisions over the primary cause and remediability of educational underachievement and the nature of the US federal system had significant effects on the final shape of Goals 2000.[101] Prima facie, Goals 2000 spoke the language of standards advocacy. It declared that "Congress finds that . . . all children can learn and achieve to high standards and must realize their potential if the United States is to prosper."[102] To qualify for the bulk of Goals 2000 funding, states had to submit a plan describing "a process for developing or adopting state content standards and state student performance standards for all students."[103]

Nonetheless, Goals 2000 was a very confused piece of legislation. The effort to forge compromise across the diverging viewpoints of antistatists, liberals, and standards advocates resulted in a mish-mash.[104] Many of the contradictions centered on the conditions of aid for states to receive Goals 2000 funding, the powers of the National Education Standards Improvement Council versus those of the National Education Goals Panel, state use of assessments, and opportunity-to-learn standards.

The Conditions of Aid. As enacted, Goals 2000 required states to submit their plans to the secretary of education for approval.[105] In order to stave off the antistatist charge that Goals 2000 usurped local control of curricula, Goals 2000 had extremely modest criteria for approval. Section 305 stipulated that a state's first-year application for aid shall "describe the process by which the State educational agency will develop a State improvement plan that meets the requirements of section 306 . . . [and] describe how the State educational agency will use funds received under this title for such year." In subsequent years, a state's application had to set out a four-year plan that

> meets the requirements of section 306, or if the State improvement plan is not complete, a statement of the steps the State will take to complete the plan and a schedule for doing so . . . [and] include an explanation of how the State educational agency will use funds received under this title.

For any of this to have any teeth, then, section 306 would have to be robust. In fact, section 306 was quite permissive. State improvement plans needed to contain "strategies" for reaching the National Education Goals, including "a process for developing or adopting State content standards and State student performance standards for all students . . . [and] a process for developing and implementing valid, nondiscriminatory, and reliable State assessments."[106] There was no deadline for having actually implemented a system of standards and aligned assessments. States only need show that they have devised "strategies" and "processes" to these ends.

Furthermore, Goals 2000 did not oblige states to have either their standards or assessments certified by NESIC. The law is quite clear on this point: "Notwithstanding any other provision, standards or State assessments described in a State improvement plan submitted in accordance with section 306 shall not be required to be certified by the Council."[107] There was, then, no obligatory federal quality control. Senator Kassebaum opposed this permissiveness but could not rally her colleagues:

> I have sent out a "Dear Colleague" letter. I have tried to see how many are willing to make standards of achievement mandatory—and there is very little response. To propose that if schools are to buy into this program, if they take the federal money, that the standards should be mandatory is not yet an idea whose time has come.[108]

This permissiveness presented states with an easy choice: either take the money and undertake the arduous task of systemic, standards-based reform, or take the money and go through the motions of standards reform. With no guarantee that Goals 2000 would be reauthorized and noncompliant states sanctioned, the latter was an expedient and obvious choice.[109] Not surprisingly, forty-seven states applied for Goals 2000 funds by mid-1995, none were denied funds, and as Chapter 2 indicated, few developed adequate standards and assessments.

The Powers of NESIC vs. the Powers of NEGP. Richard Riley, who served as secretary of education under President Clinton, wrote,

> Although the establishment of this council had been recommended by a congressionally established bipartisan commission and officials in the previous Republican administration, concerns were raised about the role the new council would play and the power it would have.[110]

Those who feared federal control over curricula saw to it that NESIC would be checked by the NEGP.[111] The latter was empowered to nominate candidates for NESIC. The NEGP also had the power to review and disapprove NESIC's "criteria for the certification of State content standards, State student performance standards, State assessments, and State opportunity-to-learn standards" and the "voluntary national content standards, voluntary national student performance standards, and voluntary national opportunity-to-learn standards."[112]

The NEGP's membership was structured in a way that greatly reduced the probability that either the national standards or the criteria for approval of state standards would be set very high. Of the NEGP's sixteen members, there would be eight governors, four state legislators, two senators, and two members appointed by the president. Thus, twelve of the sixteen members of the NEGP would be state officials. If they were to agree to rigorous approval criteria or national standards, they would risk having their own states flunk the approval process. As Senator Jeff Bingaman (D-NM), who served on the NEGP, later attested,

> Let me just say that there is great sensitivity—as you can imagine, with eight governors and four State legislators . . . on the National Education Goals Panel, to the Federal Government or the national government not being too intrusive in what the States do. This is not a problem. . . . The National Education Goals Panel is not about to run roughshod over the States because you've got twelve states represented right there.[113]

State Use of Assessments. Liberal concerns over the effects of standards and assessments on the poor and minorities made for almost Byzantine requirements for certification of assessments and standards by NESIC.[114] For example, "all students" and "all children" were defined very broadly to include those with disabilities, limited-English proficiency, and, oddly, those who had dropped out of school.[115] Title II, section 213, stated that NESIC "shall certify State assessments" only if "a State can demonstrate that all students have been prepared in the content for which they are being assessed." How a state was to meet this criterion that all students be prepared is unclear. What would constitute being prepared? Is this where opportunity-to-learn standards would come in?

Furthermore, liberals also saw to it that states could not use NESIC-certified assessments for high-stakes decisions. Title II, section 213, held: "such assessments will not be used to make decisions regarding graduation, grade promotion, or retention of students for a period of four years from the date of enactment of the Act."[116] This made creating NESIC-approved assessments a costly undertaking. A state that chose to have graduation or grade promotion exams would not be able to submit them for NESIC approval or they would no longer be usable for such; thus, a state would need to develop a second set of exams, one for submission for approval, another for high-stakes decisions.

Goals 2000 also required state assessments to be "nondiscriminatory," a standard that is simply impossible to meet if "nondiscriminatory" is defined, as some liberals seemed to suggest it should be, as having disparate impacts upon genders, races, classes, and language proficiency.[117] A state was also required to submit evidence that "the test or tests . . . are valid, reliable measures of their intended purposes, are aligned with the

State content standards, are capable of assessing the progress of all students toward learning the material in the State content standards, and are consistent with relevant nationally recognized professional and technical standards."[118] With hurdles so high, states had little incentive to submit their assessments to NESIC for certification.[119]

Opportunity-to-Learn Standards. Here we see the most obvious collision of antistatist and liberal views. Liberals saw to it that as a condition of aid, state plans had to include "standards or strategies for providing all students with an opportunity-to-learn."[120] OTL standards would address difficult-to-measure resources such as "the capability of teachers to provide high quality instruction to meet diverse learning needs in each content area to all students," and "the extent to which schools utilize policies, *curricula, and instructional practices* which ensure nondiscrimination on the basis of gender [emphasis added by author]."[121]

Even so, to satisfy critics on the right, Goals 2000 held that NESIC was to approve national standards only if they were so broadly defined that they could be adopted by "any State without restricting State and local control of curriculum and prerogatives regarding instructional methods employed."[122] The point was to prevent, as Senator Judd Gregg (R-NH) called it, the birth of a "federal methodology for teaching."[123] And Title III made a strong defense of the rights of states and localities over schooling (see Figure 4.2).[124] It reaffirmed that the federal government may not impose "directly or indirectly . . . standards or requirements of any kind . . . which would reduce, modify, or undercut State and local responsibility for control of education."[125]

The confusion is manifest. States had to submit plans to receive aid, and said plans had to include strategies for developing education standards, assessments, and opportunity-to-learn standards. And if any of these standards were to be certified by NESIC and the NEGP as "comparable or higher in rigor and quality" to national standards and assessments, they would have to meet the criteria created by NESIC. So, for example, if state OTL standards were ever to be certified as acceptable, they had to meet a number of federal criteria for adequacy, including nondiscriminatory assessments, standards applicability to all students, teacher training, and curricular materials adequacy. Yet, the federal government was not supposed to be exerting increased control over education.

The sole way to square these two contradictory imperatives would be for states to submit plans clarifying how they would raise standards and fashion opportunity-to-learn standards, but never to seek NESIC approval for these standards. Only thus could states qualify for Goals 2000 funds without allowing the federal government to increase its control over the public schools. In the end, this is what happened.[126]

Figure 4.2   Goals 2000 Prohibition of Federal Control

Title III, Sec. 318
PROHIBITION OF FEDERAL MANDATES,
DIRECTION, AND CONTROL
Nothing in this Act shall be construed to authorize an officer or employee of
the Federal Government to mandate, direct, or control a State, local education
agency, or school's curriculum, program of instruction, or allocation of State
resources . . .

Sec. 319
STATE AND LOCAL GOVERNMENT CONTROL OF EDUCATION
(a) FINDINGS. The Congress finds as follows:
(1) Congress is interested in promoting State and local government reform
efforts in education.
(2) In Public Law 96-88 the Congress found that education is fundamental
to the development of individual citizens and the progress of the Nation.
(3) In Public Law 96-88 the Congress found that in our Federal system the
responsibility for education is reserved respectively to the States and the local
school systems and other instrumentalities of the States . . .
(6) Public Law 96-88 specified that the establishment of the Department
of Education shall not increase the authority of the Federal Government over
education or diminish the responsibility for education which is reserved to the
States and local school systems and other instrumentalities of the States.
(7) Public Law 96-88 specified that no provision of a program administered by the Secretary or by any other officer of the Department of Health,
Education, and Welfare shall be construed to authorize the Secretary or any
such officer to exercise any direction, supervision, or control over the curriculum, program of instruction, administration, or personnel of any educational institution, school, or school system, over any accrediting agency or
association or over the selection or content of library resources, textbooks, or
other instructional materials by any educational institution or school system.
(b) REAFFIRMATION. The Congress agrees and reaffirms that the responsibility for control of education is reserved to the States and local school systems and other instrumentalities of the States and that no action shall be taken
under the provisions of this Act by the Federal Government which would,
directly or indirectly, impose standards or requirements of any kind through
the promulgation of rules, regulations, provision of financial assistance and
otherwise, which would reduce, modify, or undercut State and local responsibility for control of education.

Politics Hobbles Goals 2000, Part 2: The 1994 Elections and Antistatism

The election of 1994 was astonishing. The four-decades-old control of
Congress by the Democratic Party was broken. For the first time in history
a sitting Speaker of the House—Thomas Foley (D-WA)—lost a reelection
bid. Republicans gained fifty-two seats in the House, eight in the Senate,
and control of numerous state legislatures and governorships.[127] Analysts

dispute whether voters handed Republicans a mandate, but it is indubitable that Republicans proclaimed one.[128] Three hundred GOP candidates had pledged, in late September, that upon election they would carry out *The Contract with America*. Those who won election vigorously attempted to do so as soon as they took office.

The Contract itself, though calling for revolutionary reduction in the size of the federal government, had little to say on education.[129] However, by the close of the first hundred days of the 104th Congress, it was clear the Republican plan was to roll back much of what had been done in federal education policy in the previous twenty years.[130] Republicans now controlled all education committees. The powerful House Education and Labor Committee shifted from thirty-seven Democrats and twenty-three Republicans to thirty-one Republicans and twenty-one Democrats. William F. Goodling, a moderate Republican (PA), became its chair and told the press that he would review all federal education programs and would insist on "local control" of schooling.[131]

Before the 1983 publication of *A Nation at Risk* and the Reagan press conference concerning it, those who took an antistatist line against federal involvement in education made, as noted earlier, a number of different arguments for this position. Afterward, though, two other arguments predominated: that the federal government and the Department of Education, in particular was unable to make good education policy, and, to a lesser extent, that the federal government was perniciously accreting power over schools in order to force them to use progressive pedagogy and to teach children liberal, secularist values.

In early 1995, Republicans issued *Restoring the Dream*, which they described as a "sequel" to *The Contract with America*. It set out "a longer-term House strategy" for governance.[132] The Department of Education was to be folded into the Department of Labor because since "it was created, test scores and virtually every other objective measure of school performance have declined."[133] The book also provided a graph and noted

> the relationship between education spending and a standard measure of achievement—SAT scores—between 1970 and 1994. The chart calls into question whether the amount of money the schools are spending is at all related to how much our kids are actually learning. If anything, the spending/quality relationship appears to be negative.[134]

This implied causality between federal intervention and test score decline, as the reader will recall, was first enunciated by President Reagan on the release of *A Nation at Risk*.[135]

These ideas were not the sentiments of a small, radical portion of the Republican Party. They were echoed in a book the very next year, written by Haley Barbour, chairman of the Republican National Committee from 1993 to 1996.[136] Barbour declared:

> Anyone willing to think about the condition of American education without bias will be immediately struck by the negative and far-reaching effects of centralization. The centralization of our education bureaucracies in Washington, D.C., has coincided with the decline of order and test scores.[137]

Both Barbour and the House Republicans saw something nefarious in Goals 2000 and the 1994 reauthorization of the ESEA.

> The federal usurpation of state and local authority in the field of education continues. In 1994, for example, with the passage of a measure called "Goals 2000: Educate America Act," the Clinton administration came close to nationalizing American education. The proposed goals, which the Clinton administration insisted were voluntary, specify levels of "inputs" or resources local schools and school districts must meet in order to receive additional federal funding. In reality, of course, these goals are far from voluntary—if a state refuses to submit to the standards, it can lose federal dollars.[138]

Accordingly, the only proper course was to "abolish the Department of Education."[139] The belief that the federal government could not make policy to improve the schools had been bolstered by the great controversy that erupted around the American history standards a few months earlier, in autumn 1994. Diane Ravitch, who served as assistant secretary for educational research and improvement under President George H. W. Bush, writes,

> In 1991 and 1992 the Department of Education (in collaboration with other federal agencies, such as the National Endowment for the Humanities and National Science Foundation) awarded grants to organizations of scholars and teachers to develop voluntary national standards in seven school subjects (science, history, geography, the arts, civics, foreign languages, and English [the National Council of Teachers of Mathematics had already promulgated its own standards]).[140]

The department wanted the standards to represent what all children ought to learn. The standards themselves were to be reviewed by a national board, such as NESIC, which would examine them for accuracy and acceptability. If they were found wanting, they would presumably be returned to the creators unapproved, perhaps with suggestions for alterations; if accepted, states could adopt them or use them as a model for crafting their own standards. They would not be federal standards, that is, standards that would be forced upon public schools by law.

In October 1994, the history standards were ready for release. Unfortunately, NESIC, the board that Goals 2000 had created to examine the standards, had not yet been formed. Meanwhile, Lynne V. Cheney, a former head of the National Endowment for the Humanities (NEH), saw the soon-to-be-released American history standards.[141] She was aghast and wrote a very widely read op-ed for the *Wall Street Journal*, sharply criticizing the standards.[142] The standards painted a jaundiced view of the development of the United States. Many famous figures in American history were omitted; many nonwhite and arguably less influential persons were trumpeted, and the nation's sins of slavery, misogyny, and the like were highlighted. Professor Gary Nash, whose National Center for History in the Schools at the University of California at Los Angeles produced the standards, fanned the flames by declaring that one of the goals of the standards was to revolutionize the teaching of American history.[143] A debacle ensued.[144] Instead of being judiciously deliberated by a politically balanced federal council behind closed doors and quietly amended, the history standards were hotly debated in the newspapers and on radio and television.[145] A small cultural battle erupted, and it spilled over to Congress and raised doubts about the federal government's competence to make education policy.

The Clinton administration distanced itself from the history standards, and in January 1995 the Senate, with little serious deliberation, condemned the standards by a vote of 99 to 1.[146] Though the federal government had neither written nor approved the standards, the fiasco provided ammunition for antistatists who thought the federal government should not be involved in the public schools.[147]

The Senate vote against the standards was the opening shot in an effort to reduce the federal role in education and policy generally.[148] Two organizations were influential with congressional conservatives: the Christian Coalition and the Heritage Foundation. Both criticized the federal government's intrusion into the schools and called for the abolition of Goals 2000 and the Department of Education.[149] Chester E. Finn Jr., an assistant secretary of education in the Reagan administration and one of the people who was involved with the crafting of America 2000, set to work with Republican leaders to pass what was called the "ABC" bill.[150] It proposed to repeal Goals 2000, shrink the Department of Education, and devolve control and administration of many federal education programs to the states (or transform them into block grants), among other things. Republicans also began formulating policy to expand the rights of students to pray in schools and to voucherize Title I education dollars.

By late January 1995, just eight months after Goals 2000 became law, both houses of Congress were pondering bills to curtail federal involvement in education. Senator Kassebaum, who had been instrumental in getting Goals 2000 passed, offered a bill (S 323) that would abolish NESIC, terminate grants for crafting national opportunity-to-learn standards, and remove the NEGP's power to review standards submitted by states. "I do not believe it is appropriate to expand federal involvement into areas traditionally handled by states and localities," Kassebaum explained.[151] Senator Judd Gregg (R-NH) offered a similar bill (S 469), although it would have let the NEGP retain the power to certify standards. The new Speaker of the House, Newt Gingrich (R-GA), at a conference of private-college administrators, called for the abolition of the Department of Education, dismissing it as "a federal department of homework checkers."[152]

Between January and September 1995, Congress held hearings on the "proper role" of the federal government in education, Goals 2000, and education standards.[153] A clear divide had opened in the 104th Congress between those who thought the federal government should have a major role in the effort to raise education standards and those who thought it should not. Critics stressed the incompetence and even malevolence of the federal government and called for the reduction and devolution of federal education policymaking. Like *The Contract with America* and *Restoring the Dream*, antistatists often voiced an angry, populist, anti–federal government message.

At a hearing in late January, two former secretaries of education, Lamar Alexander (who crafted America 2000) and William Bennett (who served in the Reagan administration), seconded Speaker Gingrich's call to shutter the Department of Education.[154] In their joint statement before the House, they argued that the department should be abolished because it was incompetent and often spawned policies that were at best, ineffective, and at worst, "actually do harm."[155] Bennett asserted that this was not merely the wish of the right wing of the Republican Party; rather, the public "very much" wanted to see the Department of Education abolished.[156] Both men repeatedly called the department and the federal government "arrogant" and said that the bureaucrats in Washington thought they were "smarter" than the governors, teachers, principals, and parents. They also claimed that the federal government was impeding a grassroots movement to improve educational achievement. Local schools were being coerced by the federal government, which was "defining family, defining art, [and] making suggestions about sex education. . . . [The federal government also instructs] little boys and girls what to think of each other . . . [and has set] what the weapons policy ought to be in every public school in America."[157]

Bennett testified that in his visits to schools, "I saw the results of federal education [policies] and they are not good." He asserted that there was "a tremendous corruption in the educational system today. It is run by powerful education brokers, powerful special interests; they have their hands all over the US Department of Education." To break this "stranglehold," both men suggested that the department should be abolished, all programs should be reviewed to see if they ought to be cut, and any programs that were found worth keeping should be transferred to another department to administer.[158] They also, notably, suggested that educational achievement could be improved through the privatization of some schools, and, in the spirit of localism, asserted that children would learn more if power was devolved from both the federal government and the states to localities. These sweeping assertions, not backed up by any evidence, were indicative of the new climate in Congress. There had been a large influx of first-term conservative Republicans who earnestly believed in local control and its superiority to federal involvement, no matter how modest.[159]

Those at the hearings who favored Goals 2000 and federal policy to raise standards, meanwhile, argued that the federal government was aiding, not impeding, school reform. They also attempted to dispel the notion that Goals 2000 was a malevolent federal power grab. Representative Thomas Sawyer (D-OH) quoted a circular published by the Council of Chief State School Officers (CCSSO) that explained,

> Goals 2000 does not federalize education. It does not establish a national curriculum or the equivalent of a national school board. . . . It does not dictate to states how much money to spend, how to utilize its teachers or what text books to use. Goals 2000 does not establish school-based health clinics, nor does it mandate values-based or outcomes-based education.[160]

Sawyer then asked why these state education officials held a view of Goals 2000 so different from that of Bennett and Alexander. After professing all due respect to the CCSSO, Alexander said that "they are wrong" and went one step further, saying that education should be devolved all the way down, from state officials to citizens themselves.[161] Mario Cuomo, Democratic governor of New York, contested the notion that states were laboring under an overbearing federal presence. "I don't feel any intrusion from the Department of Education, any intrusiveness or anything but helpful cooperation."[162]

At a House hearing in March, Senator Jeff Bingaman (D-NM), Albert Shanker (president of the American Federation of Teachers), Diane Ravitch, and Pascale Forgione (who served on the NEGP) spoke in favor of Goals 2000 and federal involvement in raising education standards.[163] A number of members of Congress questioned Senator Bingaman about the controversial history standards. Bingaman emphasized that the standards had not been accepted or approved by the government and that the NEGP existed to do just this. Bingaman also emphasized that the NEGP was by statute a bipartisan body composed largely of state officials.[164]

Shanker and Ravitch testified that education standards were already being produced by textbook companies and education researchers, labeled "national standards," and marketed to localities and states.[165] That being so, parents, teachers, and administrators faced a bewildering task in trying to choose which standards to use. Shanker noted that state education departments, teachers, and principals simply could not, on their own, discern what constituted world-class education standards. Comparing one set of standards to those of, say, Germany or Japan is a complex task. It is made more difficult by the dearth of research. "There's almost no literature on it," he explained.[166] Furthermore, Shanker said, the United States was an increasingly mobile society. Parents often changed residences, which moved their children from one school to another. The tradition of local control over curricula can make such moves troublesome for children and educators alike. The children face a disruption in their education because they are subjected to shifting curricular demands. Teachers are placed in the difficult position of having to alter their teaching to accommodate large numbers of children with different educational backgrounds.[167]

Ultimately, only a small portion of Congress took to the idea of abolishing the Department of Education.[168] The amount of federal spending on education, though, was hotly contested. Whereas the Senate was amenable to modest cutbacks in education spending generally, the House favored radical cuts.[169] The House passed HR 1158 by a nearly party-line vote of 235 to 189 in May 1995. The bill would have cut nearly $4 billion (over 12 percent) of the Department of Education's yearly budget and included large reductions in Goals 2000 funds. The House Committee on Economic and Educational Opportunities passed HR 1045, which would have eliminated NESIC. Clinton threatened to veto HR 1158 and countered with a proposal to cut all nonmandatory federal spending, education and defense excepted, by 20 percent.

As for the federal role in raising education standards, Congress put off offering nominees for NESIC and generally supported scaling back federal influence. The Clinton administration saw that it had to acquiesce. The White House calculated that it had to reduce federal involvement and oversight if it was to preserve any federal role in raising standards. Accordingly, Secretary Riley testified before the Senate that the administration was amenable to the abolition of NESIC, which had been a target for antistatist criticism.[170] Through 1995 and early 1996, Congress and the president grappled over the federal role in education.

On April 26, 1996, President Clinton signed an omnibus spending bill (which included education funds) that Congress had passed overwhelmingly the day before.[171] Surprisingly, PL 104-134 maintained the budget of the Department of Education at its 1995 level.[172] It did, though, have profound effects on the federal government's power to raise standards. The NEGP, which by virtue of its membership might have seemed safe from antistatist ire, had its 1996 budget cut from $2.3 million to $1 million. Goals 2000's funding was reduced slightly. More important, though, was that PL 104-134 further weakened this already permissive law.[173] Among other things, the measure abolished NESIC, removed all mention of opportunity-to-learn standards from the Goals 2000 legislation, and ended the requirement that states must submit their reform plans to the secretary of education to receive Goals 2000 funding.[174] Now, states merely had to promise to spend the money in accordance with the rules of the program, not show how they planned to do so. Some conservative critics of Goals 2000 had complained the law's first goal that "all children start school ready to learn" might embolden the federal government to begin inspecting parents' homes in order to see whether they were carrying out their parental duties. To placate these critics, the spending measure included a provision that stipulated Goals 2000 did not "require or permit any state or federal official to inspect a home, judge how parents raise their children, or remove children from their parents."[175] To further appease conservatives, PL 104-134 also provided that no state or locality would be forced by Goals 2000, as a condition of aid, to adopt an outcomes-based education curriculum or fund school health clinics.[176]

Nevertheless, some on the right remained outraged. Phyllis Schlafly, president of the Eagle Forum, a conservative "pro-family" interest group, applauded the changes but maintained that it "would be better if they'd repealed the whole law" and decried the "Clinton master plan to take over education."[177] Robert G. Morrison, an education policy analyst at the conservative Family Research Council, denounced Goals 2000 and the standards movement generally as "an Orwellian exercise in government-approved truth."[178] Indeed, antistatist antipathy toward Goals 2000 was so intense that when Clinton sought to appoint Marshall S. Smith as deputy education secretary in 1996, Republicans refused to accede. They held up the vote on his appointment for more than two years because Smith had advocated national standards, assessments, and modest opportunity-to-learn standards.[179]

Conclusion

Goals 2000 was the Clinton administration's first legislative effort to use federal power to raise education standards. With Congress stacked in its favor, it had managed to get Goals 2000 enacted into law. This victory was indicative that the new politics of education, which included a strong coalition of quality schools advocates, was not ephemeral. Raising standards to raise achievement was widely regarded as a rational policy. Yet, this did not mean that the education politics of old had disappeared. Liberals and antistatists remained, and both exacted great compromises that weakened Goals 2000's power to raise standards. The 1994 elections, which sent numerous antistatists into Congress, resulted in a further gutting of Goals 2000 and even greater challenges for standards-based reform.

Notes

1. US Congress, House of Representatives, Subcommittee on Elementary, Secondary, and Vocational Education of the Committee on Education and Labor, *Hearings on HR 1804—Goals 2000: Educate America Act,* April 22, 1993, p. 32.

2. Cooper, "For Democrats a New Ball Game," p. A8, as quoted in Jennings, *Why National Standards and Tests?* p. 43. Ford, as will be seen, quickly returned to playing defense. One insider who asked to remain unnamed describes how Ford "jerked around" a number of members of the Clinton team during a meeting in February. Ford's motivation was "to show he had power and had to be dealt with." Author interview: anonymous source.

3. There was one independent in the House.

4. Come 1994, John F. Jennings, a liberal who served as the top aide on education in the House for nearly three decades and attacked America 2000, confessed, "I do believe in standards now; I didn't a few years ago." Pitsch, "Education Aide Leaves 27-Year Legacy of Quiet Influence."

5. Miller, "Election 1992: Candidates Education and Related Policies at a Glance," p. 22.

6. Clinton, "The Clinton Plan for Excellence in Education," p. 134.

7. Mathematics standards had already been drawn up by a private group of educators and scholars. The funding of the projects was done through discretionary monies. Their fate is described herein. Ravitch, ed., *Debating the Future of American Education*, p. 6. Diane Ravitch, personal correspondence, October 26, 2001.

8. US Congress, Senate, Committee on Labor and Human Resources, *Examining the Need to Improve National Education Standards and Job Training Opportunities*, February 24, 1993.

9. Ibid., pp. 11–14. For more of Reich's thinking on economic changes and the need for government to invest in human capital, see Reich, *The Work of Nations: Preparing Ourselves for 21st-Century Capitalism.*

10. Some industries atrophied; others, such as textiles, were shifting from the United States to nations like Mexico, leaving American textile workers unemployed and often unemployable.

11. US Congress, Senate, Committee on Labor and Human Resources, *Examining the Need to Improve National Education Standards and Job Training Opportunities*, February 24, 1993, p. 12. This proposal later became Title IV of the Goals 2000: Educate America Act.

12. Ibid., pp. 6–11.

13. Ibid., p. 9.

14. Ibid., pp. 7, 9.

15. Ibid., p. 9.

16. Ibid., p. 10.

17. Ibid., quote at p. 19, testimony at pp. 18–22.

18. Ibid., p. 25.

19. Ibid., pp. 1–2.

20. Smith and O'Day, "Systemic School Reform," pp. 233–267.

21. Based on testimony by the aforementioned senators at US Congress, Senate, Committee on Labor and Human Resources, *Examining the Need to Improve National Education Standards and Job Training Opportunities*, February 24, 1993, pp. 22–39.

22. Miller, "Democrats' Objections Spur E.D. to Delay Reform Bill."

23. Author interview: Thomas Wolanin, December 18, 2002.

24. Miller, "Administration Readies Reform Bill."

25. Dale Kildee (D-MI), who served with Ford, describes this in "Enacting Goals 2000: Educate America," pp. 27–46. See also Ravitch, *National Standards in American Education*, p. 150.

26. Ravitch notes that whereas Clinton campaigned for creating national exams, he did not include them in Goals 2000, "probably in deference to key allies" on the left, including "the National Education Association, civil rights groups, and leading Democrats on the House Education and Labor Committee." Ravitch, *National Standards in American Education*, p. 148.

27. Clinton, *Proposed Legislation—"Goals 2000: Educate America Act," Message from the President of the United States*, Title I, sec. 102, (3)A and (4)A.

28. Ravitch notes that originally the administration wanted to call the council NESAC, for National Education Standards and Assessment Council. The word *assessment* was dropped in favor of *improvement* to placate liberals who worried over the use of tests as a policy tool. Ravitch, *National Standards in American Education*, p. 154.

29. Clinton, *Proposed Legislation—"Goals 2000: Educate America Act,"* Title III, sec. 306.

30. Ibid., Title III, sec. 303.

31. Riley, "Reflections on Goals 2000," p. 385.

32. Clinton, *Proposed Legislation—"Goals 2000: Educate America Act,"* Title III, sec. 306(d).

33. Ibid., Title II, sec. 213(d), 4c, and Title V, sec. 502.

34. On the complexity of defining and measuring opportunity-to-learn standards, see Porter, "Defining and Measuring Opportunity-to-Learn Standards," pp. 33–73.

35. That is, Goals 2000 was not an amendment to existent legislation, nor did it explicitly aim to amend any current federal education policies.

36. Congress disagreed with this less political appointment process and transformed it into a very political process whereby the president would appoint all nineteen members but would receive nominations from the secretary of education, the NEGP, and leaders of both houses of Congress, and nominees would have to be chosen from a number of groups, including civil rights organizations and educators. PL 103-227, Title II, sec. 212.

37. Ibid., Title III, sec. 305–306, pp. 40–41. This included developing education standards, performance assessments, and opportunity-to-learn standards.

38. Not surprisingly, this author has failed to locate one instance of a state being denied Goals 2000 funding on reapplication, in spite of numerous state failures to create educational frameworks and standards (see Chapter 2).

39. Author interview: Thomas Wolanin, December 18, 2002.

40. Why the Senate behaved similarly is unclear. The historical record is silent on this point.

41. Hearings Before the Subcommittee on Elementary, Secondary, and Vocational Education of the Committee on Education and Labor, US House of

Representatives, *Hearings on HR 1804—Goals 2000: Educate America Act*, April 22, May 4, and 18, 1993, p. 4.

42. Ibid., p. 4.

43. Ibid., p. 18.

44. Ibid., pp. 12–13, 15–16, 33–35.

45. Ibid., pp. 13–14, 20–32. One representative did gingerly inquire about the possible effects of raising standards on American Indians, females, and nonwhites. But the subject was not debated.

46. US Congress, Senate, Committee on Labor and Human Resources, *Goals 2000: Educate America Act*, S 846, May 4, 1993, p. 6.

47. Ibid., pp. 38–39, 43–49.

48. Ibid., pp. 41–43, quotes at p. 42.

49. US Congress, Senate, Committee on Labor and Human Resources, *Goals 2000: Educate America Act*, May 4, 14, 1993, p. 1.

50. Ibid., pp. 4, 16–17, 21–23, 25–28.

51. Thurmond did say he was "concerned" Goals 2000 "supports the development of a national curriculum," but he did not grill Secretary Riley on this issue. Ibid., pp. 2, 23–25, 28–30, quotes at pp. 23–24.

52. Ibid., pp. 12, 15, 56–57.

53. Sroufe and Knutson, *OIA Info Memo,* p. 7.

54. Congressional Quarterly, *Congressional Quarterly Almanac 1993*, p. 405.

55. Romer and Campbell, it is important to note, were chair and vice chair, respectively, of the NEGP.

56. As quoted in Ravitch, *National Standards in American Education,* p. 151.

57. Ibid., quote at p. 152.

58. The NEA had vigorously supported candidate Clinton. Shortly after the election, future secretary of commerce Ron Brown told NEA members at a breakfast event, "We would not be here without you." As quoted in Sroufe and Knutson, *OIA Info Memo,* p. 12.

59. Even the often-liberal research group, the American Educational Research Association, sneered at this list, asking, "Anybody missing?" because it seemed to dole out federal largesse to everybody employed by the public schools. See Sroufe and Knutson, *OIA Info Memo,* p. 11.

60. Goodling became so exasperated with the Democrats and their support of the Reed Amendment that he unleashed a five-minute tirade while pounding the dais. Pitsch, "Sharply Divided House Panel Amends 'Goals 2000.'"

61. Jennings, *Why National Standards and Tests? Politics and the Quest for Better Schools*, pp. 60–62.

62. US Congress, House of Representatives, *Goals 2000: Educate America Act, Report of the Committee on Education and Labor to Accompany HR 1804*, p. 16.

63. Jennings, *Why National Standards and Tests? Politics and the Quest for Better Schools*, pp. 79–80; Congressional Quarterly, *Congressional Quarterly Almanac 1983*, p. 407.

64. School clinics were a source of controversy because in some of them students could receive sexual behavior counseling and contraceptives without parental permission or knowledge.

65. Jennings, *Why National Standards and Tests?* p. 65.

66. As quoted in ibid., p. 70.

67. National Governors Association, *The Debate on Opportunity-to-Learn Standards*, statement and quote at p. 360.

68. Jennings, *Why National Standards and Tests?* p. 83.

69. As quoted in Editorial, "An Education Standards Bill," p. A16.

70. "This should put to rest the concern that we were going to dictate [opportunity-to-learn standards] from the federal government," said Goodling. Congressional Quarterly, *Congressional Quarterly Almanac 1983*, p. 406.

71. Clinton, "Let Us Resolve to Continue the Journey of Renewal," *Public Papers of the Presidents*, available at http://www.nexis.com.

72. New Standards Project, *Listening to the Public*.

73. S 846 was replaced with the text of HR 1804 and renamed S 1150 on February 8, 1994. The Senate debated on February 2, 3, 4, and 8 and passed it on February 8.

74. *Congressional Record*, February 2, 1994, pp. S608–S609.

75. *Congressional Record*, February 3, 1994, p. S701. Senator Judd Gregg (R-NH), a conservative who was quite critical of Goals 2000, nonetheless agreed: "Nobody is satisfied with what is happening in education. That is unquestionably the case. We are all very concerned that as a nation our children are not able to compete in the international economy or the global marketplace"; quote on p. S619.

76. Secretary Riley noted that three debates impinged on the passage of Goals 2000: the role of the federal government in education, opportunity-to-learn standards, and the pressure of time imposed by budgetary considerations. Riley, "Reflections on Goals 2000," p. 384. Anderson's reading of the debates finds likewise. Anderson, *Ideology and the Politics of Federal Aid to Education, 1958–1996*, chapter 8.

77. *Congressional Record*, February 2, 1994, p. S606.

78. Ibid., p. S611.

79. Ibid., p. S615. On eugenics and testing in the early twentieth century, see Ravitch, *Left Back*.

80. *Congressional Record*, February 2, 1994, p. S619.

81. *Congressional Record*, February 8, 1994, quotes at pp. S1152, S1153, S1154.

82. *Congressional Record*, February 2, 1994, p. S621.

83. Kozol, *Savage Inequalities: Children in America's Schools*.

84. *Congressional Record*, February 2, 1994, p. S629.

85. There were also brief outcries that Goals 2000 was mandating outcomes-based education (OBE), an approach to schooling that became in the eyes of the far right a plot to dumb down academics and force children to learn liberal social attitudes. For an example of this viewpoint, see Holland, *Outcomes-based Education*. This column was inserted into the *Congressional Record* on February 2, 1994, by Senator Larry Pressler (R-SD).

86. For an overview of the social issues, see Congressional Quarterly, *Congressional Quarterly Almanac 1994*, pp. 397–399. On Grassley and the surveys, see *Congressional Record*, February 4, 1994, pp. S859–S882.

87. On November 29, 1993, Muhammad, in a speech at Kean College, unleashed a torrent of epithets, calling, for example, Jews "bloodsuckers" and the Pope "a cracker." The Senate voted 97–0 in favor. *Congressional Record*, February 2, 1994, pp. S634–S636, S640–S642.

88. *Congressional Record*, February 3, 1994, p. S724.

89. In recent years, students have, for example, been sanctioned by schools for mentioning God in graduation valedictories or daring to write biographical reports on religious figures. For an introduction to the Supreme Court's decisions on religion and public schools, see Epstein and Walker, *Constitutional Law for a Changing America: Rights, Liberties, and Justice*, pp. 178–202.

90. ADA scores are assigned to members of Congress by the liberal interest group Americans for Democratic Action. They are based upon the votes members of

Congress cast on twenty key votes each year. A score of 0 is extremely conservative, and a score of 100 is extremely liberal. For further details see http://adaction.org. Author's tabulation confirms the results of Anderson, *Ideology and the Politics of Federal Aid to Education: 1958–1996*, p. 166.

91. Author's tabulation confirms the results of Anderson. Ibid.

92. Chapter 3 traced the role antistatism played in earlier education debates and the quality schools movement.

93. Their reflexivity may be rooted in either principle or in their conservative disposition. Harbour, *The Foundations of Conservative Thought: An Anglo-American Tradition in Perspective.*

94. The fear that the federal government will use schools to indoctrinate children in noxious ideas goes back to at least the 1880s. The Clinton administration had to rebut the charge that Goals 2000 was a pernicious effort to teach children secular values. Author interview: William Galston, deputy assistant to the president for domestic policy in the Clinton administration, May 29, 2002.

95. Smith, "Education Reform in America's Public Schools: The Clinton Agenda," p. 19.

96. Conservatives won a few small victories against Goals 2000. For example, they penned Title X, sec. 1018, which required that federal programs that funded the distribution of contraceptives in the schools develop procedures to see that the families of those receiving contraceptives were involved in the decision. They also added Title X, sec. 1017, which forbade federal dollars being used to fund surveys of student social, sexual, and political attitudes without parental consent.

97. E.g., Senator Wellstone, *Congressional Record*, February 2, 1994, p. S629. Recall that the Democratic platform of 1994 condemned the "savage inequalities" between US schools.

98. Beyond the aid provided in Title III, which they insisted be more targeted at poor school districts, liberals saw to it that Goals 2000 included funds for midnight basketball programs for poor children and minority-focused civics education grants. See PL 103-227, Title III, sec. 309; Title VIII; and Title X, part D. They also supported the creation of Title IV, which created grants for education centers for parents who needed instruction in child rearing.

99. For a similar typology, see Finn, "Education and the Election," pp. 44–48.

100. Goals 2000 was a stinging rebuke to those seeking federal funds for private school choice. It provided none. Section 1020 holds that "Except as provided in Section 310, nothing in this Act shall be construed to authorize the use of funds under title III of this Act directly or indirectly to any school other than a public school." Section 310 held that states were required to make information about state standards and assessment reforms available to private schools and allow their administrators and teachers to attend state and local standards reform training seminars. Title III, sec. 308(I) did allow for state subgrants to be spent on "promoting public magnet schools, public 'charter schools,' and other mechanisms for increasing choice among public schools, including information and referral programs which provide parents with information on available choices." Such is the only mention of school choice in the legislation.

101. Author interview: Chester E. Finn Jr., April 17, 2002; author interview: Richard Elmore, June 4, 2002; and author interview: William Galston, May 29, 2002. See also Stedman and Riddle, *Goals 2000: Educate America Act Implementation Status and Issues*; and Kildee, "Enacting Goals 2000: Educate America," pp. 27–45.

102. PL 103-227, Title III, sec. 301(1).

103. Ibid., sec. 306a.

104. This is to say nothing of the permissive interpretation of the statute by the Department of Education. See US Department of Education, *Guidelines for Reviewers for Reviewing Comprehensive Plans Developed Under the Goals 2000*.

105. As will be explained later, antistatists deleted this provision in 1996.

106. Title III, sec. 306c.

107. Title III, sec. 316.

108. *Congressional Record*, February 2, 1994, p. S625.

109. As it happened, Goals 2000 was not renewed.

110. Riley, "Reflections on Goals 2000," *Teachers College Record*, p. 38.

111. Reflecting their concern that standards would hurt some children, House liberals sought to expand the membership of the NEGP and NESIC to include experts on school finance and the needs of the poor, minority, disabled, and limited-English-proficient children. See Kildee, "Enacting Goals 2000: Educate America," pp. 35–37.

112. Title II, sec. 203(1A), (1B).

113. US Congress, House of Representatives, Subcommittee on Oversight and Investigations of the Committee on Economic and Educational Opportunities, *Hearing on Education Standards*, March 22, 1995, 104th Cong., 1st sess., p. 10.

114. And, again, states were not obliged to submit their standards or assessments for certification.

115. *Goals 2000: Educate America Act, Section 3, Definitions*.

116. After four years, states were free to do so if they pleased.

117. Title III, sec. 306(1B).

118. Ibid.

119. No states did so because none had the chance. As described later, NESIC's members never were selected and sat.

120. Title III, sec. 306d.

121. See Title II, sec. 213 generally.

122. Ibid., Title II, sec 213(5e).

123. *Congressional Record*, February 2, 1994, p. S615.

124. It reiterated the prohibition in PL 96-88, the law that created the Department of Education in 1980, of any federal control over school curricula.

125. This amendment to the Goals 2000 bill came from Representative William Goodling (R-PA). Kildee, "Enacting Goals 2000: Educate America," pp. 39–40.

126. As will be seen, NESIC's members were not seated, and it was abolished.

127. This gave Republicans a 230 to 204 advantage in the House and a 53 to 47 advantage in the Senate.

128. On Republican speed and unity in passing bills in the House, see Jones, *Clinton and Congress, 1993–1996*, pp. 103–115.

129. See also Gingrich, *To Renew America*, pp. 71–110.

130. Jones, *Clinton and Congress*, pp. 119–122.

131. Pitsch, "New Committee Chairman Outlines Agenda, Basks in the Spotlight."

132. Moore, ed., *Restoring the Dream*, p. vii.

133. Ibid., p. 121.

134. Ibid., p. 174.

135. Neither at this time nor during Reagan's term did this line of reasoning take well with the media (see Chapter 3).

136. They were later echoed by Representative John Boehner (R-OH), who served on the House education committee: "Despite decades of federal aid and

higher spending for education, problems with public schools appear only to get worse." Boehner, "The Unmaking of School Reform," p. 48.

137. Barbour, *Agenda for America*, p. 128.

138. Ibid.

139. Ibid., p. 131.

140. Ravitch, *Left Back*, p. 432.

141. Previously, Cheney had been involved in the history standards project. See Linda Symcox, *Whose History? The Struggle for National Standards in American Classrooms*. Meanwhile, Symcox served as assistant director for the national standards project and clearly was upset by Cheney's actions.

142. Cheney, "The End of History." As chair of the NEH, Cheney had supported the funding of standards. When the history standards emerged, she changed her mind, saying that the lousy standards showed that the federal government ought to get out of education altogether because it was a captured agency, controlled by the "education establishment." Pitsch, "House Panel Launches Series of Hearings on National Standards." For a critical (and less than impartial) view of Cheney's role in the history standards project, see Symcox, *Whose History?*

143. Ravitch, *Left Back*, p. 434.

144. This was the second standards debacle. In a less politicized and publicized incident, the previous spring the Department of Education had ceased funding the groups working on the English-language standards. The standards were found, among other things, to be too vague to be of much use to educators. Diegmueller, "English Group Loses Funding for Standards."

145. Ravitch, *Left Back*, pp. 434–436.

146. Senate Resolution 66, January 20, 1995.

147. For example, Representative John Boehner (R-OH) blamed the NEGP for the standards and called for more local control of education. Boehner, "Goals 2000: Subcommittee Favors Local Control," Talking Points, House Republican Conference, July 12, 1995. See also Diegmueller, "Backlash Puts Standards in Harm's Way."

148. Senate Majority Leader Robert Dole (R-KS) declared during a ceremony opening the new Congress, "Reining in our government will be my mandate—and I hope it will be the purpose and principal accomplishment of the 104th Congress." As quoted in Pitsch, "GOP Begins Reign, Makes Changes in Panel."

149. Schwartz and Robinson, "Goals 2000 and the Standards Movement: The Limits of Federal Policy Building in a National Education Strategy," p. 198. The Heritage Foundation's *The New Member's Guide to the Issues* urged members to end "many of the harmful education programs of the last 30 years." As quoted in Olson, "Undo School Programs, Heritage Urges."

150. Pitsch and Miller, "Down to Work: Congress Sets a New Course."

151. Olson, "Bills to Scrap NESIC Likely to Hold Sway."

152. Staff, "Gingrich Goes on the Record: Abolish the Education Department."

153. US Congress, House of Representatives, Committee on Economic and Educational Opportunities, *Hearing on the Proper Federal Role in Education Policy*, January 12, 1995; US Congress, House of Representatives, Subcommittee on Oversight and Investigations of the Committee on Economic and Educational Opportunities, *Hearing on Reexamining Old Assumptions*; US Congress, House of Representatives, Subcommittee on Oversight and Investigations of the Committee on Economic and Educational Opportunities, *Hearing on Education Standards*, March 22, 1995; US Congress, Senate, Subcommittee of the Committee on Appropriations, *Goals 2000*, September 12, 1995.

154. US Congress, House of Representatives, Subcommittee on Oversight and Investigations of the Committee on Economic and Educational Opportunities, *Hearing on Reexamining Old Assumptions*, pp. 5–12.

155. Ibid., quotes at p. 6.

156. A search of polling data failed to locate any evidence to substantiate this claim. In light of the data suggesting that Americans have a generally sanguine view of federal involvement in education, this claim is highly suspect. On polling data, see Chapter 3.

157. US Congress, House of Representatives, Subcommittee on Oversight and Investigations of the Committee on Economic and Educational Opportunities, *Hearing on Reexamining Old Assumptions*, pp. 6–7. Setting aside the hyperbole and exaggerations, Alexander's and Bennett's argument is not persuasive, as the various intrusive policies they mention were not created by the department but were penned into law by Congress—in which case abolishing the department and transferring its duties to another agency would not make these problems end.

158. Ibid., pp. 10–11.

159. Representative Thomas Sawyer, who was present at the hearing, described the Alexander and Bennett speeches as "pure ideology" and as an effort at whipping up sentiment in Congress and among the public for the House Republican agenda. Author interview: Thomas Sawyer, June 14, 2002. Seeing government schooling as a failure, some on the right insisted privatization was the only sensible policy. For example, Representative David Weldon (R-FL) said, "As long as we have the government running education, even at the local level . . . it will never be a system where excellence comes to the surface." To this Alexander replied, "I agree with you." US Congress, House of Representatives, Subcommittee on Oversight and Investigations of the Committee on Economic and Educational Opportunities, *Hearing on Reexamining Old Assumptions*, p. 28.

160. Ibid., p. 23.

161. Ibid., pp. 23–24.

162. Ibid., p. 50.

163. US Congress, House of Representatives, Subcommittee on Oversight and Investigations of the Committee on Economic and Educational Opportunities, *Hearing on Education Standards*, March 22, 1995, pp. 13–17, 48–51, 65–69.

164. Ibid., pp. 3–13.

165. Ibid., pp. 65–69.

166. Ibid., p. 49.

167. Ibid., p. 50.

168. Importantly, Chairman Goodling was not impressed with the idea. Pitsch, "Former Secretaries Urge Abolishing E.D."

169. The result was that Congress often was divided against itself: the House would circulate bills to greatly reduce or zero out certain education programs while the Senate would restore most of the funds.

170. US Congress, House of Representatives, Subcommittee of the Committee on Appropriations, *Goals 2000*, September 12, 1995, p. 10.

171. The House passed the appropriations and rescissions bill 399 votes to 25; the Senate, 88 votes to 11.

172. Education Appropriations, Fiscal 1996; Goals 2000; DC School Reform, PL 104-34 (1996); and Stedman and Riddle, *Goals 2000*, pp. 3–4, 12–13.

173. Stedman and Riddle, *Goals 2000*, pp. 13–15.

174. PL 104-134, Title VII, sec. 701, 703, 705.

175. PL 104-134, sec. 706a. See also Pitsch, "To Placate Conservatives, Measure Alters Goals 2000."

176. Outcomes-based education was a form of pedagogy that conservatives reviled, believing that it was a pernicious form of progressivism that deemphasized academic rigor in favor of inculcating liberal, secular values in children. Health clinics, as noted in the previous chapter, were suspect to social conservatives because they might serve as contraception distribution centers, unbeknownst to parents. PL 104-134, sec. 706a. On OBE, see Ravitch, *National Standards in American Education*, pp. 161–168.

177. Pitsch, "Supporters Worry That Goals 2000 Changes Hurts Standards Efforts"; Schlafly, "The Clinton Master Plan to Take Over Education."

178. Morrison, "An Exercise in Government-Approved Truth."

179. Sack, "Smith to Leave the Education Department in January."

5

Title I and Voluntary National Tests

We want to foster an "ethic of learning" across America. This ethic begins with a straightforward premise: high standards will replace minimum standards—high standards for ALL children.
—Clinton Administration Plan for ESEA Reform, September 1993[1]

Education is now one of the dominant points of debate in the country. Across America, parents, teachers, and local officials are in hand-to-hand combat over who controls the education agenda in their community.
—Terry Holt, spokesman, House Republican Conference, 1997[2]

Goals 2000 was a small but bold initiative, and it ran aground on liberal-antistatist politics. Though frustrated, the Clinton administration would try twice again. On the heels of Goals 2000 it offered the Improving America's Schools Act (IASA), a proposal to reform the federal government's largest elementary and secondary aid program, Chapter 1.[3] During his second term, President Clinton also moved to create voluntary national tests (VNTs). Both were aimed at using federal power to raise education standards, but in a manner less direct than creating national standards outright.

The Politics of Reforming Chapter I

The Call for Change

During the 1980s, mounting evidence indicated Title I was not working as hoped. The initial criticism of Title I primarily came from researchers. Other policy network members were not particularly quick to respond. Liberals and public school lobbies were mostly content with the program since it served as "a vehicle to get federal dollars to resource-starved school districts"; members of Congress were likewise content.[4] In great part, Chapter 1's popularity was a function of its funding formula, which was from day one constructed to deliver funds to nearly every congressional district. This gives members of the House of Representatives a strong incentive to direct their energies toward ensuring that the disbursement formula steered as much money as possible to their home districts.[5] Until recently, then, congressional reauthorizations of Chapter 1 have been more an exercise in hashing out who gets what and less an effort to improve policy.

Yet, the evidence in favor of fundamental change was seeping into Congress and the White House. In November 1991, the Bush administration created a task force to consider revisions to Chapter 1. Directed by William Hansen of the Office of Management and Budget, the task force delivered its recommendations to the secretary of education, Lamar Alexander, in September 1992. The task force report suggested a number of reforms, including school choice (i.e., voucherizing Chapter 1 funds) and greater flexibility in state use of funds. The report also advocated better targeting of the funds to the poorest districts and, significantly, requiring states as a condition of aid to set challenging curricular frameworks for all public school children (including Title I students) that would be based on "world-class standards."[6] Because the ESEA was not up for reauthorization until 1993, the Bush administration had no opportunity to get a Democrat-controlled Congress to even consider such sweeping changes.

Two major studies of Chapter 1 were released on the cusp of President Clinton's entry to office. The first was *Making Schools Work for Children in Poverty*, which appeared in December 1992.[7] The report was authored by the Commission on Chapter 1, a group of twenty-eight school officials, business people, and advocates for children and education. It included a number of individuals who were well respected in the education policy network in Washington, DC, such as Phyllis McClure, Kati Haycock (director of the Education Trust), and Diane Piche (director of the Citizens' Commission on Civil Rights), to name a few. Two of the commission's members, Marshall Smith and Sharon Robinson, would go on to serve in the Clinton administration as undersecretary and assistant secretary of education, respectively.

The commission concluded that Chapter 1 was in need of fundamental reform. As Kati Haycock and David Hornbeck, two of its members later explained, "the commission quickly came to the conviction that virtually all children can learn at high levels. We believed that low performance among poor children often was attributable to low standards and expectations, which were actually encouraged by then current law."[8] The report suggested a number of reforms, such as targeting more Chapter 1 funds to schools with high percentages of students from impoverished families. It also urged that more schools be allowed to use funds not just for programs to aid poor pupils but to overhaul the entire academic program of schools. The main thrust of the suggested reforms, though, was standards. All students should be required to meet the same high standards, more funds should be spent to train teachers in the standards, and schools that lifted achievement should be rewarded while those that did not should be restructured.

The commission recognized that the dramatic reform they were suggesting would be "rather frightening to many in the traditional Chapter 1 community. . . . After all, 28 years of thinking in remedial [education] terms makes it hard to comprehend all this talk about high standards."[9] To this end, the commission held institutes and briefings with stakeholders and members of Congress to deliver the message that change was needed and to inform them about standards-based reforms and other strategies for reworking Chapter 1. The report itself proved very newsworthy, generating stories in many periodicals. Over 30,000 copies of the report were distributed.[10]

Shortly after the publication of *Making Schools Work for Children in Poverty* came *Reinventing Chapter 1: The Current Chapter 1 Program and New Directions.*[11] The Department of Education released it to the public in February 1993. The study was composed by the Independent Review Panel (IRP), a group that included university scholars, state and local school administrators, and representatives from the Department of Education.[12] *Reinventing Chapter 1* was mandated by the National Assessment of Chapter 1 Act of 1992 (PL 101-305) and examined the efficacy of Chapter 1 and the effects of 1988 Hawkins-Stafford amendments thereto.[13] *Reinventing Chapter 1* drew on over twenty studies of Chapter 1 and came to the conclusion that "a new vision" for the compensatory education program was needed.[14] The 1988 Hawkins-Stafford amendments "began to move the Chapter 1 program toward concern with the educational quality of the projects it funded." However, they did not "carry the weight needed to move state and local school personnel toward higher standards. . . . Chapter 1 remains a program in which the teaching of basic skills is the norm and instruction in higher order thinking skills the exception."[15]

The report was unequivocal on the subject of opportunity-to-learn standards: there was no simple correlation between resources and educational achievement. It even noted that high-poverty school districts often had higher average per-pupil expenditures than low-poverty districts.[16] Despite the apparent plenitude of resources, high-poverty schools saw a student grade failure rate that was 2.5 times higher than that of low-poverty schools, and just 8 percent of pupils in high-poverty schools were high-achievers in reading (compared with 40 percent in low-poverty schools).[17]

In part, *Reinventing Chapter 1* offered self-help and economic justifications for overhauling Chapter 1. It argued that every citizen ought to be able to financially support him- or herself. It then noted the economy had grown more complex, technological, and competitive. Thus, if individuals were to be able to find work, the schools had to give them the skills they needed. Because the schools were not doing this, government needed to make them do so by establishing "ambitious national standards of what all children, particularly those most at risk for failure, should know and be able to do."[18]

The report's examination of the efficacy of Chapter 1 was damning:

> Although there is clear evidence of relative improvement in the perform-
> ance of at-risk students since 1970, the gap separating the outcomes of
> students in high- and low-poverty schools remains large. . . . Moreover,
> the achievement gap appears to widen as students move through the
> grades.[19]

As was explained in Chapter 3 of this book, the raison d'être for the Chapter 1 program was to dramatically reduce, if not erase, the achievement gap between pupils.[20]

Since there was no clear single cause for the lower performance of poor children, *Reinventing Chapter 1* reasoned that no one magic bullet reform could be urged. Rather, what was needed was "comprehensive and systemic reform," a "radical" reworking of Chapter 1.[21] As it was then structured, Chapter 1 was a compensatory education program. The thinking behind it was that lower-income and minority students came to school ill-prepared in the basics. Thus, they needed compensatory schooling in the rudiments. As implemented, typically Chapter 1 pupils were pulled out of class each day for less than a half an hour, drilled in the rudiments, then returned to class. Thus, while other children were back in the classroom learning more advanced material, Chapter 1 students were being trained in the basics. Michael Kirst, who served on the Independent Review Panel, noted that Chapter 1 was structured against educating poor students to high standards. Instead of curriculum and teaching being driven by high standards and aligned assessments, Chapter 1 programs prepared children to take federal multiple-choice tests that only assessed "low-level skills," the rudiments.[22] Worse, these federally mandated assessments were not aligned with state curricula and exams, and they were norm-referenced, which meant that the scores they produced were measures of students' achievement vis-à-vis other students, not curricular standards.[23]

Congress Considers Reforming Chapter 1

Congress held hearings on the reauthorization of the Elementary and Secondary Education Act from winter through summer 1993. The Clinton administration, meanwhile, withheld its ESEA reform proposal until late autumn, fearing that releasing it earlier might get its Goals 2000 bill shelved.[24]

The themes for reform enunciated in *Reinventing Chapter 1* and the call for crafting standards dominated the 1993 hearings on Chapter 1.[25] In part, this was due to the House Subcommittee on Elementary, Secondary, and Vocational Education's choosing.[26] It picked witnesses, such as members of the Independent Review Panel, who could be expected to testify in favor of making Chapter 1 a standards-based program. So, Michael Kirst of IRP appeared at the very first hearing. Phyllis McClure, who chaired IRP, and Alan L. Ginsburg, also of IRP and the acting assistant secretary at the Department of Education's Office of Planning and Policy, were at the third hearing, which was devoted to "reform proposals for Chapter 1."[27]

Yet, it was not just IRP members who emphasized standards reform. Other respected experts agreed that Chapter 1 had not lived up to its promise and needed repair. David Hornbeck, a former superintendent of schools who chaired the twenty-eight-member Commission on Chapter 1, testified forcefully. "The results [of our research are] . . . clear . . . very significant changes are called for. . . . Nearly all the gains . . . between rich and poor, minority and nonminority kids, nearly all of them, have occurred at very low skill levels."[28] Hornbeck further reported that the commission's first suggestion for fixing Chapter 1 was that states should be "asked to set clear, high standards for what all students should know and be able to do. And they should be the same for all kids: rich and poor, minority and white."[29] Thomas A. Romberg, on behalf of the Advisory Committee on Testing and Chapter 1, similarly emphasized the importance of making Chapter 1 a standards-based program.[30] "The time is now appropriate for Chapter 1 testing to concentrate more on promoting student learning and less on measuring regulatory compliance."[31]

Because Chapter 1 was the major grants-in-aid education program, states, local school agencies, and school administrators clearly had a huge interest in any changes to it. They too endorsed the notion of basing Chapter 1 on high standards and aligned, criterion-referenced assessments. Don Ernst, director of Education Policy for the State of Indiana, spoke on behalf of the National Governors Association:

> Reformers now conclude that a massive transformation of the entire educational system is required to produce a nation of learners. There appears to be a growing consensus on what needs to be done to create an education system that will support the nation's expectations for higher student outcomes. . . . The first step is to establish higher standards for students and educational systems.[32]

Representatives from the American Association of School Administrators, National School Boards Association, Council of the Great

City Schools, and other groups testified in favor of standards-based reform of Chapter 1.[33] Dissenters, such as the National Education Association, were few. These interest groups didn't so much object to standards as they expressed concern over what types of assessments would be used, to what ends, and possible race and gender bias in the assessments.[34]

However, as might be expected, states also asked for fewer federal regulations and more freedom to consolidate program funds to use as they saw best.[35] Republicans, including their ranking member on the House education committee, William Goodling, joined them in this call for increased flexibility. Both states and Republicans contended that the proliferation of programs to assist low-income children over the years, administered by different departments (e.g., Education, Health and Human Services, and Agriculture), created a regulatory tangle that inhibited the coordinated delivery of student services.[36] Different programs had different definitions and categories for who was eligible to receive what, different paperwork and procedures to follow, and so forth. Ad hoc problem solving over decades had resulted in collective incoherence and staggering amounts of red tape.[37]

The Clinton Proposal and Congress

In September 1993 the Clinton administration offered its bill for reforming the ESEA. The Improving America's Schools Act was quickly introduced in the House by Dale Kildee (D-MI), chairman of the Subcommittee on Elementary, Secondary, and Vocational Education; the committee's top two Republicans, Bill Goodling and Steve Gunderson; and some fourteen other cosponsors.[38]

The administration's proposal was crafted, in great part, by Marshall S. Smith, undersecretary of education. Not surprisingly, it contained many of the attributes that Smith had argued for in his widely read article on systemic reform and the aforementioned reports by the Commission on Chapter 1 and IRP.[39] To qualify for aid, a state would, as with Goals 2000, have to show that it was adopting challenging standards and aligned assessments that all children, including those served by Title I, would be expected to meet. States that had created standards under Goals 2000 could submit these standards to meet the conditions of aid of the new Title I. States would also have to test students to see if they were making "adequate yearly progress" in "at least mathematics and reading or language arts." Students were to be tested "at some time during" grades three through five, six through nine, and ten through twelve. States and school districts both would be obliged to take corrective action if schools receiving Title I funds failed to improve.[40] The legislation, then, broke sharply with the past. It would:

- Transform Chapter 1/Title I from a pull-out compensatory aid program to a standards-based program.[41]
- Make this standards-based reform the basis for systemic reform, which would require reworking other titles of the ESEA so that they "help tie teacher preparation, certification, and ongoing professional development" to the standards and aligned assessments.[42]
- Use Title I as general aid; that is, use it to improve the education of all children by conditioning acceptance of the aid on states enacting standards-based reform for all schools.[43]

Unlike America 2000, there was no talk of national standards; too many in the education policy network were still smarting from that battle. Instead, as with Goals 2000, control over curricula would remain with states and localities.

Congress showed little antipathy to this federalism-sensitive standards-based proposal for reform.[44] A close examination of the hearings on Chapter 1 in 1993 and 1994 indicates that members of Congress rarely voiced any objections to standards. Indeed, the record reflects that they were quite supportive of the idea. Whereas conservatives in Congress had raged against federal usurpation of local control during the debates on Goals 2000, they did not raise this argument against the Clinton plan for making Chapter 1 a standards-based program.

This, though, is not to say that there was no disagreement. Beyond a bevy of social issues (school prayer, education aid to the children whose parents brought them to the United States illegally, sex education), there was intense disagreement over two subjects. As in the past, senators and representatives grappled over the funding formula for Title I. And, once again, opportunity-to-learn-standards split the left and the right.

The Title I Funding Formula. Congress was generally pleased that the president had requested an increase in funding for Chapter 1, some $700 million the first year alone. But "who got what" was a topic of hot debate in Congress.

The Chapter 1 formula for sending federal dollars to localities has always been quite complex.[45] Yet its general contours can be sketched out without doing too much violence to the facts. There were two sorts of Chapter 1 grants, Basic Grants and Concentration Grants. About 90 percent of Chapter 1 dollars were devoted to Basic Grants, the remainder to Concentration Grants. The federal government allotted funds thus:

1. The federal government allocated Basic Grant funds to each county based on the number of poor children each has.[46]
2. Said funds were then sent to state departments of education.

3. Each state department of education allocated money to counties based on the number of children from low-income families.
4. Counties, with some discretion, then distributed the funds to individual schools based on two criteria:
   (a) eligibility for aid (the number of poor children they have), and
   (b) low achievement rates among a school's children.

Counties where 15 percent (or 6,500 or more) of the children were impoverished were eligible for Concentration Grants. Basic Grant funds went to nearly every county.

This formula has some obvious problems. For one, the funds a school receives are partly contingent on student achievement levels. Therefore, if a school is effective and raises student achievement relative to the norm, it might lose Chapter 1 funding. The converse also holds true: schools where student achievement slides can receive more and more funds. Moreover, whereas the federal government apportions Chapter 1 Basic Grants on the basis of poverty, counties disburse funds on the basis of poverty and achievement. Chapter 1 is not an entitlement like, say, welfare. All of those eligible are not legally assured of funds because of their status.[47] Add to this problematic formula the many years of congressional bargaining so that the formula would send more Chapter 1 aid to individual districts, and the result, Secretary Riley testified, was less than ideal.

> The current Chapter 1 formula distributes funds to virtually all counties in the nation, 93 percent of all school districts, and two-thirds of the nation's schools, yet leaves many of the country's poorest children in the poorest schools unserved. . . . Thirteen percent of high-poverty schools, for example, do not receive any Chapter 1 funding, and a third of the low-achieving children in high-poverty schools do not receive Chapter 1 services.[48]

Under HR 6 the percentage of Title I dollars for Concentration Grants for the poorest districts would increase from 10 to 50 percent. The bill would also raise the percentage of children in poverty that counties must have in order to qualify for Concentration Grants. The point of the reforms, clearly, was to focus more Title I funds on districts with extremely high rates of poverty.

Because the proposed formula would favor districts with high poverty concentrations, states with large urban areas would benefit. Meanwhile, sixteen states with large rural areas would lose funding. Indeed, all states would see a shifting of Title I funding away from rural counties to high-density urban counties, and affluent counties that served small numbers of poor children would also lose federal dollars.[49] The response in Congress was swift. The first day the administration presented its proposal to Congress (September 23), the second-ranking Republican, Representative

Steve Gunderson, welcomed the plan, but added, "I also know I speak for every Republican that . . . cosponsoring this bill doesn't mean we endorse the Chapter 1 formula that is in the proposal."[50] The haggling over the new formula began immediately and carried on through autumn and into winter. In February 1994, the Democrat-dominated House Subcommittee on Elementary, Secondary, and Vocational Education voted down the Clinton funding proposal and replaced it with a compromise worked out among its contending members. Title I's funding formula would remain the same, but funding beyond the current $6.6 billion level would be increasingly targeted to the poorest districts. Though negotiations over the funding formula continued through summer and into early autumn, this agreement essentially held.[51]

Opportunity-to-Learn Standards. Opportunity-to-learn standards briefly imperiled passage of the Improving America's Schools Act. During the hearings in 1993, the topic received scant discussion. The subject did come up in hearings before the Senate Subcommittee on Education, Arts, and Humanities in 1994. However, Secretary Riley and the committee's chairman, Edward Kennedy (D-MA), and top Republican member, Nancy Kassebaum (R-KS), quelled the issue by presenting a united front. They strongly cautioned colleagues against any effort to make an issue of OTL standards.[52]

In the House, though, opportunity-to-learn standards nearly flickered into a firestorm. During a meeting of the House Education Committee, Representative Major Owens (D-NY) attached an OTL amendment to Title I. The amendment passed 26 votes to 16. All but one Democrat voted for it, and all but one Republican voted against it. Republicans were outraged and threatened to do everything they could to stonewall the bill. Before February's end, Democrats, seeing that Republicans would not compromise on OTL standards, replaced the provision with a nearly symbolic one. State plans would be required to include

> such other factors the State deems appropriate (which may include opportunity-to-learn standards or strategies developed under the Goals 2000: Educate America Act) to provide students an opportunity to achieve the knowledge and skills described in the challenging content standards adopted by the State.[53]

Remarkably, the matter ended there. Though further complaints were raised over the Title I formula and there were skirmishes over a number of social issues, these matters were settled with relative ease. On March 24, the House passed HR 6 by a vote of 289 to 128. The Senate followed suit on August 2, voting 94 to 6 in favor. Conferees ironed out the differences between the two bills with relative ease, and both houses agreed to the report by October 5. President Clinton signed PL 103-382 into law on October 20, 1994.

The Effects of Politics on IASA's Revisions of Chapter I

The Clinton administration had hoped Goals 2000 and IASA would induce states to adopt systemic, standards-based public schools reform. States that participated in Goals 2000 would craft standards and aligned assessments; then, to meet the new conditions of aid under Title I of the ESEA, they would be allowed to submit these standards and assessments. The result would be that all public school children would be held to high standards.

However, politics intervened and Goals 2000 ended up as a permissive program with little power to push states to do anything they did not care to do. Much the same could be said for IASA. Unlike Goals 2000, Title I was not significantly altered when the Republicans took over Congress in January 1995. PL 104-134, the spending act that abolished NESIC, in fact, slightly raised Title I spending. Yet, thanks to antistatist-liberal politics, the new Title I, like Goals 2000, was permissive. In particular, IASA's short-comings were to be found in the statute's provisions on measuring state compliance and the Clinton administration's oversight thereof.

Measuring State Compliance

Goals 2000 and the new Title I were, in tandem, to create incentives for states to craft standards. Title I held that:

> If a State has State content standards or State student performance stan-
> dards developed under Title III of the Goals 2000: Educate America Act
> and an aligned set of assessments for all students developed under such
> title . . . the State shall use such standards and assessments, modified, if
> necessary, to conform with the requirements [of Title I].[54]

Title I's conditions of aid for state reform plans stipulates a number of criteria that if followed would set states on the path to systemic reform. Figure 5.1 indicates that the law required states to create content standards, performance standards, and aligned assessments. Assessments were to be given at different schooling levels, roughly corresponding to elementary, middle, and high school, and states were to define at least three levels of student performance on these assessments: advanced, proficient, and partially proficient. The data collected from this testing was to be compiled to indicate how each local school district and school is doing at educating children to the state standards.[55]

Figure 5.1   Title I State Accountability System Requirements

---

Sec. 1111(b)(1)(D)
Standards under this paragraph shall include—

(i) challenging content standards in academic subjects that—
    (I) specify what children are expected to know and be able to do;
    (II) contain coherent and rigorous content; and
    (III) encourage the teaching of advanced skills;

(ii) challenging student performance standards that—
    (I) are aligned with the State's content standards;
    (II) describe two levels of high performance, proficient and advanced, that determine how well children are mastering the material in the State content standards; and
    (III) describe a third level of performance, partially proficient, to provide complete information about the progress of lower performing children toward achieving to the proficient and advanced levels of performance.

(3) Assessments. Each State plan shall demonstrate that the State has developed or adopted a set of high-quality, yearly student assessments . . . in at least mathematics and reading or language arts. . . . Such assessments shall—

(A) be the same assessments used to measure the performance of all children . . .

(B) be aligned with the State's challenging content and student performance standards and provide coherent information about student attainment of standards; . . .

(D) measure the proficiency of students in the academic subjects in which a State has adopted challenging content and student performance standards and be administered at some time during—
    (i) grades 3 through 5;
    (ii) grades 6 through 9; and
    (iii) grades 10 through 12;

(6) (A) A State that does not have challenging State content standards and challenging State student performance standards, in at least mathematics and reading or language arts, shall develop such standards within one year of receiving funds under this part after the first fiscal year for which such State receives such funds after October 20, 1994.

(B) A State that does not have assessments that meet the requirements of paragraph (3) in at least mathematics and reading or language arts shall develop and test such assessments within four years (one year of which will be use for field testing such assessment), of receiving funds under this part after the first fiscal year for which such State receives such funds after October 20, 1994 . . .

These were challenging requirements. Perversely, states most in need—those with the least developed educational agencies, limited tax resources, and strong traditions of local control—faced the greatest challenges.[56] That said, the federal government faced fundamental obstacles to oversight. In keeping with the tradition of no federal control over curricula, the 1994 reworking of Title I fenced off school curricula from federal examination.

> Each State plan shall demonstrate that the State has developed or adopted challenging content standards and challenging student performance standards that will be used by the State, its local educational agencies, and its schools, except that a state will not be required to submit such standards to the Secretary [for approval].[57]

And,

> The Secretary has authority to disapprove a State's plan . . . but shall not have the authority to require a State, as a condition of approval of the State plan, to include in, or delete from, such plan one or more specific elements of the State's content standards or to use specific assessment instruments or items.[58]

This raises obvious hurdles to federal oversight: What, specifically, was a state to submit to the federal government to demonstrate that it had developed or adopted challenging content standards without submitting the standards themselves? Or, to put it from the perspective of the Department of Education: How was it to discern if states were developing or had adopted challenging standards and aligned assessments if it could not compare them with touchstones for what constitutes adequate standards and assessments? The law provided no hint as to what constituted "challenging standards" and "aligned assessments." With no NESIC to judge the quality standards and assessments, how could the federal government be sure states really were creating good standards and tests?

The Department of Education struggled with this chore, and it was not until 1997 that it issued to states its *Guidance on Standards, Assessment, and Accountability*.[59] The guide was remarkable in its opacity on what state reform plans had to include. "This guidance sets general principles intended to be interpreted in the context of each State rather than specifying detailed procedures to be followed."[60] Instead of clear benchmarks for adequacy, the guide gave vague suggestions and a menu of types of evidence states might submit to show they are undertaking standards reform. For example, the guide asked, "What considerations are relevant as a State determines whether its standards are challenging?" Unable to answer the question directly, it then posed some rather obvious questions for States to ask themselves in order to answer this question, including: "Do the standards reflect the best professional judgment of content specialists? Is the State setting challenging enough standards? Are they balanced, accurate, and sound?" The guide then explained that a state "may wish to include in its plan information that responds to these questions" but added this was not mandatory.[61] Another Title I guide issued by the department in 1999 to peer reviewers of the adequacy of state assessments suffered from the same problem. Lacking a national assessment to use as a yardstick for adequacy and the power to review state assessments, peers had to, for example, judge the alignment of assessments by looking at "evidence that [a state] has studied the alignment of the assessment and standards and, if gaps exist, that it has identified additional measures to adequately assess the standards."[62]

Weak Federal Oversight of State Compliance

Julie Roy Jeffrey notes that among those who crafted Title I in 1965,

> it was recognized that the presence of an established bureaucracy was a factor inhibiting change. . . . Although planners . . . sensed the nature of the educational bureaucracy and recognized that local power structures had long ignored the poor and were educationally conservative, they feared the local control issue could defeat their bills. So they had chosen to give local areas substantial and important powers. [Francis] Keppel and other departmental planners thought that federal funds could instigate reforms in attitude and practice, could infuse the whole educational structure with a desire for change. . . . [Yet the] different titles of the ESEA, in fact, allocated most or all money on an automatic formula basis, leaving the Office of Education with only the powers "to coax and cajole localities" to change their practices.[63]

Three decades later, little had changed. Federal power to compel state compliance to federal requirements remained weak. The 1994 reauthorization provided that only "the Secretary may withhold funds for State administration and activities . . . until the Secretary determines that the State plan meets the requirements of this section."[64] State administrative funds make up a small portion of the total Title I funds; moreover, in light of the political response an administration might receive from members of Congress representing a noncompliant state and its voters, the Department of Education has a clear incentive to avoid withholding funds. Michael Cohen notes an often-told tale in Washington, DC:

> When Doc Howe was Commissioner of Education under LBJ [President Lyndon Johnson], he attempted to withhold federal education funds from Chicago because it failed to comply with certain desegregation require-

ments. Upon receipt of formal notification from HEW [the Department of Health, Education, and Welfare], Mayor Daley called LBJ directly to complain. Doc Howe was gone by the next day. And no one has been foolish enough to try anything like that since.[65]

Howe's removal began a tradition of benign neglect. Presidents did not make Title I oversight a priority.[66] Neither did Congress. It might be expected that the Democrats (who controlled Congress during all but two years from 1965 to 1994) would have been especially interested in whether Title I funds were being used to raise achievement and lift children out of poverty. This, though, was not their primary concern. Because they saw public schools—especially those in poor communities—as starved for funds and resources, they viewed Title I as a sort of general aid to schools, to be used as districts and schools saw fit. This, then, left a few weak stakeholders, such as civil rights groups, futilely urging stricter oversight of Title I funds and program efficacy.[67] Indeed, the federal government never withheld any funds from any state. Phyllis McClure of the National Association for the Advancement of Colored People (NAACP), a longtime observer and advocate for increased Title I funding, points out the long-term effect of lax federal oversight: "Nobody believes that money will actually be terminated. . . . These states, they know the game."[68]

The Clinton administration failed to break this tradition of lax oversight. It did not press states to conform to the new mandates of Title I. In part, the administration suffered from the same problem as previous administrations: the political pitfalls of strict oversight. Marshall Smith noted, "It's hard to take money away from any state. The argument against it is you're taking money away from poor kids. . . . We never worked through that [conundrum] in the way that we should."[69] Representative George Miller (CA), the ranking Democrat on the House Education Committee, was blunt on the matter: "Its implementation was fudged by the administration."[70]

The cause for this, in large part, was political.[71] Shortly after the new Title I was enacted, Republicans took control of both houses of Congress. John F. Jennings, who served as a legislative aide to the Democrats for nearly three decades, notes that after this,

> the Clinton team was worried about just keeping the federal government in the game. . . . They thought if they pressed hard on states to comply with the new law, they would be shaking the foundations of the federal role in education, and giving ammunition to the far right [who] wanted to eliminate any federal role.[72]

Michael Cohen concurs: "Efforts in Congress to abolish both Goals 2000 and the Education Department . . . contributed to a widespread view that tough enforcement would be a particularly hazardous course of action for the Department to pursue."[73] Victor F. Klatt III, education and human resource policy coordinator for the Committee on Education and the Workforce in the US House of Representatives at the time, agrees that the Republican Congress would have raised a stink if the Department of Education applied the law vigorously.[74]

Thus, when the Department of Education drew up its guidelines for Title I, it interpreted the law in a manner that put very few demands upon the states. There are a number of examples of this.[75] However, for the purposes of this chapter, one example is particularly pertinent.

Title I stipulated:

> Each State plan shall demonstrate that the State has developed or adopted a set of high-quality, yearly student assessments, including assessments in at least mathematics and reading or language arts, that will be used as the primary means of determining the yearly performance of each local educational agency and school served under this part in enabling all children served under this part to meet the State's student performance standards.
>
> Such assessments shall—
>
> (A) be the same assessments used to measure the performance of all children, if the State measures the performance of all children;
>
> (B) be aligned with the State's challenging content and student performance standards and provide coherent information about student attainment of such standards; . . .
>
> (D) measure the proficiency of students in the academic subjects in which a State has adopted challenging content and student performance standards; . . .
>
> (E) involve multiple up-to-date measures of student performance, including measures that assess higher order thinking skills and understanding.

The law also stated, "Each State plan shall demonstrate that the State has developed or adopted challenging content standards and challenging student performance standards that will be used by the State, its local educational agencies, and its schools." Reading these in tandem, it might reasonably be inferred to have required criterion-referenced exams that are aligned to a single set of challenging state standards. Indeed, as noted earlier, three of the great criticisms against the old Title I was that it used norm-referenced exams that did not reveal information about students' learning of curricula, that these tests covered rudimentary skills and knowledge, and that the tests encouraged schools to provide a "dumbed down" curriculum to Title I students. However, the Department of Education took a more permissive interpretation. Its guide declared:

> "Must State content and performance standards be uniform throughout a State for Title I purposes?"

> "No. Title I requires that each State develop or adopt challenging content and student performance standards. It does not require that a single set of content or performance standards be applied uniformly to every LEA within a State."[76]

The department further held that assessments need not be uniform statewide; localities could develop their own assessments. And criterion-referenced tests were not required. Indeed, the Department of Education interpreted the phrase "multiple up-to-date measures of student performance" to mean that any number of assessment types might be used, including norm-referenced tests, criterion-referenced tests, portfolios, and so forth. Additionally, states were not, the department stated, legally obliged to use more than one test type (norm-referenced, for example) in any one subject area.[77]

The Clinton administration's failure to enforce the standards and assessments requirements of the new Title I contributed to the slow response to the law by states. Under the conditions of aid, states were to:

- Develop/adopt challenging content standards and performance standards by the 1997–1998 school year.
- Develop/adopt aligned assessments by the 2001–2002 school year.

The deadline for full implementation was the conclusion of the five-year reauthorization period. The vast majority of states failed to meet the law's deadlines for compliance. Few states, as indicated in Chapter 2, have created rigorous, useful standards.[78]

Raising Standards Through Voluntary National Tests

Politics had hobbled both Goals 2000 and the IASA reauthorization of Title I. Despite this, President Clinton again tried to make federal policy to raise standards. The idea of voluntary national tests was not new. As was indicated in Chapter 3 of this book, the first President Bush had proposed them. So did Clinton early in his first term. But both presidents backed off national tests because they saw great resistance in Congress from the left and the right.

The notion behind using VNTs as a tool for raising standards in the public schools was this: the federal government would fund the creation of challenging academic examinations. States, eager to show the public and the business community that their schools were good, would have their children take the examinations. States that did well could brag about it;

states that did poorly would need to rework their standards to be aligned with the high standards inherent to the VNTs.

After securing a second term in office, Clinton quickly moved to fashion VNTs. The president announced his proposal for voluntary national tests during his February 4, 1997, State of the Union Address. It was part of his Call to Action for American Education.

> I have a plan, a Call to Action for American Education, based on these 10 principles. First, a national crusade for education standards—not federal government standards, but national standards—representing what all our students must know to succeed in the knowledge economy of the 21st century. Every state and school must shape the curriculum to reflect these standards, and train teachers to lift students up to them.

Again, rather than have the federal government commission actual standards, a less direct (and hopefully less politically explosive) approach would be taken. Clinton continued:

> To help schools meet the standards and measure their progress, we will lead an effort over the next two years to develop national tests of student achievement in reading and math. Tonight, I issue a challenge to the nation. Every state should adopt high national standards, and by 1999, every state should test every fourth grader in reading and every eighth-grader in math to make sure these standards are met.[79]

The administration soon thereafter actuated its complex plan to devise national tests. The Department of Education contracted with the Council of Chief State School Officers (CCSSO) and a consulting firm, MPR Associates (MPRA), to draft the basic specifications of the assessments (e.g., number of questions, mix of questions that would be multiple choice and open-ended, the amount of time students would have to take the exams, etc.).[80] The CCSSO was chosen, in part, because it had worked on the frameworks used to create the NAEP reading and TIMSS math tests, which the VNTs were to resemble. The Department of Education also created a sixteen-member national test panel of state education officers, teachers, national education interest groups, scholars, and business persons to examine and vote on the specifications drafted by the CCSSO and MPRA. The national test panel would also hold hearings to get input from parents, educators, and others before choosing the final formats of the exams and creating the test questions.

At an April hearing before the House Subcommittee on Early Childhood, Youth, and Families, Secretary Riley made a case for the national exams and sought to fend off the accusation that the federal government was creating a national school board. The benefits, he argued, were manifest. First, in contrast to the often unreliable, norm-referenced state and local assessments, VNTs would be of high quality. They would be modeled on the widely respected NAEP and TIMSS exams. Students taking these tests would receive a rating like those given on NAEP exams: not proficient, proficient, and advanced.[81] This would mean parents, schools, and state policymakers all across the United States would have a good measure of the educational progress of individual children.[82] Different districts could compare their students' achievement, as could different states. Moreover, the scores students received on the exams could be compared to exams given by states. If student scores on the state exams were higher than those on the VNTs, it might provoke policymakers to raise state standards, toughen exams, and better align their curricula with the national exams. Those students taking the math exam would also have a measure of their learning relative to that of students in other nations. Riley also stated that

> our decision to test fourth-grade reading and eighth-grade math was very deliberate. We chose these grades very carefully. Reading and math are the core basics, and fourth and eighth grades are critical transition points in a child's educational experience. We know, for example, that being able to read independently by fourth grade is the prerequisite for all other learning. . . . The latest NAEP results tell us, however, that many of our fourth-graders (42%) [are unable to read adequately].[83]

The case was similar for geometry and algebra, which, Riley noted, students should learn by the eighth grade if they want to have a good chance at learning any higher math.

To placate conservatives, Riley emphasized that the tests were voluntary,

> and the decision to use these tests . . . must be made by state and local authorities. . . . States and localities will not lose one penny of federal funding if they choose not to participate. These proposed tests are an opportunity, not a requirement, a national challenge, not a national curriculum.

Riley also noted that a few states had already asked to take the exams and that 240 leaders of technology companies (including Lou Gerstner of IBM and Steve Case of America Online) supported federal action to raise education standards. Speaking to concerns about student privacy held by both conservatives and liberals, Riley explained that the federal government was not going to know which kids took the tests or how individual students performed. "No data from individual students will come to the US Department of Education. . . . We will not keep records on any individual test scores." States and localities would administer the exams, and private contractors would score them.

There were, obviously, legitimate policy reasons to be concerned about the administration's proposal. It was not clear, for example, whether the national reading exam was to test reading or reading in English.[84] Indeed, the Hispanic caucus in Congress raised this very issue, fearing millions of ESL children would be either excluded from the exams or forced to take a test they were likely to do poorly on. Yet, the question of national tests, like national standards, tapped into long-standing concerns about federal power over school curricula and the education of poor and minority children.[85] The administration's plan allowed the appearance if not the actual politicization of the tests. As Chester E. Finn Jr. and Diane Ravitch argued, the NAEP exams were overseen by the independent and bipartisan National Assessment Governing Board (NAGB).[86] In terms of experience and competence, the NAGB was well equipped to handle the task of national exams. In terms of politics, being heavily staffed with governors from both parties, it would be hard for anyone to accuse the NAGB of being a national school board or against poor and minority children. Instead of choosing the NAGB, the Clinton administration proposed putting the Department of Education—long loathed by the right as an incompetent, leftist agency—in charge of the VNT program. Thus, whoever served as secretary of education would have the power to revise the tests to suit his or her particular politics. Worse, the administration antagonized the Republican Congress by attempting to bypass it entirely. The administration moved quickly to use discretionary funds to create the exams. By August 1997, the Clinton team had already held meetings and awarded contracts, and the national test panel had held meetings.

The result was a political firestorm that lasted two years and resembled the battles over America 2000, Goals 2000, and the 1994 reauthorization of Title I. Liberals and antistatists responded as they had to standards legislation previously.[87] Members of the House's black caucus, led by Major Owens (D-NY), were nearly unanimously opposed. They and other liberals said they would not even consider national tests until the United States had national opportunity-to-learn standards. "You can't do one," said Owens, "without the other."[88] The question of the primary cause of student underachievement returned. Liberals again argued that testing was unfair to poor and nonwhite children because their schools lacked sufficient resources. On the right, the philosophical issue of the extent of federal power resurfaced. Representative Robert Schaeffer (R-CO) circulated a letter against the exams along with another letter signed by eleven conservative groups, including the Eagle Forum and the Christian Coalition. They objected to the tests because they would lead to more federal control.[89] House education committee chair William Goodling (R-PA), for his part, denounced national testing generally and insisted that any national tests would require congressional authorization.

By early September, amendments had been offered in both houses of Congress that would require explicit congressional authorization for the development of any tests. To add to the stakes, opponents of testing attempted to attach these amendments to the hulking $286 billion Departments of Labor, Health and Human Services, and Education, and Related Agencies appropriations bill. This would force the president to sign the bill and drop his bid for testing or to veto a spending bill loaded with federal dollars for the poor and middle classes (a politically risky move). In the more moderate Senate, the amendment was turned back, and another amendment was attached that shifted control over the development of national tests to the NAGB.[90] The Senate passed the amended bill by a vote of 87 to 13. In the House, though, members voted 295 to 125 in favor of Goodling's amendment to prohibit the Department of Education from spending funds on VNTs. More than a third of the Democrats had supported the Republican amendment on September 16, 1997, the same day that the national education panel voted in favor of the national test specifications. President Clinton threatened to veto the whole bill if it disallowed national tests. Representative Peter Hoekstra (R-MI), who served on the Education and Workforce Committee, responded, "If he wants to veto it over national testing, people on our side of the aisle are fine with that. For many of us, it's a matter of principle."[91]

The opposition to VNTs, especially from the right, grew. Gary Bauer and his Family Research Council lobbied against them. Senator John Ashcroft (R-MO) vowed to filibuster any bill with national tests and united thirty-five Senate Republicans against them. In October the rancor over national testing grew still more intense. Representative Goodling refused to move on President Clinton's $2.7 billion reading initiative unless Clinton ceased pushing for the national tests. In order to avoid appearing as a "do-nothing" party on education, Republicans then rolled out their "Republican Agenda for the American Learner," an amalgam of policies that centered on increasing parental school choice. Intriguingly, the Republicans justified their choice policies in the language of standards: "We want to take out ideas for expanded parental choice beyond the beltway and create the kind of competitive environment that will improve standards in schools," Terry Holt, a House Republican and conference spokesman, told the press.[92] They also continued to emphasize the importance of federalism and the impropriety of federal control over schooling.[93]

The wrangling over testing continued until a conference committee forged a complex compromise that was signed by Clinton on November 13, 1997.[94] Both sides claimed victory with PL 105-78, the Departments of Labor, Health and Human Services, and Education, and Related Agencies Appropriations Act of 1997. However, if the decision was between voluntary national tests and no tests at all, then the White House clearly lost. Under the agreement:

- The National Academy of Sciences would investigate whether national tests were even necessary by studying whether the individual state tests used could be calibrated to a common national metric. Its report was due by June 1998.
- Field testing of any VNTs could not begin until autumn 1998.
- Republicans would hold hearings on the advisability of VNTs.
- The NAGB would review the work that had been done thus far to develop VNTs.

In February 1998 the NAGB, to the disappointment of the administration, announced it would not be able to field test any exams until March 1999 and 2000, which meant the tests could not actually be used until at least 2001. That same month, though, the likelihood of national tests in 2001 dropped precipitously. The House, at the urging of Representative Goodling, passed a bill by 242 votes to 174 that required Congress to "specifically and explicitly" authorize the development of a national test beyond 1998. Just two of 219 Republicans were against the bill, and twenty-five Democrats joined them.[95]

The NAS delivered its report in June 1998. Its conclusions supported the Clinton administration's argument for national tests:

> If there is any common ground shared by advocates and opponents of national testing, it is the potential merits of bringing greater uniformity to Americans' understanding of the educational performance of their children. Advocates of VNT argue that this is only possible through the development of a new test, while opponents have suggested that statistical linkages among existing tests might provide a basis for comparability.[96]

The authors came down squarely against the latter position.

1. Comparing the full array of currently administered commercial and states tests to one another, through the development of a single equivalency or linking scale, is not feasible.
2. Reporting individual student scores from the full array of state and commercial achievement tests on the NAEP scale and transforming individual scores on these various tests and assessments into the NAEP achievement levels is not feasible.[97]

In short, any effort at either of the above had an unacceptably high risk of producing scores that inaccurately portrayed student learning. Accurate assessments are an essential element in standards-based reform, so this was a blow to the "leave it to the states" position on testing.

Congress did not take issue with the report or accuse it of being politically biased. Instead, it simply ignored its findings. By October 1998, Representative Goodling told the press that national tests were "dead, dead, dead."[98] Under an omnibus spending law inked that month, the NAGB was allowed to continue developing the tests but was not authorized to field test the exams. In 1999, Congress did not authorize further funds for development of national tests.[99]

Conclusion

The 1990s saw major legislative efforts to use federal power to raise the education standards of the public schools. These efforts were not wholly in vain. Goals 2000 did, for example, help some states better their accountability systems.[100] The federal pushes for standards helped get the states speaking the language of standards-based reform for all children. The same might be said for the 1994 reauthorization of Title I.

Yet, for all the effort, at the decade's end the United States remained without national standards and assessments. When the year 2000 came, Goals 2000 expired.[101] The nation fell far short of reaching the national goals it had set.[102] The National Education Goals Panel, which had helped focus the nation's attention on the efforts to achieve the goals and a steadfast advocate for raising education standards, quietly expired in 2002. With no national goals, the panel had little to do.[103] Unconnected to any national test or condition of aid, the national standards funded by George H. W. Bush's administration failed to draw much interest from the federal government or the states.[104]

During the hearings on the reauthorization of ESEA, Iris C. Rotberg of RAND quipped, "in the past few years we have talked a lot about accountability and standards. It's hard to oppose them in theory. They have a ring of motherhood and apple pie."[105] This was true. Standards were rarely attacked as bad policy by members of Congress. Yet, for all the public support, for all the sound policy arguments that were advanced, national standards did not come to be. Politics trumped popular demand and good policy, and the very idea of national standards fell from favor in Washington.[106] The resistance to using federal power to establish or raise standards came in many forms. Raw partisanship and power politics played a role, and on occasion, there were honest differences of opinion on the wisdom of standards.

But, the big story is that standards proposals ran up against political resistance with deep historical roots. As Chapters 3 through 5 have described, this resistance stemmed from antistatists who were skeptical of involving the federal government in the public schools. Meanwhile, those who favored an increased federal role—and who ought to have favored using federal power to raise standards—were divided. Liberals were unable to agree on the primary cause of educational underachievement, and so they fought one another over which was more important, higher standards or increased resources for schools.

The 1990s, then, were filled with both promise and disappointment for quality-schools advocates who favored standards. In order to have an educational system that focused on results and measured its progress thereto, high standards were needed. States mostly had failed to create high standards. Thus, the federal government was obliged to step in and see to it that all children could attend schools with high standards. A flurry of federal standards initiatives commenced, and, unfortunately, all the policies were frustrated by politics. None could ensure that high standards were fashioned. So the federal dollars continued to flow by the billions, states proclaimed their commitment to systemic reform, but high standards, the sine qua non for helping children to learn more, remained the exception to the rule.

Notes

1. US Department of Education, *Improving America's Schools Act of 1993*, p. 2.

2. As quoted in Chaddock, "Brinkmanship over National Tests Could Prompt Washington Shutdowns."

3. The proposal also sought to reform the other parts of the Elementary and Secondary Education Act of 1965. The concentration here, though, is on standards, which fell under Chapter 1/Title I. Originally named Title I, the 1988 reauthorization renamed it Chapter 1. The IASA changed its name back to Title I.

4. Haycock and Hornbeck, "Making Schools Work for Children in Poverty," p. 78.

5. In Lowi's terms, Chapter 1 politics has been distributive; it is characterized by bargaining among members of Congress to see that each gets his or her share. Lowi, "American Business, Public Policy, Case Studies, and Political Theory," pp. 686–715.

6. Hansen, "Elementary and Secondary Education Reauthorization," as quoted in Vinovskis, *The Development and Demise of the National Education Goals*, p. 179.

7. Commission on Chapter 1, *Making Schools Work for Children in Poverty*.

8. Haycock and Hornbeck, "Making Schools Work for Children in Poverty," p. 79.

9. Ibid., p. 81.

10. Ibid., pp. 81–82.

11. National Assessment of Chapter 1 Independent Review Panel, *Reinventing Chapter 1*. This study echoed much of what was written in the independent (but not government commissioned) report, *Making Schools Work for Children in Poverty*.

12. Phyllis McClure and David Hornbeck served on both IRP and the Commission on Chapter 1.

13. PL 100-297.

14. National Assessment of Chapter 1 Independent Review Panel, *Reinventing Chapter 1: The Current Chapter 1 Program and New Directions*, p. 13.

15. Ibid., p. 2.

16. Ibid., pp. 25–31.

17. Ibid., pp. 36, 39.

18. Ibid., p. 14.

19. Ibid., p. 45.

20. This was not the first report to cast doubt on the value of Chapter 1, and before the year's end, preliminary data from the congressionally mandated *Prospects* study raised further questions about the efficacy of Chapter 1. Carter, "The Sustaining Effects Study of Compensatory and Elementary Education," pp. 5–13. *Prospects* was a longitudinal study that compared the educational achievement of Chapter 1 students versus similarly situated children who did not participate in Chapter 1. Its initial results were released after the Clinton administration had formulated and offered its plan for reform. Moss and Puma, *Prospects*. See also Riddle, *Title I: Education for the Disadvantaged*.

21. Independent Review Panel, *Reinventing Chapter 1: The Current Chapter 1 Program and New Directions*, pp. 45, 19.

22. US Congress, House of Representatives, Subcommittee on Elementary, Secondary, and Vocational Education Subcommittee of the Committee on Education and Labor, *Hearings on HR 6*, February 2, 1993, p. 29.

23. "A norm-referenced test is an objective test that is standardized on a group of individuals whose performance is evaluated in relation to the performance of others. Criterion-referenced tests are assessments that measure the mastery of specific skills or subject content and focus on the performance of an individual as measured against a standard or criterion rather than the performance of others taking the test." See General Accounting Office, *Title I: Education Needs to Monitor States' Scoring of Assessments*, p. 5.

24. The administration thought that Congress would be more interested in working on the ESEA renewal because it involved more than ten times as much money per annum. However, its ideas about how to reform Chapter 1 were sketched out by January 2003 and were similar to that urged by the IRP and the Commission on Chapter 1. See Presidential Transition Team, Education, Labor, and Humanities Cluster, *Report of the K–12 Transition Team to the Incoming Assistant Secretary for Elementary and Secondary Education*.

25. US Congress, House of Representatives, Subcommittee on Elementary, Secondary, and Vocational Education Subcommittee of the Committee on Education and Labor, *Hearings on HR 6*, February 2, 4, 1993; February 18, 1993; February 25, 1993; May 13, 25, June 10 and 30, 1993; Subcommittee on Elementary, Secondary, and Vocational Education Subcommittee of the Committee on Education and Labor, *Hearings on Reauthorization of HR 6*, March 4, 18, 23, 31, April 21, and 27, 1993; Subcommittee on Elementary, Secondary, and Vocational Education Subcommittee of the Committee on Education and Labor, *Hearings on HR 3130*, September 23, 1993.

26. Other committees did not hold hearings until 1994 or were excluded because they studied aspects of the ESEA other than Chapter 1 (e.g., technology for education, antidrug programs, etc.).

27. Phyllis McClure returned as a witness at a later hearing; and Secretary Riley, who agreed with the commission's findings, appeared at three hearings and

emphasized the need for standards. Nobody at this hearing expressed a different approach for reforming Chapter 1 than standards-based reform.

28. Subcommittee on Elementary, Secondary, and Vocational Education, *Hearing on HR 6: Reform Proposals for Chapter 1*, February 25, 1993, p. 3.

29. Ibid., p. 4. See also Subcommittee on Education, Arts, and Humanities, Committee on Labor and Human Resources, US Senate, *ESEA: Framework for Change*, March 18, 1994, pp. 144–151.

30. The Advisory Committee on Testing and Chapter 1 was appointed by the secretary of education to advise Congress and the Department of Education on how to improve Chapter 1 assessment practices.

31. Subcommittee on Elementary, Secondary, and Vocational Education, *Hearing on HR 6*, February 18, 1993, pp. 24–26, quote at p. 24.

32. Subcommittee on Elementary, Secondary, and Vocational Education, *Hearing on HR 6*, February 4, 1993, p. 98.

33. Subcommittee on Elementary, Secondary, and Vocational Education, House of Representatives, *Hearings on the Reauthorization of HR 6*, March 4, 1993, pp. 3–5, 28–30; and March 18, 1993, pp. 102–105.

34. For example, see Bob Chase, then vice-president of the NEA, at ibid., March 4, 1993, pp. 55, 61. On gender bias and assessments, see the testimony of Marcia D. Greenberger of the National Women's Law Center, Subcommittee on Elementary, Secondary, and Vocational Education, *Hearings on the Reauthorization of HR 6*, April 21, 1993, pp. 473–477, plus insert at p. 478. In regard to 1994, see Jackie DeFazio, president, American Association of University Women, US Congress, Senate, Subcommittee on Education, Arts, and Humanities, Committee on Labor and Human Resources, *ESEA: Framework for Change*, May 5, 1994, pp. 602–605.

35. This is a perennial tension in grants-in-aid programs. The federal government has goals it wants achieved, and states want the freedom to choose the means to achieve the goals—which, it is worth adding, they often prefer to define themselves.

36. E.g., were children that qualified for Title I assistance also qualified to receive Medicaid? If so, at what age? An entire hearing was dedicated to this topic. See Subcommittee on Elementary, Secondary, and Vocational Education, *Hearings on the Reauthorization of HR 6*, March 31, 1993, pp. 317–414.

37. One witness testified that Minnesota public schools faced some fifty-two mandates regarding social service delivery, including programs for school lunches, health, day care, drug education, parental education, counseling for dropouts, AIDS prevention, and suicide prevention. "Each program enacted for education has its own mini-bureaucracy . . . its own regulations, objectives, and turf defenses. Beyond these are adjacent programs such as AFDC, Immunization, and others which impact education." Subcommittee on Elementary, Secondary, and Vocational Education, *Hearing on HR 6*, February 6, 1993, pp. 83–85, quote at p. 85.

38. HR 3130, later HR 6 and S 1513.

39. Smith and O'Day, "Systemic School Reform." The September 1993 draft of the administration's reform plan for Chapter 1/Title I cites the Smith and O'Day article and the Commission on Chapter 1 and IRP studies. US Department of Education, *Improving America's Schools Act of 1993*, pp. 21, 23–24.

40. See Title I, sec. 1111, for the specific requirements of state plans.

41. Smith would later testify that the current Title I program "only goes to contribute about 10 minutes a day to a student's achievement. That seems crazy. . . .

What we need to do is influence the entire school." Subcommittee on Elementary, Secondary, and Vocational Education, Committee on Education and Labor, *Hearing on HR 3130: Improving America's Schools Act of 1993*, September 23, 1993, p. 20.

42. US Department of Education, *Improving America's Schools Act of 1993*, p. 3.

43. Thomas Wolanin notes that the liberals' strategy for fixing the schools was to attempt to make the federal government bear a larger share of the percentage of dollars spent on schooling (say, 12 or 15 percent) and to attach conditions of aid to specify how that amount was spent. The Clinton administration, in contrast, sought to use the 7 percent of funds that the federal government contributes to schooling to influence the way the remaining 93 percent was spent by localities and states. Author interview: Thomas Wolanin, December 18, 2002.

44. This finding is derived from examination of the 1993 and 1994 hearings on Chapter 1, which include U.S. Congress, Senate, Subcommittee on Education, Arts, and Humanities, Committee on Labor and Human Resources, *ESEA: Framework for Change*, March 2, 16, 18, 24, April 12, 14, 21, 26, and May 5, 1994. The 1993 hearings are listed at footnote 25. Secondary sources were also consulted: *Congressional Quarterly,* 1993 and 1994; *Education Week,* 1993 and 1994; and Jennings, *Why National Standards and Tests?* pp. 111–153.

45. On the complexities, see National Assessment of Chapter 1 Independent Review Panel, *Reinventing Chapter 1*, pp. 50–52.

46. This number is then adjusted based upon state average per pupil expenditures relative to the national average. This is supposed to compensate for differences in the cost of education among states but in fact has the perverse effect of decreasing the funds received by states that have low per-capita education funding.

47. Thus, if parents of a school-age child should suddenly become impoverished, they cannot go to an AFDC-like agency and apply for aid for their child. As Albert Shanker, president of the American Federation of Teachers, noted, a sudden rise in the number of poor children in the United States did not result in more Title I dollars being sent to the states. Moreover, at the time, measures of the number of impoverished children were drawn from the decennial census. Subcommittee on Elementary, Secondary, and Vocational Education, Committee on Education and Labor, *Hearings on HR 6*, May 13, 1993, pp. 12–13.

48. Secretary Riley, testimony in Subcommittee on Elementary, Secondary, and Vocational Education, Committee on Education and Labor, *Hearing on HR 3130*, September 23, 1993, p. 6.

49. In a few cases, the amounts were dramatic: Iowa would see a decrease of 29 percent, Maine, 28 percent. Pitsch, "E.D. Officials Begin Marketing Proposal to 'Reinvent' ESEA"; and Pitsch, "Chapter 1 Formula Plan Hot Topic in States, Districts."

50. Subcommittee on Elementary, Secondary, and Vocational Education, Committee on Education and Labor, *Hearing on HR 3130*, September 23, 1993, p. 2.

51. On the complexities of the funding formulas considered and the debates thereon, see Congressional Quarterly, *Congressional Quarterly Almanac 1994*, pp. 383–391.

52. Subcommittee on Education, Arts, and Humanities, Committee on Labor and Human Resources, US Senate, *ESEA: Framework for Change*, March 2, 1994, pp. 19–27, 33. Two letters, one from Governor Carroll Campbell and the other a response from President Clinton affirming their agreement against federal opportunity-to-learn standards, were also submitted to the record. See pp. 50–52.

53. Title I, sec. 1111, B8.

54. PL 103-382, Title I, sec. 1111(b)(1)(C). States that refused to participate in Goals 2000, meanwhile, only had to submit a plan that included "a strategy and schedule for developing State content standards and State student performance standards for elementary and secondary school children served under this part."

55. States were also to establish a measure of "adequate yearly progress" (AYP) to discern whether students were progressing as quickly as they should. For a discussion of AYP, see Piche et al., *Title I in Midstream*.

56. US General Accounting Office, *Title I: Education Needs to Monitor States' Scoring of Assessments*, pp. 12–13.

57. PL 103-382, Title I, sec. 1111(b)(1)(A).

58. Title I, sec. 1111, (d)(1)(F).

59. US Department of Education, *Guidance on Standards, Assessments, and Accountability*.

60. Ibid., pp. 3–4.

61. Ibid., p. 7.

62. US Department of Education, *Peer Reviewer Guidance for Evaluating Evidence of Final Assessments Under Title I of the Elementary and Secondary Education Act*, p. 28.

63. Jeffrey, *Education for Children of the Poor*, p. 78.

64. Title I, sec. 1111, (d)(2).

65. Michael Cohen, "Implementing Title I Standards: Lessons from the Past, Challenges for the Future," p. 10.

66. Author interviews: Phyllis McClure, December 6, 2002; and Scott Hamilton, December 6, 2002.

67. Author interview: Richard Elmore, June 4, 2002.

68. Robelen, "States Sluggish in Execution of 1994 ESEA," p. 26. Michael Cohen, who became an assistant secretary for elementary and secondary education near the end of the Clinton years, echoed this sentiment. "It became very clear to me that there was widespread assumption [among states] that the deadline for those requirements would come and go, and nothing much would happen." It is also true, though, that some states could not comply quickly due to legitimate legal and financial issues. Alabama, for example, had a law that mandated an assessment system that did not meet Title I's testing requirements. And Montana has had difficulty appropriating sufficient funds to cover the costs of altering its accountability system.

69. Robelen, "States Sluggish in Execution of 1994 ESEA."

70. Gorman, "Bipartisan Schoolmates," pp. 37–38.

71. Dianne M. Piche and the Citizens Commission on Civil Rights argue that managerial problems were partly to blame, but that politics was key: "The Clinton administration, once a prime advocate of standards-based reform, has since had a massive failure of will and nerve. That failure has been manifested by a refusal to insist that states comply with fundamental provisions of the law." Piche et al., *Title I in Midstream*, p. 27. Richard Elmore suggests that the failure goes beyond the efforts of the Department of Education. The larger problem is that the department and the Office of Title I were handed an enormous oversight task but given grossly inadequate resources. Author interview: Richard Elmore, June 4, 2002.

72. Robelen, "States Sluggish in Execution of 1994 ESEA," p. 26.

73. Cohen, "Implementing Title I Standards: Lessons from the Past, Challenges for the Future," p. 11.

74. Author interview: Victor F. Klatt, June 12, 2002.

75. See further examples in Piche et al., *Title I in Midstream*.

76. US Department of Education, *Guidance on Standards, Assessments, and Accountability*, p. 10.

77. Ibid., pp. 16–18.

78. General Accounting Office, *Title I: Education Needs to Monitor States' Scoring of Assessments*. Astonishingly, as of April 2002, only nineteen states were in full compliance with the 1994 Title I assessment requirements. Robelen, "States, Ed. Dept Reach Accords on 1994 ESEA," p. 1.

79. Clinton, State of the Union Address, February 4, 1997.

80. The CCSSO and MPRA put together two committees of educators, one of which handled the math exam, the other, the reading exam.

81. For details on these exams, see Chapter 2.

82. The NAEP and TIMSS exams, in contrast, do not collect child-specific data.

83. This and the following quote are from the US Department of Education, *Voluntary National Tests for Reading and Math, Statement by Richard W. Riley*, April 29, 1997.

84. The question raised was whether children might be tested on their ability to read in their native languages or in English. The thinking was that if testing influences what teachers teach, then the choice of testing students in their native versus English language could have repercussions for English as a second language (ESL) instruction, to say nothing of the failure rates on the tests. And failure rates among a nonmajority demographic, such as ESL children, raise equity concerns.

85. Author interview: Richard Elmore, June 4, 2002.

86. Finn and Ravitch, "A Yardstick for American Students"; and Ravitch, "National Tests: A Good Idea Gone Wrong."

87. Harris, "Clinton Defends National Testing Plan."

88. Hoff, "Clinton Team Pulls Out Stops for Test Plan."

89. Lawson, "Feds Position on National Tests on Fast Track."

90. The agreement also required the expansion of the NAGB to twenty-five members, adding two mayors, one from each party, along with more business representatives and another governor (from the party that did occupy the Oval Office). Sanchez, "Senate Backs Modified Plan for National Student Tests."

91. Hoff, "Compromise Is Next Step in Test Odyssey."

92. Chaddock, "Brinkmanship over National Tests Could Prompt Washington Shutdowns."

93. Thus, Holt's contention that "education is now one of the dominant points of debate in the country. Across America, parents, teachers and local officials are in hand-to-hand combat over who controls the education agenda in their community." Ibid.

94. On the various proposals considered and rejected, see Pianin, "Hill Negotiators Compromise on Plan for National Student Tests"; Pianin, "Deal on National Testing Crumbles Under Pressure"; and Pianin and Sanchez, "Compromise Reached on Testing Plan."

95. Bill quoted in Hoff, "To Administration's Dismay, House Passes Test Bill."

96. Feuer et al., *Uncommon Measures*, p. 1.

97. Ibid., p. 4.

98. Hoff, "National Testing Plan Appears Headed for Perilous End."

99. According to Ray Fields of the NAGB: "In August 2001, the Governing Board determined that test development for the VNT [voluntary national tests] was completed and notified the contractor that the contract would terminate at the end of

the performance period (September 22, 2001). NAGB also had determined that the test questions that had been developed for the VNT were appropriate for use in the National Assessment of Educational Progress. The Governing Board transferred those test questions to the National Center for Education Statistics solely for use in the National Assessment." Author correspondence: July 2, 2002.

100. It is highly probable that the improvements were at best modest and tended to occur in states that were well on their way to creating standards-based systems. Schwartz and Robinson, "Goals 2000 and the Standards Movement," pp. 183–184.

101. Although Goals 2000 the statute expired, the matter of Goals 2000 funding is more complex. According to Thomas Skelly of the Department of Education, "Goals 2000 had an authorization until fiscal year 2000 that allowed Congress to appropriate money for fiscal year 2000. The 2000 appropriation became available to the Department of Education to obligate to states on July 1, 2000. States are supposed to use their Goals 2000 grants for their next academic year. That means they could use it for the three months of fiscal year 2000 and the next nine months of fiscal year 2001. What's more complicated, by virtue of another education law, if states make an obligation during the academic year, say to place an order for books or materials, they can effectively use the federal money for a longer period by taking longer to request cash payment for the grant they received. Some of our grants take four to five years to be paid off entirely." Author correspondence: July 23, 2001.

102. Hoff, "Goals Push for 2000 Falls Short."

103. Diane Ravitch, who served on the panel, noted that beyond losing its mission the panel had long had a precarious existence. It "didn't really have any interest groups to keep it alive," and Congress had never been enamoured of it because it was "a forum for governors." Author correspondence: March 20, 2002. On congressional resentment of the NEGP, see Chapter 6.

104. The English standards were defunded and the history standards were condemned by the Senate. Meanwhile, the science, civics, math, and fine arts standards were finished. They can be accessed via http://www.education-world.com/standards/.

105. Subcommittee on Education, Arts, and Humanities, Committee on Labor and Human Resources, US Senate, *ESEA: Framework for Change*, March 18, 1994, p. 167.

106. Chester E. Finn Jr., for example, notes that at present "nobody wants" national standards and the idea "isn't even being discussed" among policymakers. Author interview: April 17, 2002.

6

The No Child Left Behind Act

We believe that education is a national priority but a local responsibility.
—George W. Bush[1]

The New Consensus: A Larger, Limited Federal Role

The 1996 Election: Antistatism on the Decline

During the twentieth century, one or the other of the major parties positioned itself against an expanded federal role in education. The Democrats were the party of antistatism and "of federal control over schools" until the 1930s; with the rise of Franklin D. Roosevelt, the parties realigned, and antistatism began moving to the Republican Party.

At first view, the 1996 presidential race seemed like a continuance of the old liberal-antistatist divide. The Democratic candidate, President Clinton, stumped for deeper federal involvement in the schools. Robert Dole, the Republican nominee, ran on a platform that declared,

> The American people know that something is terribly wrong with our education system. The evidence is everywhere: children who cannot read, graduates who cannot reason, danger in schoolyards, indoctrination in classrooms.
>
> To this crisis in our schools, Bill Clinton responds with the same liberal dogmas that created the mess: more federal control and more spending on all the wrong things. . . .
>
> Americans should have the best education in the world. We spend more per pupil than any other nation. . . . Our goal is nothing less than a renaissance in American education, begun by returning its control to parents, teachers, local school boards, and, through them, to communities and local taxpayers. . . .
>
> The federal government has no constitutional authority to be

involved in school curricula or to control jobs in the work place. That is why we will abolish the Department of Education, end federal meddling in our schools, and promote family choice at all levels of learning. We therefore call for prompt repeal of the Goals 2000 program.[2]

Ross Perot, who again was the presidential nominee of the Reform Party, often struck a similar note during his campaign. For example, Perot told supporters at the convention that US schools had been the best in the world in 1960, but once the federal government got involved in them they became worse.[3]

Despite the resemblance to elections past, the 1996 election was not the same old battle between an antistatist candidate and a liberal pro–federal action candidate. Both major parties offered enormous education policy planks in their presidential platforms.[4] Both believed students were learning less than they should and that the crisis declared by *A Nation at Risk* in 1983 remained.[5] Dole, despite railing against federal "meddling," was not an old-fashioned antistatist who championed leaving education policy to the states. He stumped for a federal school choice policy to raise achievement.[6] All three candidates supported higher education standards. Much was the same, yet different.

Though Dole and the leaders of the Republican Party voiced antistatist rhetoric, lay members of the party and the public felt differently.[7] A poll by the National Education Association found that most registered Republicans wanted to keep the Department of Education and to increase federal education spending.[8] The public also saw a difference between the parties. A September 1996 *USA Today*/CNN/Gallup poll revealed that more voters (59 percent) believed Clinton was more apt to make policy to improve the schools than Dole (30 percent).[9] By a margin of 44 percent to 27 percent, the public felt the Democratic Party was more interested in improving public education than was the GOP.[10]

President Clinton, who was both a vigorous supporter of increased federal education spending and sensitive to the polls, advocated an astonishing number of education programs during the campaign. In doing this, he further legitimized the idea that the federal government ought to be involved in fixing the public schools.[11]

Clinton won an overwhelming victory over Bob Dole. To the surprise of few, exit polls found that on the education issue, voters preferred Clinton to Dole.[12] The leaders of the GOP, who were often the most vocal advocates of the antistatist position, got the message. Looking back to 1996, Chester E. Finn Jr. explained, "There's been a huge change in the Republican view of the federal role. . . . There's no doubt that Republicans learned that to be for less federal involvement in education is a mistake." The reason is simple: the public "is not interested in abstract arguments about federalism." If there is a national educational emergency, then the federal government should do something about it.[13] Shortly after Dole's defeat, Texas governor George W. Bush remarked, "There's no question that from a political perspective, [Clinton] stole the [education] issue and it affected the women's vote. . . . Republicans must say that we are for education."[14]

The 2000 Election: The New Consensus Emerges

In the 2000 election primaries, George W. Bush faced a number of candidates, though only three had sufficient funds or public recognition to mount a formidable challenge: former vice president Dan Quayle, Malcolm S. "Steve" Forbes, and Senator John McCain (R-AZ). Like many Republican candidates before them, none of Bush's challengers advocated expanding the federal role in education. Candidate Forbes unabashedly favored abolishing the Department of Education. Senator McCain was uncomfortable with national standards and favored block-granting most federal education monies.[15] Bush, meanwhile, antagonized many Republicans when he advocated an expansion of the federal role in education. His position, which resonated with voters, was a mix of quality-schools advocacy and liberalism and was in keeping with his campaign theme of "compassionate conservatism."[16] Bush stumped for a $1 billion a year compensatory reading program. Bush urged that Title I be reformed to increase accountability with standards and assessments that would serve as the bedrock of the accountability system. He argued that all students in grades three through eight who attend schools receiving Title I aid should be tested to see if they are making educational progress. He also proposed to reward or punish states financially based on whether they raised test scores and reduced the test score gap between whites and nonwhites, the poor and nonpoor. States would also be required to publish school report cards that broke down the test score data by district, school, and student race, ethnicity, and gender. Bush also advocated allowing that children who attended schools receiving Title I funds should be permitted to transfer to a public or private school and take $1,500 in Title I funds with them if their school failed to raise test scores. He also advocated spending $3 billion to upgrade and create new charter schools.[17] Though trumpeting school choice pleased the right, Bush sought to further shore up conservatives' favor by advocating more freedom for states to use federal dollars as they deem fit. In the tradition of "Ed-Flex" and the many other Republican bills offered in the previous two decades, which sought to devolve more spending discretion to local authorities, Bush urged that over sixty federal, categorical education programs be lumped into five block grants.[18]

Governor Bush's opponent in the general election, Clinton's vice president, Albert Gore Jr., favored policies that mixed the liberal education politics of old with a little quality-schools advocacy. Gore's initial education plan favored a large increase in federal spending on the public schools. Gore wanted $115 billion over a decade directed toward creating smaller schools and lower pupil-to-teacher ratios, upgrading schools and their computers, and more before- and after-school education programs.[19] When his proposal failed to poll strongly, Gore followed Bush by emphasizing higher standards, increased accountability, and expanded student testing.[20]

The Gore and Bush plans, despite their differences, shared a similar vision for the federal government. The federal role would be enlarged, with more money and more state accountability for improved achievement. Title I would serve as the main vehicle for standards-based reform. Both men urged that consequences (e.g., rewards or penalties) for states be attached to student performance on the National Assessment of Educational Progress (NAEP).[21] Yet, neither Bush nor Gore would have the federal government create standards or even review the quality of state standards. State and local control over curricula would remain. This was the new paradigm for federal policy. It marked both the triumph and defeat of education standards. Higher standards carried the day, but national standards were dead.

The No Child Left Behind Act

No Child Left Behind: Sealing the New Political Consensus

Upon entering office in January 2001, President George W. Bush was in a precarious political position. On the one hand, he was more fortunate than his father, George H. W. Bush, who had faced a House and Senate dominated by Democrats. George W. Bush confronted an evenly divided Senate (50 Republicans, 50 Democrats) and had the House behind him (221 Republicans, 212 Democrats).[22] On the other hand, Bush had lost the popular ballot but won the electoral vote, which had not happened since 1888.[23] He could not, obviously, credibly proclaim a mandate. Moreover, large numbers of Bush's own party and supporters had long opposed expanding the federal role in public education and so were uneasy with the new president's activist position. President Bush did have the upper hand against the antistatists in his own party. He had made increased federal spending on education and federally mandated testing the centerpiece of his campaign. He could not, on taking office, shrink back from his commitment for bold reform without losing what public support he had. Indeed, to have done so would have made it easy for Democrats to tell voters that Bush was like previous Republican presidents: an antistatist who was not interested in doing anything to solve the problem.

Furthermore, the Republicans had seen the polls and knew that the public was concerned about education and wanted something done. One long-time Republican adviser noted, "The federalism debate is a within-the-Beltway issue. People don't care who fixes the problem, they just want it fixed."[24] The public desire for action, moreover, was not going to disappear. The same veteran of the education policy battles of the 1990s observed, "It seems like you are always seeing stories in the newspapers about how bad the schools are doing, how low the tests scores are. Parents see this and are concerned."[25] If the Republican Party was to keep control of Congress and hold the presidency, it had to reach out to women voters and moderates. This meant taking a proactive stance toward federal involvement in public education. Yet, with an almost evenly divided Senate and a narrow majority in the House, the president could not force through an education reform bill that blatantly offended the Democrats. The political situation was, as a number of commentators said, ripe for either true bipartisanship policymaking or gridlock.

Though it took nearly a year to pass, HR 1, the No Child Left Behind Act of 2002 (hereafter, NCLB), was a compromise between the parties that sealed the new consensus on standards and the federal role. The final votes in both houses of Congress were overwhelmingly in favor: 381 to 41 in the House, 87 to 10 in the Senate.[26] The celebratory tour of the United States by the politicians who forged NCLB was telling. On the same platform, hands raised together, were two of the most liberal members of Congress, Senator Ted Kennedy (D-MA) and Representative George Miller (D-CA), and two of the most conservative, Senator Judd Gregg (R-NH) and Representative John Boehner (R-OH). Between them stood George W. Bush—a Republican president from Texas—the new middle ground in federal education policy.[27]

The five men had agreed on much: Educational achievement was less than it ought to be, especially for many low-income and nonwhite children.[28] Many schools were underserving their students. Education standards in the schools were too low, and federal power had to be used to raise them.[29] They also agreed that it was unacceptable to require children to stay in schools with low test scores year after year. John F. (Jack) Jennings, an aide who worked on education issues in the House for three decades, observed that the debates around the Bush proposal were less rancorous than in previous years. A couple of factors were at work. Jennings notes it is important to recall that "who proposes a policy is almost as important as what the policy is. . . . The right was not about to jump on George W. Bush because he is their guy." Beyond partisan politics, though,

> the conversation about reform has moved forward. Now the states are more used to the idea that they will have standards . . . that there will be state testing. Teachers in many states are more used to states testing than they were before. Even though they may not like it, they see it as a fact of life.

Jennings also points out that education chairman George Miller, though liberal, does not hold the same views as his Democratic predecessors. Augustus Hawkins and William Ford were "civil rights" and "blue-collar union" liberals, whereas Miller is a "more modern, intellectual liberal." Whereas Ford was "extremely skeptical" of standards and "very close to the educational establishment," Miller is not.[30] Another observer reports that Miller, like his father (who served in California's state legislature), is "pro–public education" but "hasn't been hesitant to criticize teachers' shortcomings" and school systems.[31]

The new Bush administration's proposal to expand testing and to use NAEP as an audit of state testing results might have been expected to meet attacks from the left and right. However, the attacks were few and had little effect. Many Republicans were loath to attack their own president, especially since he had won office in large part due to his education plan. There was dissent, though. Lisa Bos, who worked for a member of the House Education and the Workforce Committee and was involved in the negotiations over NCLB, notes that the right was unhappy with the accountability provisions. "Adequate yearly progress" (AYP) and the use of NAEP raised federal issues:

> The debate on HR 1 did end up focusing a great deal on federal versus state/local control of education. HR 1 included significant new federal mandates for states and local schools, primarily new testing requirements in Title I. This led conservatives to fight to get as much flexibility as possible within those mandates. For example, the bill included a new requirement that all states must participate in the National Assessment of Educational Progress. In the House bill, conservatives succeeded in getting language inserted . . . that allowed states to use either NAEP or an equivalent test (like the Stanford 9 or Iowa Test of Basic Skills), giving flexibility to states who may have already been using one of these alternate assessments. Unfortunately, this provision was removed in the final conference report.[32]

Bos also notes that testing united the far right and the far left, as had been the case in years past.

> An interesting coalition of moderate and conservative Republicans and liberal Democrats joined in an effort to remove all of the new K-8 annual testing from the bill, which pitted them against an administration that viewed the testing as the centerpiece of their accountability system. The coalition of members who opposed the new assessment mandates had varying reasons (tests don't accurately measure what students know, teachers will teach to the test, tests are biased against minority students, requiring more tests is an expensive mandate for states).[33]

In the House, six conservative members of the House's Education Committee voted against the bill, three going so far as to write dissents to the conference report, and thirty-three conservative members, including Majority Whip Tom DeLay (R-TX), voted against the conference report. However, Bos concurs with Jennings: "I personally believe that many more Republicans voted for the bill very reluctantly because the president was so passionate about getting the bill passed. Had it been President Clinton offering the same bill, I think the vote would have been very different."[34]

Similarly, the attacks from the left, as one might have expected, were less sharp and widespread. In part, this was due to the president offering to drop private school choice from his plan. This impressed the liberals, showing them that Bush was willing to work with them. But, importantly, Miller and Kennedy were quick to agree with the president that testing was a key component to systemic reform. Brian Jones, who worked as a congressional aide for much of the 1990s and more recently as a vice president of the pro-reform Education Leaders Council, notes that "Miller and Kennedy from the start said that they believed in testing children frequently. When they did that, they left the critics on the left with nobody [in Congress or the White House] to turn to."[35] The National Education Association and other liberal organizations that had fought standards reform and testing were left with less of a voice in the debate. Jennings says that "Clearly, the unions are the most powerful force in elementary and secondary education, but the tenor of the times is to demand more accountability . . . so they were fighting the spirit of things."[36] Moreover, the Council of Chief State School Officers (CCSSO) was not the force that it had been in recent years.[37] During much of the 1990s, the CCSSO and its influential leader, Gordon Ambach, had been intimately involved in federal policy negotiations and had lobbied against testing. Near the end of the Clinton presidency Ambach and the CCSSO parted ways, and its new leader hinted that the group was going to cease lobbying against quality-schools type reforms.[38]

That said, Miller, Kennedy, Gregg, Boehner, and Bush were not in perfect agreement on the question of the primary cause of educational underachievement. As in the past, legislators grappled mightily over the Title I funding formula. At the request of Congress, the Congressional Research Service (CRS), a government thinktank, ran computer simulations to forecast "who got what" under different formulae.[39] Liberals like Miller and Kennedy did emphasize the lack of money and insufficient resources, especially for those children in poor and nonwhite school districts. Gregg and Boehner, as in previous years, emphasized that the schools themselves were performing inadequately. Thus, the solution was to coerce them either through raising standards or by creating an education market through school choice. Rather than wrangle over primary causes, the two sides agreed to disagree and produced a policy that was an amalgam of all three solutions: more money, school choice, and standards-based reform.[40]

An Overview of NCLB Policies:
More Money, School Choice, and Standards

More Money and School Choice. President Bush and Congress agreed to a dramatic increase in Title I funding from fiscal year 2001 to 2007. Table 6.1 shows the leap in authorizations, from less than $10 billion in the final year of the Clinton presidency to $13.5 billion during the first full year of the Bush administration and to $25 billion in fiscal year 2007. Liberals were pleased with the large funding increases. Quality-schools advocates who favored choice got some of what they wanted. They were disappointed that President Bush very early in his negotiations with Congress indicated he would back away from private school choice.[41] However, NCLB does have potent public school choice provisions. Title V, section 5201, notes that in order to "increase national understanding of the charter schools model," Title V would provide "financial assistance for the planning, program design, and initial implementation of charter schools." States, and under special conditions, local education agencies (LEAs), may apply for some of the $300 million available in short-term start-up funds for use in crafting a charter school's curricula and assessments, acquiring educational materials and supplies, professional development for its instructors, and other "initial operational costs."[42] To receive funds, a charter school must provide "a description of the educational program . . . [showing] how the program will enable all students to meet challenging State student achievement standards."[43]

But the real catalyst for public school choice is Title I, which empowers parents as consumers in three ways:

1. It requires states and local education agencies to provide easily understood information on student and school performance.
2. It grants parents of children in failing schools the right to intradistrict public school choice.
3. It requires local education agencies to grant parents of children in failing schools the right and power to choose among supplementary educational service providers for their children.[44]

NCLB builds on the 1994 IASA reforms for informational reporting. NCLB requires states and local education agencies to provide parents with annual school report cards, detailing the educational performance of students on state assessments. Parents are to be informed how well their children performed on state assessments, how well the school performed, and

**Table 6.1   Title I Grants to Local Education Agencies, 2001–2007
($ billions)**

Fiscal Year	Authorizations	Appropriations
2001	$9.7	$8.76
2002	$13.5	$10.35
2003	$16.0	$11.69
2004	$18.5	$12.32
2005	$20.5	$12.74
2006	$22.75	NYA
2007	$25.0	NYA

Source: US Office of the Federal Register, *United States Statutes at Large.* Washington, DC: GPO. http://memory.loc.gov/ammem/amlaw/lwsl.html.
Note: NYA = Not yet appropriated.

how well other schools in their local school district did. Student perform-ance data must be broken down on the basis of gender, major racial and ethnic groups, student disability and economic disadvantage status, and English proficiency or the lack thereof.[45] Parents are also to be informed if their child's school is failing, why it has been deemed failing, and of their options for remedies, to which we now turn.[46]

Section 1116 of the 1994 reauthorization of Title I required local edu-cation agencies

> to review annually the progress of each school served under this part to determine whether the school is meeting, or making adequate progress as defined in section 1111(b)(2)(A)(i) toward enabling its students to meet the State's student performance standards described in the State plan.[47]

Schools that failed to make "adequate progress" for two years were to be defined as being in "school improvement" status.[48] Schools that failed to make adequate progress toward raising achievement for more than two years fall into "corrective action" status. Under the 1994 law, states were obliged to take some form of action to attempt to improve achievement at such schools. However, if such actions failed to remedy the problem, noth-ing more had to be done. Meanwhile, the children in these schools remained there, falling further behind their peers in nonfailing schools.

NCLB dramatically revised this. Title I now mandates that children in a school with school improvement or corrective action status must be per-mitted by the LEA to transfer to other nonfailing public schools in that dis-trict.[49] Local education agencies must also provide funding for transporting these students to their new schools.[50] Furthermore, students in schools undergoing corrective action must also be provided with supplemental educational services by local educational agencies. These services are not to be offered by the failing school; instead, parents are to be provided with a list of state-approved service providers from which they can choose. These providers can be nonprofit or private entities, such as Sylvan Learning Centers, private schools, or a public school making adequate yearly progress.[51] Importantly, LEAs must pay for these services.

Standards-Based Reform. NCLB continued the transformation begun in 1994. Title I funds would continue to be targeted toward low-income children, but Title I would no longer be a compensatory education grant program that pulled poor and minority children from classrooms.[52] The new law expanded the 1994 reform, making Title I a tool for encouraging states to fashion standards-based education systems that aimed, as NCLB puts it, to ensure "all children" attend schools where the curricula is based on "challenging State academic achievement standards and state academic assessments."[53]

NCLB's reform of Title I is a mixture of the favorite ideas of the political left and right. It largely embodies the idea of standards-based systemic reform as first enunciated by Marshall Smith and Jennifer O'Day.[54] There are to be high academic standards for the sake of accountability, as the quality-school advocates and those on the right sought. But, to the pleasure of the left, there is more spending, much of which is to be directed toward bolstering resources. Yet, NCLB did not simply "leave the money on the stump for the taking." In accordance with Smith and O'Day's vision of systemic reform, NCLB funding for resources is to be spent to ensure (1) that instruction and resources are aligned to the academic standards, and (2) that schools that failed to educate children were assisted or coerced into reform.[55]

Standards and assessments. Title I of NCLB further solidified the movement away from national education standards in favor of state standards. NCLB did not reinvigorate the controversial National Education Standards and Improvement Council (NESIC), which Goals 2000 had charged with certifying state standards. Nor did NCLB preserve the National Education Goals Panel, which had examined the progress of the nation toward the national education goals and was to serve as a check on NESIC's certification process.[56] Indeed, NCLB gives the federal government no role at all in the crafting of education standards.[57]

Moreover, as before, NCLB has not created any federal oversight for examining the quality of state education standards and assessments. As always, the federal government is expressly forbidden from tampering with state standards and curricula:

> Each State plan shall demonstrate that the State has adopted challenging academic content standards and challenging student academic achieve-

ment standards that will be used by the State, its local educational agencies, and its schools to carry out this part, except that a State shall not be required to submit such standards to the Secretary.[58]

NCLB carries other prohibitions against federal involvement with curricula (see Figure 6.1).[59] NCLB reiterates IASA's requirement that each state must develop standards and assessments in math and reading and language arts. NCLB adds that each state needed to do the same for science by the 2005–2006 school year.[60] NCLB also mandates that by the school year 2005–2006 each state had to test annually all students in grades three through eight in English and math and to begin testing some grade levels of students in science.[61]

Figure 6.1   Prohibitions on Federal Control over State Standards and Curricula

---

LOCAL CONTROL—Nothing in this section shall be construed to . . . authorize an officer or employee of the Federal Government to mandate, direct, review, or control a State, local educational agency, or school's instructional content, curriculum, and related activities;

And,

GENERAL PROHIBITION—Nothing in this Act shall be construed to authorize an officer or employee of the Federal Government to mandate, direct, or control a State, local educational agency, or school's curriculum, program of instruction, or allocation of State or local resources, or mandate a State or any subdivision thereof to spend any funds or incur any costs not paid for under this Act. . . .

(b) PROHIBITION ON ENDORSEMENT OF CURRICULUM— Notwithstanding any other prohibition of Federal law, no funds provided to the Department under this Act may be used by the Department to endorse, approve, or sanction any curriculum designed to be used in an elementary school or secondary school.

(c) PROHIBITION ON REQUIRING FEDERAL APPROVAL OR CERTIFICATION OF STANDARDS—

(1) IN GENERAL—Notwithstanding any other provision of Federal law, no State shall be required to have academic content or student academic achievement standards approved or certified by the Federal Government, in order to receive assistance under this Act.

Source: PL 107-110, Title IX, Sections 9526 and 9527.

Standards and assessments are to be the foundation of a state's education system. School curricula are to be based upon state standards and assessments; teacher and paraprofessional education and continuing professional development are to be aligned with state standards and assessments.[62] And, as will be described, state standards and assessments are to serve as the foundation of states' quality measurement and corrective action of failing schools.

Adequate yearly progress and corrective action. Systemic reform, as required by NCLB, bases the measurement (in part) of student, teacher, principal, school, and LEA quality on student achievement on state student assessments. This measurement is called "adequate yearly progress." Put simply, each state is to use data from its 2001–2002 school-year assessments to establish a "starting point." It must be set at "the State's lowest achieving group of students" or "the school at the 20th percentile in the State, based on enrollment, among all schools ranked by the percentage of students at the proficient level," whichever is higher.[63] The goal is for all students to score at the proficient or advanced levels by the end of twelve years. Therefore, each state devises a timeline of improvement, one that creates yearly improvement goals in the percentage of students scoring proficient or advanced. Adequate yearly progress for a state is, then, the targeted rate in the percentage of students who score at said state's definition of academic proficiency.[64]

Each school must show AYP each year for all students (in aggregate) and for each of the demographic measures listed previously (e.g., race and ethnicity, gender).[65] If a school as a whole or any of these groups individually fails to show adequate yearly progress in either math or English for two years, the school will fall into school improvement status.[66] As noted earlier, school improvement status requires a failing school's LEA to provide its students with the option to transfer to another nonfailing school. Beyond this, the law mandates that an LEA must work with the school to devise a two-year "school improvement plan" that includes commitments to devote more Title I funds toward teacher retraining, an extended school day, programs for increasing parental involvement, and mentoring for teachers by better or more experienced teachers.[67] If a school continues to fail to reach adequate yearly progress, it falls into corrective action status and the severity of the required reforms increase. LEAs are forced to choose between options, such as replacing the failing school's staff, implementing a new curriculum, extending the school year, and reopening the school as a charter school with new management and staff.[68]

NAEP and federal auditing of state AYP. The federal government is empowered by NCLB to monitor a state's adequate yearly progress in two ways: through reports to the secretary of education and through the use of the NAEP. As a condition of aid, a state drawing Title I funds must provide an annual report to the secretary of education. This report must include the data on student achievement (in aggregate and disaggregated by the afore-mentioned demographics), AYP for the state and LEAs individually, along with "the number and names of each school identified for school improve-ment, why it was so identified, and the measures taken to address the achievement problems" of those schools.[69]

The law further requires that as a condition of aid, a participating state must have a portion of its students take the fourth- and eighth-grade NAEP reading and mathematics exams.[70] The objective of this policy is to enable the federal government to audit the integrity of a state's reports of state-level AYP.[71]

Conclusion

Though often touted as a revolution, the No Child Left Behind Act is more of an evolution. It builds upon the reforms of years past and, generally speaking, gives the federal government more authority over schooling.[72] NCLB, more so than the Improving America's Schools Act of 1994, requires states to show they are enacting systemic reform. Merely creating timelines and plans to reform are no longer sufficient. Politically, NCLB is quite significant. With it we see the convergence of the two major parties on the subject of education. No longer does either believe that the federal government should limit itself to small programs of underserved children and leave the rest of schooling to the states. Both agree that the federal gov-ernment should make policy to see that all children receive a rigorous edu-cation. This is entirely new.[73]

Yet, the concerns about federal control have not subsided. Although the right has conceded more and more ground to the federal government, American schooling very much remains a local and state enterprise. As will be seen in the concluding chapter, though the No Child Left Behind Act did give the federal government much power over schooling, it left the heart of education, curricula, where it always has been: in the hands of localities and states.

Notes

1. As quoted on the No Child Left Behind website at http://www.nclb.gov.
2. Republican National Party Presidential Platform 1996.
3. Congressional Quarterly, *Congressional Quarterly Almanac 1996*, p. D-57.
4. This is important, as it implies that both the parties feel they must tell the

voters that they recognize there is a problem with the schools and will do something about them.

5. This trend, whereby politicians and candidates for office feel obliged to say something about what should be done about educational underachievement, continues to this day. Bronner, "Better Schools Is Battle Cry for Fall Elections"; Preston and Crabtree, "Parties Vie for Edge on Education"; and Robelen, "GOP, Democrats Vie for Education Bragging Rights."

6. Though Dole did not say, presumably any federal programs would be administered by a department other than the Department of Education.

7. This is unsurprising: since Michel's research appeared in 1915, sociologists and political scientists have found that party leaders often are more ideological than their membership. Michel, *Political Parties*.

8. Hoff, "NEA Poll Finds GOP Leaders at Odds with Their Voters," p. 4.

9. As cited in Jennings, *Why National Standards and Tests?* pp. 173–174.

10. Lightfoot-Clark, "Opposition to Vouchers May Be Dissipating," pp. 1, 3, 5–6.

11. Finn, "Education and the Election," p. 45.

12. Ceasar and Busch, *Losing to Win*, pp. 164–167.

13. Author interview: Chester E. Finn Jr., April 17, 2002.

14. Balz, "Stands on Education Cost GOP Among Women, Governors Told," p. A6.

15. Robelen, "McCain's Views on Schools Becoming Clearer."

16. Robelen, "Bush Leading Republicans in New Direction."

17. Dao, "Gore Would Link Federal Aid to School Performance." Bush later pushed his party to drop language advocating the abolition of the Department of Education from the 2000 platform. Rudalevige, "The Politics of No Child Left Behind," p. 65.

18. Candidate Bush's website said that he would "restore local control." George W. Bush for President official website, http://georgewbush.org.

19. Note the traditional liberal emphasis on school resource spending and compensatory education as opposed to policy to alter school management and governance.

20. Hoff, "NAEP Weighed as Measure of Accountability, President, Candidates Pursue High Stakes"; Gore 2000, Inc., *Al Gore's Education Blue Book*; and Dao, "Gore Would Link Federal Aid to School Performance."

21. President Clinton also cottoned to this idea. Feinberg, *Rewards for NAEP: Proposals and Consequences, Background Paper*.

22. Republican control of the Senate would soon slip away when liberal Republican Jim Jeffords (VT) left the Republicans and announced himself an independent in May 2001.

23. Benjamin Harrison tallied nearly 95,000 fewer votes than Grover Cleveland yet won the electoral college vote 233 to 168. Langley and Peirce, *The Electoral College Primer 2000*, p. 34.

24. Author interview: Victor F. Klatt III, June 12, 2002.

25. Author interview: Victor F. Klatt III, June 6, 2002.

26. This was the vote on the final conference bill. Previously both houses had passed a version of the NCLB by nearly identical margins: 384 to 45 and 91 to 8.

27. Boehner, interestingly, a few years earlier had condemned the federal government's involvement in education and advocated the abolition of the Department of Education. On the legislative haggling on the NCLB, see Rudalevige, "No Child Left Behind: Forging a Congressional Compromise."

28. Though popular among education school professors and liberal literati, the arguments that low achievement was a "manufactured crisis" simply did not resonate with members of Congress or the public. Berliner and Biddle, *The Manufactured Crisis*; Rothstein, *The Way We Were?*

29. Kohn, a virulent critic of the standards movement, has conceded that a political consensus exists in favor of high standards: "Today, it is almost impossible to distinguish Democrats from Republicans on [standards]." Kohn, "The Case Against Tougher Standards."

30. Author interview: John F. (Jack) Jennings, December 18, 2002.

31. Author interview: Denis Doyle, December 18, 2002.

32. Author interview: Lisa Bos, December 4, 2002.

33. Ibid.

34. Ibid.

35. Author interview: Brian Jones, December 13, 2002.

36. Author interview: John F. (Jack) Jennings, December 18, 2002.

37. Gerald Sroufe of the American Educational Research Association suggests that the CCSSO lost power in part because its members became more philosophically diverse. In recent years, chiefs who were quality-school advocates had joined the groups and therefore were unhappy that the CCSSO fought many of the reforms it favored. Author interview: Gerald Sroufe, December 12, 2002.

38. G. Tom Houlihan, as quoted in Richard, "State Chiefs' Groups Readies for New Direction." It is the case that the CCSSO has, of late, faced competition from groups such as the Education Leaders Council.

39. Congressional Research Service, *Annual Report Fiscal Year 2001*, p. 11.

40. The discussion here focuses on the NCLB's reform of Title I, particularly Part A. However, the portions of Titles IV and V that are related to the reforms set forth in Title I are described.

41. David Hess, "Bush School Bill Moves to Floor Despite Conservatives' Ire."

42. Title V, sec. 5204f. The $300 million is for FY 2002; thereafter, Title V authorizes Congress to provide "such sums as may be necessary." See sec. 5211a. Title V also provides funds for helping new charter schools acquire or construct facilities. See subpart 2.

43. Title V, sec. 5203(3)(A)(i). This is an example of a middle way between school choice and government-enforced standards policy: private operators run the schools, and a governmental authority audits their work to ensure quality.

44. Title I, sec. 1116(a)(b), 1116(b), and 1116(e), respectively. Senator Judd Gregg (R-NH) had, with little success, advocated choice throughout the 1990s. One Capitol Hill observer notes that the supplementary schools provision was very important to Gregg. Author interview: Brian Jones, December 13, 2002.

45. Ibid., 1111(b)(2)(C).

46. 1116(b)(6).

47. 1994 Title I, sec. 1116(a)(2).

48. Adequate progress referred to the academic achievement of students as measured by state assessments that were aligned to state standards. More on this is below.

49. Section 1116(b)(1)(E). Under the 1994 reauthorization, states were permitted to allow students in schools in corrective action to transfer to another school in the same district, but they were not required to do so. See Title I, section 1116(5)(B)(VII).

50. Section 1116(b)(9).

51. Section 1116(b)(7).

52. That said, it must be noted that Title I remains, in part, a compensatory education program. The NCLB revised Title I, Part B, which, had been a grant program that directed funds toward improving the literacy of poor children and their parents. It became a "reading first" program that provides money for compensatory reading programs for kindergarten through third-grade children. Part B also mandates that any reading programs utilized by states and LEAs be "scientifically based," which has provoked some to protest of improper federal involvement in pedagogy.

53. PL 107-110, Title I, sec. 1001.

54. Smith and O'Day, "Systemic School Reform."

55. And states are also able to dangle carrots before LEAs by offering rewards for reaching AYP. See Title I, sec. 1117.

56. On the roles of NESIC and the NEGP, see Chapters 4 and 5.

57. Whereas, for example, Title II of the NCLB provides funds for grants to improve the teaching of American history, it leaves the actual content to the states. See Title II generally for the federal programs designed to bolster the education levels and competence of teachers. It must be noted that the NCLB does give the federal government influence over reading curricula in schools. Title I, Part B, which creates the Reading First program, requires that states use reading programs that are "scientifically based." Though prima facie innocuous, this phrase theoretically could be used by the federal government to, say, disapprove of a state application for funding if it is based on the whole-language approach as opposed to phonics.

58. Section 1111(b)(1)(A).

59. ESEA has carried prohibitions since its inception; however, the NCLB's prohibitions are more extensive than those found in the IASA or earlier iterations of ESEA.

60. Yet, as before, the federal government was not given the power to verify if states' standards are high, if they test "higher order thinking skills" as NCLB requires, and if standards and assessments are aligned.

61. The 1994 reform of Title I, in contrast, required that states test only some of these grades each year. See NCLB Title I, sec. 1111(b)(3).

62. The NCLB mandates that states raise education requirements for paraprofessionals. It also requires that all teachers in schools receiving Title I funds be "highly qualified" by the school year 2005–2006. This was done to answer the liberal concern that schools in poor neighborhoods tend to have high numbers of less-qualified and uncertified classroom personnel than other schools. As before, the liberal position is that if children are to be held to higher standards, they must have an opportunity to learn. Teacher qualifications are a form thereof.

63. On the rules for setting a baseline and AYP, see Title I, sec. 1111(b)(2)(E) through sec. 1111(b)(2)(I).

64. Department of Education, *The Facts About . . . Adequate Yearly Progress*, retrieved from http://www.nclb.gov/start/facts/yearly.html. That said, AYP is also to factor in graduation rates and other measures that states find useful. This has led to confusion as to which other factors would be acceptable to the Department of Education (to which measures of AYP must be submitted for approval) and how many may be included.

65. This feature of the legislation speaks to long-standing liberal concerns that school systems tend to discriminate against lower-income, nonwhite, and LEP students. It aims to coerce states and LEAs into paying attention to the academic achievement of these students so that, as the law's title says, no child will be left behind.

66. Schools, meanwhile, are to be provided with data reports that detail their shortcomings so that they can see where they need to improve their services. Title I, sec. 1111(b)(10).

67. Title I, sec. 1116(b)(2)(A); and Secretary of Education Rod Paige, *Dear Colleague Letter Regarding Implementation of the No Child Left Behind Act*, July 24, 2002.

68. Title I, sec. 1116(b)(7)–(8); and Paige, *Dear Colleague Letter*, July 24, 2002.

69. Title I, sec. 1111(h)(4).

70. Title I, sec. 1111(c)(2).

71. In the conference report on the NCLB, Congress failed to explain its intent. However, a fact sheet released by the conference committee chairman, John Boehner (R-OH), stated that NAEP would "verify the results of statewide assessments." Boehner, *Fact Sheet on HR 1*, January 2002.

72. Before Bush entered office, a number of proposals to reform Title I along similar lines were being circulated by Democrats. In particular, a white paper by Andrew Rotherham, of the Democratic Leadership Council's Progressive Policy Institute, sparked major discussion and served as an outline for reform proposals. Rotherham, *Toward Performance-Based Federal Education Funding*; see also Rudalevige, *No Child Left Behind.*

73. On the shifting of the parties on education, see Hess and McGuinn, "Seeking the Mantle of 'Opportunity.'"

7

Improving Federal Standards Policy

This study has offered both a political and policy analysis. Chapter 1 made the case that there was a social problem in need of remedy: student under-achievement. Chapter 2 offered a policy analysis, arguing there was a compelling policy rationale for federal action to raise education standards in the public schools. The evolving political constraints were taken up in Chapters 3 through 6. These chapters showed there have long been philosophical dif-ferences among members of Congress and presidents over the wisdom of increased federal involvement in the public schools. They also revealed that despite widespread public and policy network support for higher education standards, political constraints thwarted all the efforts in the 1990s to do this at the federal level.

Now it is appropriate to offer suggestions for policy reform, its pre-scriptions teased out from the tension between advisable policy (robust fed-eral standards policy) and the political constraints (antistatism and local control over curricula).[1] The recent elections and reform of Title I confirm the new direction for federal standards policy and politics that developed in the 1990s. They also indicate that the federal role in education is growing. However, states will retain control over education standards and assess-ments. This political reality greatly limits the possibilities for further feder-al policy to raise education standards for the sake of advancing student learning.

No Child Left Behind and Standards

To begin, it is worth pondering what effects NCLB may have on standards. There are, again, three sorts of standards: content standards, performance standards, and opportunity-to-learn (OTL) standards. The possible effects of NCLB on each of the standards is considered in turn, beginning with OTL standards.

Opportunity-to-Learn Standards

NCLB does not require states to alter their school funding formulas to more equitably fund schools, nor does it require states to create OTL. However, NCLB does carry provisions to better the educational resources of low-performing schools. Under Marshall Smith and Jennifer O'Day's narrow definition of OTL, which includes factors clearly related to enabling teachers to teach to the standards, NCLB has two provisions that can improve OTL. First, NCLB requires that beginning with the 2002–2003 school year, all newly hired teachers must be "highly qualified."[2] Teachers already on the job must be certified as highly qualified by the 2005–2006 school year. If faithfully carried out, this could improve the quality of education received by all students, in particular pupils in failing schools. Furthermore, Title I students sometimes have been taught by paraprofessionals who have little academic or pedagogical training. NCLB addresses this problem by requiring increased educational training for teacher's aides.[3] To improve the quality of instruction of Title I students, NCLB mandates that local education agencies (LEAs) assure that "low-income students and minority students are not taught at higher rates than other students by unqualified, out-of-field, or inexperienced teachers."[4] NCLB also requires LEAs to work with schools that fail to meet adequate yearly progress. They must create "school improvement" plans and, if necessary, reconstitute schools that do not improve.[5] Although this does not necessarily mean a state or LEA must increase the funding of underperforming schools, it does mean that underperforming schools are supposed to be reworked to improve the quality of education they deliver.

If we use a broader definition of OTL, we find NCLB does offer some aid to improve schools. Beyond Title I, NCLB has nine titles, many of which provide resource aid, such as professional development for teachers, school technology, high school dropout programs, and English-language acquisition programs. The Even Start program, for example, offers literacy courses to low-income children (up to age seven) and literacy and parenting programs to their parents. NCLB improves Even Start by more sharply focusing it on literacy and introducing accountability provisions to ensure that participants are improving their reading skills.[6] Most of these programs and services are supposed to be structured to help schools teach children to state standards. The funding for these programs is modest. Although they cannot be expected to remedy underfunding entirely, they can ameliorate the resource deprivation in some schools. NCLB does, then, have the potential to raise the OTL standards at schools.

But "possible" should not be confused with "probable." NCLB allows states considerable leeway in defining what "highly qualified" means. More fundamentally, despite efforts to target more money to the poorest schools, NCLB is effectively general aid. Nearly all school districts get a slice of the pie. NCLB is not designed to even the resource distribution between schools. It does not require states to be sure that every school has up-to-date, challenging textbooks or, even, roofs that do not leak. Nor does NCLB force states to stop district bureaucracies from absorbing money that should be spent on classroom needs. The distribution of school resources and opportunities afforded thereby remain largely a function of property taxes and therefore within the policy province of states and localities.[7] Thus, the ability of NCLB to improve opportunity-to-learn standards appears quite limited.

Content Standards and Performance Standards

Content standards, the reader will recall, are the education standards themselves. Performance standards are the levels at which students are to demonstrate learning to the standards. States, as mandated by IASA and NCLB, are to have at least three performance standards: not proficient, proficient, and advanced.

NCLB gave neither the secretary of education nor any federal officer the power to review state content standards (or assessments, for that matter) to see if they are, as the law requires, "challenging," "high quality," and contain "rigorous content."[8] Nor does the law allow the federal government to prescribe the level of performance standards. But there are two aspects of NCLB that may have effects on content and performance standards: adequate yearly progresss (AYP) and the use of the National Assessment of Educational Progress (NAEP) as an audit of AYP.

Adequate Yearly Progress

To review, as a condition of aid states are required to draw up a twelve-year timeline during which they raise the achievement of all students to the performance standard of "proficient" or higher. States must:

1. Set a percentage of the students in each school that need to score at proficient or better. This is the "starting point" or baseline. It must be set at "the State's lowest achieving group of students" or "the school at the 20th percentile in the State, based on enrollment, among all schools ranked by the percentage of students at the proficient level," whichever is higher.
2. "Establish statewide annual measurable objectives" in mathematics

and English that "shall be the same for all schools" and "shall identify a single minimum percentage of students who are required to meet or exceed the proficient level."

3. Create "intermediate goals for annual yearly progress" for the state as a whole that "increase in equal increments over" twelve years, reaching 100 percent.

4. For a school to make AYP and avoid falling into "school improvement status," it must:
   - Meet or exceed the "single minimum percentage" of students at or above proficiency.
   - The school's population as a whole must meet the "intermediate goals" for the school.
   - Every racial and economic subgroup must meet the "intermediate goals."[9]

These AYP rules will likely have implications for state performance standards. As Kane and Staiger have pointed out, if states are to raise every student to proficiency, then states have a strong incentive to set their definition of "proficient" low.[10] For example, a state might declare that any student who correctly answers 25 percent of the questions on a reading examination is proficient. Why? The answer is simple: to avoid the political and financial consequences occurring when schools fail to make AYP (e.g., providing intradistrict choice, supplementary services). This fear is real: a recent survey of state education leaders found their greatest fear about NCLB is that its AYP demands will result in an enormous percentage of schools being declared "in need of improvement."[11] Not surprisingly, some states have gamed the system by lowering their definition of "proficient."[12]

There already are indications some states are considering doing this.[13] Michigan, which has challenging content and performance standards, heatedly debated lowering standards when 1,513 of its schools fell into school improvement status or worse.[14] Colorado, meanwhile, has contemplated fashioning a dual system of proficiency measurement. The state would continue to use its definition of proficiency but wants to create a lower definition for the purpose of federal reporting.[15]

On the whole, clear incentives exist for states to lower their performance standards. Quite probably, this temptation varies for differently situated states. In states where schools are close to reaching AYP goals, political leaders may bet that they can reach the targets without lowering performance standards; in states where the fear of failure is great, political leaders may find irresistible the temptation to lower the definition of "proficient."

The effect of the AYP rules on content standards is less direct and clear. Systemic reform argues that children will learn more by being taught to high standards and tested thereon. Indeed, assessments serve to check whether students are learning to high standards, teachers are teaching to high standards, and so forth. They serve, in short, as a measure of quality control and motivate all interested parties (teachers, students, administrators) to work harder. Therefore, it is possible—if states feel the need—to redefine the definition of "proficient" on assessments.[16] The result might be similar to what happened with the minimum competency movement in the 1980s: curricular leveling. Students in poor and failing schools would be taught to standards higher than previously; students in better schools would see their standards and assessments made easier. This might be more equitable than the status quo, but it certainly falls short of high standards for all. Kerry Mazzoni, the secretary of education in California, notes that the need to make AYP has given California a strong incentive to soften its demanding standards. "The federal government has put us in a bind. We're never going to be able to meet the 100 percent mark."[17] California's department of education, therefore, openly pondered reclassifying 1.5 million nonproficient students to proficient in order to avoid penalties.

Preliminary evidence has appeared that may indicate improvement in content standards in some states. However, both studies were simple correlative studies that sought to see if the quality of standards improved after the implementation of NCLB. They made no attempt to examine whether these apparent increases were a function of NCLB or other variables.[18]

The Use of NAEP as an Audit of State AYP

NCLB requires that states that accept Title I funds participate in the NAEP state-level assessments. These examinations produce data that offer a statistical picture of student achievement in each state. One might imagine that this NCLB requirement will have the effect of raising state performance and content standards. The logic runs thus: the use of NAEP as an audit of state test scores will encourage a state to align its assessments and content standards to the rigorous NAEP exams. This will occur because state leaders fear having their test scores indicate improvement while NAEP shows otherwise.

Unfortunately, the situation is more ambiguous than this. First, there are practical difficulties. Aligning state standards and assessments with NAEP is a technically complex task. It is true, anyone may download a small number of old NAEP questions from the website of the National Center for Education Statistics (NCES) and acquire copies of some of the NAEP frameworks, which provide an outline of the "domain of coverage" of the exams.[19] Moreover, both NCES and the National Assessment Governing Board (NAGB) have been instructed to provide information on NAEP to states that request it.[20] However, it is a large leap from possessing a number of old NAEP questions and the frameworks to having well-structured academic standards that can be used by teachers to fashion curricula and lesson plans.[21] Considering the challenges states and others (e.g., university consortia) have faced trying to create good content standards, it is unlikely that the ready availability of NAEP questions will greatly ease the process.[22]

Beyond this, though, is the critical matter of motivation. A state, as noted earlier, has strong incentives to lower standards. But what are the consequences of doing so? First, there is the law. Under NCLB, a state that fails to implement an adequate accountability system can be penalized with the loss of a portion of its administrative funds.[23] However, the secretary of education is unlikely to do that except in the most egregious cases of divergence between state and NAEP scores. The complex, technical nature of assessing the educational achievement and progress of hundreds of thousands, if not millions, of children makes taking a strong position perilous.[24] According to the NAGB, a host of variables might account for differences in state AYP and NAEP reports of learning trends, including, "definitions of subgroups, changes in the demography within a state over time, sampling procedures, standard-setting approaches, reporting metrics, student motivation in taking the state test versus taking NAEP, mix of item formats, test difficulty," and, importantly, different content coverage between state exams and NAEP.[25] The latter possibility—that NAEP and a state's exams test different skills and knowledge—is particularly pertinent, for it directly undermines any federal argument in favor of punishing a state for this.[26] By what right can the federal government punish states for failing to teach curricula that comports with the NAEP exams? Once again, the fundamental issue of state and local control over curricula returns, and federal law clearly supports that control. Additionally, there are incentives resulting from electoral calculations. Title I is widely perceived as a program to help low-income children in resource-poor schools. Any effort to reduce federal funds looks like punishing poor children and schools.[27] A president seeking reelection, or the election of a successor from his party, has clear incentives not to have his or her administration associated with the withholding of Title I dollars. The former deputy secretary of education in the Clinton administration, Marshall Smith, points out that "No president is going to sanction a state governor in his own party, particularly as an election is nearing."[28]

Also worth considering is the matter of public exposure. In the past, states leaders were enraged when test data emerged showing their public schools were faring worse than those in other states and, critically, worse than purported. In the mid-1990s, Mark Musick of the Southern Regional Education Board wrote a seven-page paper comparing the percentages of children in states that scored proficiently on state exams and NAEP exams.[29] The paper showed that the percentages of proficient students varied wildly within states on the two exams. For example, Georgia's exams found 83 percent of eighth-graders learning math at grade level. NAEP showed 16 percent of Georgia's eighth-graders to be proficient. The implication of this disparity was that states like Georgia were setting their standards low. This was embarrassing. NCLB requires all states receiving Title I to participate in state NAEP exams. As that data pours in, it can be used to truth-test states' content and performance standards. Indeed, this appears to have been intended by some of the crafters of NCLB.[30] If the percentage of a state's pupils scoring proficiently on NAEP is far below the percentage scoring proficiently on the state exams, there may be a public outcry that creates political pressure to better align state standards to NAEP.[31] Of course, a state can, as pointed out previously, simply shrug at the results and tell the public that the tests cover different subject matter. Whether the public buys this or not is difficult to predict; so, then, are prospects for embarrassing states with NAEP.

Incremental Reforms

The political and policy analysis presented in this study uncovered serious impediments to the use of federal power to raise education standards. Creating national standards and assessments was and is politically unacceptable.[32] Though times have changed and antistatism has declined, there is little evidence that members of Congress are itching to give the federal government great sway over school curricula any time soon. In terms of policy, the 1994 reform of Title I and the recent No Child Left Behind Act have set the federal government and the states far down the path toward a new policy paradigm: the states will fashion their own education standards and assessments, and the federal government will attempt to exert some indirect quality control over them. These reforms are valuable insofar as they prod states to make their school systems more rationally organized and accountable.

But what of the ultimate goal of creating high education standards in the schools in order to raise academic achievement? For all the effort to raise education standards through federal action—Goals 2000, and the 1994 and 2002 reformulations of Title I—the development of high standards has been uneven and often stunted. The federal government cannot impose high standards on the schools, it cannot force states to raise standards, and, as described earlier, states lack clear, strong incentives to elevate standards.

From the perspective of the advocates of a national system of standards or robust federal policy to raise standards, it would appear that politics has triumphed over advisable policy. The federal government has settled into a very limited role vis-à-vis the states and their standards. Accordingly, any improvements to federal policy to raise education standards must be incremental, working within the constraints of the present federal politics of education and the new paradigm of federal-state relations erected by the 1994 and 2002 reforms of Title I.

Suggestions for Further Reform

Without fail, political resistance has defeated or weakened general aid proposals to inefficacy (such as Goals 2000). The federal government should not attempt to create (through legislation) national exams, even if they are voluntary. As a number of education policy network members have said, the VNT battles of the late 1990s left deep wounds. Any push for national tests risks reopening these wounds.

Although of uneven and often unimpressive quality, most states have crafted standards in some subject areas. The federal government can, though, continue to help raise student achievement by encouraging states to improve their state standards and assessment systems and assisting them with these tasks. There are many steps the federal government can take toward these ends that avoid the longstanding political pitfalls described by this study.

Step One: State, not Local, Standards

The federal government should tighten up regulatory language to require states to have a single set of standards and assessments that are used by all LEAs. Under the 1994 reauthorization of Title I, the language of section 1116 seemed to imply states must have a single set of standards:

> IN GENERAL—Each State plan shall demonstrate that the State has adopted challenging academic content standards and challenging student academic achievement standards that will be used by the State, its local educational agencies, and its schools to carry out this part, except that a State shall not be required to submit such standards to the Secretary.

The Department of Education later interpreted the statute to mean that a state needed only to have a single accountability system, one that enabled a state to audit the progress of LEAs and schools against either state or locally devised standards. This meant that LEAs that had for years failed children (typically poor children) by refusing to hold them to rigorous academic standards could continue to do so. The 1994 reauthorization insisted that LEA-created standards be at least as rigorous as any state-created standards. Yet, it was implausible that states could tease out a common metric to oversee a diversity of LEA-fashioned standards and assessments.[33]

The language of the NCLB statute is stronger. It reiterates the preceding language, then adds, "SAME STANDARDS—The academic standards required . . . shall be the same academic standards that the State applies to all schools and children in the State." The Department of Education ought to interpret this new language to mean that LEAs must adopt state-created standards in reading, math, and science (in 2006). Indeed, the whole thrust of the NCLB reform of Title I is to create in each state a statewide accountability system. If, as President George W. Bush says, the "bigotry of low expectations" is to be expelled from the schoolhouses, then LEAs must be held accountable for the quality of their curricula. Because politics will not allow the federal government to impose standards, the federal government must demand that states impose state-made education standards on LEAs.

Step Two: Limit Standards-Raising
Policies to Mathematics, Reading, and Science

The federal government should limit its standards-raising to three subjects: mathematics, reading, and science. These subjects are, for the most part, not controversial.[34] Moreover, boosting student learning in mathematics, reading, and science can be justified as a bona fide national interest demanding a national response (see Chapter 2). This is not to say that history, the arts, and other subjects are not important; they are, however, by their nature much more value-laden and hence political. To avoid provoking an antistatist backlash (be it legislative or in compliance with present laws), respect should be given to the tradition of state and local control of curricula other than reading, math, and science. The federal government can encourage schools to improve their teaching in these other areas by creating voluntary grant initiatives modeled on NCLB's Teaching American History Grants program.[35] This program allows schools to apply for extra funding to improve the knowledge of teachers in American history (by sending them to history institutes, graduate seminars, etc.). Variants of this program focusing on the arts, world history, and more would be welcomed by the states and would please those who worry that NCLB's emphasis on English and mathematics risks crowding other subjects out of schools' curricula.

Step Three: Require States to Use
Aligned, Criterion-Referenced Assessments

Both the IASA and NCLB reforms of Title I told states to use multiple measures of student achievement. This language should be retained so states are not discouraged from using diverse forms of assessments, such as portfolios and oral exams that can provide richer information on student knowledge. Yet, all states should be required to utilize criterion-referenced exams as part of their assessment systems. It makes little sense to attempt to measure student learning toward standards only by comparing student achievement relative to other students. The results are deceptive: some students always score in the proficient range, some always fail, and it is difficult to tell just how much the students really know.[36]

Moreover, these assessments must be aligned to the state standards. The current law places great time pressures on states to put assessments in place. This gives them a strong incentive to purchase, as opposed to develop, a test from a commercial test company. These "off the shelf" exams "tend to focus on what is easiest to assess" and are unlikely to be aligned with state standards.[37] Indeed, by buying a test and judging the schools on the basis of the test results, states will be placing schools in a position where they will feel obliged to realign their curricula and teach to the test, regardless of the quality. This is the inverse of what is desirable: that rigorous standards be created first and tests then be fashioned based thereon.

The Department of Education needs to provide disincentives for states to follow this test-first, fashion-standards-later course. Requiring criterion-referenced exams is one measure. The federal government might also encourage states to develop their standards first by offering short-term waivers (perhaps three years) from Title I assessment requirements provided states develop standards, have them benchmarked (see following item), then fashion aligned assessments.

Step Four: Encourage States to Have Their Standards Benchmarked

States have struggled to devise good standards and face incentives to create low standards. The federal government can help states help themselves by establishing a grant program that would pay the costs for states to have their standards benchmarked. Benchmarking is the process of taking an organization's efforts and comparing it to the work of a firm recognized for its excellence. Texas and Maryland already had their standards benchmarked by Achieve, an independent, bipartisan, nonprofit organization. Achieve was founded by a group of governors and CEOs following the 1996 National Education Summit for the purpose of helping states to raise standards and improve accountability.[38]

Step Five: Align Teacher Collegiate Education with State Standards

The logic of standards-based reform holds that a state should have content standards and said standards should be manifested in the curricula taught to students. Teachers are an essential link: teachers who have not learned the standards cannot teach their students to the standards. Moreover, it is not fair to school administrators and teachers to have their performance graded on the basis of their students learning to standards if they themselves have not been trained in the standards.

Title II of the Improving America's Schools Act of 1994 required state plans to

> describe how the State requirements for licensure of teachers and administrators, including certification and recertification, support challenging State content standards and challenging State student performance standards and whether such requirements are aligned with such standards.[39]

Obviously, this requirement had little effect on teacher education and training. NCLB attempts to put more teeth in the requirement by mandating that states must develop a plan "to ensure that all teachers teaching in the core academic areas . . . are highly qualified not later than the 2005–2006 school year."[40]

NCLB requires all schools to have highly qualified teachers. Disappointingly, in a nod to state control, NCLB largely permits states great discretion in defining what training and certification make a teacher "highly qualified."[41] Clearly, this leaves open the door for states to define away the problem of teachers' lack of preparation in content standards in order to avoid any penalties.

A long-term strategy is needed. The present teacher corps can be improved through state-run training seminars that teach the content of the standards—something that few states are actually doing (states often exempt veteran teachers from demonstrating that they are "highly qualified").[42] But what of the teachers of tomorrow? To prepare them, teachers colleges need to be pushed into training their students to the standards.[43] To this end, Title I should mandate state teacher license exams to include standards-based sections. Thus, for example, aspiring English teachers in Louisiana might be required to take a general teaching exam and one that tests their knowledge of the material covered in the Louisiana state standards for English.

Finally, certification standards for teachers and substitute teachers should be made the same. Amazingly, some states permit individuals with only a general equivalency diploma (GED) to teach school.[44] This loophole must be closed, or states will feel a strong temptation to attempt to dodge the federal "highly qualified" standard by utilizing underprepared substitutes.

Step Six: Analyze the Capabilities of State Departments of Education to Carry Out Systemic Reform and Offer More Technical Assistance

Nearly all state departments of education have moved to create education standards and aligned assessments. Yet, most states have not been able to do so competently. State standards are often vacuous, and assessments are seldom aligned. Moreover, states have only begun putting into place quality assessment, feedback, and response systems. As Marilyn Peterson, an education official in Nebraska, said of AYP, "We've never done anything like this before."[45]

States need help. The federal government ought to assess why some states have been able to enact standards-based accountability systems and other have not. The Department of Education should also commission best practices research, which is then distributed to the states, and conferences that highlight state successes at standards reform. The Department of Education ought to increase the number of people it employs who provide technical assistance to state administrators.

The Department of Education has antagonized some states by taking a hard line toward reform while being slow to issue regulations to guide reform.[46] States do need to feel that the days of unpunished noncompliance have passed.[47] However, the former secretary of education's demonization of states that are pondering lowering performance standards and heavy-handed statements by other department officials invite a compliance backlash.[48] Indeed, Nebraska's school chief and Utah legislative leaders have vowed to fight some of the mandates in NCLB and openly contemplated opting out of Title I. Schools in Vermont and Connecticut have refused Title I funding, and other states have rattled sabers and threatened noncompliance and lawsuits.[49]

Meeting the complex and multitudinous demands of the new Title I is challenging states.[50] Many states must rework and significantly upgrade their accountability systems, find new schools for tens of thousands of children being declared eligible for school choice, create report cards of student achievement for parents, recruit "highly qualified" teachers, and more.[51] And states have to do this while suffering from budget shortfalls.[52] The Bush administration should provide as much technical assistance as it can to states and fund Title I at the promised authorizations levels.[53]

Step Seven: The Return of the Wall Chart

The power of embarrassment is real. During the 1980s, Secretary Terrel Bell infuriated state leaders by annually holding news conferences where he showed reporters a "wall chart" of state scores on the SAT.[54] He was not ordered to do this by President Ronald Reagan; he did it using his authority as secretary. Historically, the mission of the Department of Education has been to collect statistics on schooling and education in the United States, and Bell's presentations of the data were in line with this tradition. He did not threaten to withhold funding from states or localities or to justify new federal policies. The point of the press conferences was to focus media and public attention on the condition of educational achievement in the states. Bell's wall charts elicited numerous media stories and goaded state officials to come up with policy responses.

Such use of the bully pulpit is appropriate to the nature of the executive office and the Department of Education. Thanks to NCLB mandates, the secretary is receiving a trove of state and NAEP exams data.[55] The present secretary and his successors should present it at an annual press conference in the hope that this would embarrass states that lowball their standards to reform.[56]

Step Eight: Rework AYP to Reduce Overidentification of Underperforming Schools

Although all the numbers are not yet in, it is clear that large numbers of schools are failing to make adequate yearly progress. One survey indicates that over 10,000 schools have failed to reach their targets; another claims the number is about 26,000.[57] In Florida, to take a particularly shocking example, approximately 90 percent of elementary and middle schools failed to make AYP.[58] Some liberals suggest that these results were intended by the policymakers who crafted the AYP provisions. AYP, the conspiracy theory goes, was designed to result in many schools being labeled "failing," which would open the door (how, it is not clear) to privatization of all schools.[59]

Historically, this accusation is not accurate.[60] In fact, it was the liberals in Congress and their aides who vigorously advocated the AYP subgroup provisions. Recall, a school can fall into school improvement status or worse if all children or any racial, ethnic, or linguistic subgroup in the student body fails to make AYP. Thus, schools with many ethnic subgroups have failed to make AYP disproportionately. The left favored this policy because it worried that if schools were asked only to make AYP for the majority of the student body, schools likely would focus their test-score–raising efforts on the children who were performing at a mediocre level (the thinking being that it is easier to raise a student who is just below proficient to proficient than one that is scoring poorly).[61]

That said, the AYP provisions of NCLB do need to be reworked.[62] There are a number of scenarios under which good schools teaching to high standards may be penalized under AYP. For example, a school that has a spike in enrollment (due to immigration or due to children from underperforming schools being allowed to attend it under NCLB's choice provision) may slip from making AYP to school improvement status. A school where students gain a little (say, from 83 percent at proficient to 85 percent) but not quite enough to make AYP will fall into school improvement status. A school with limited English proficient (LEP) students may also fall into

AYP because students who learn English well graduate from LEP (leaving behind those who are struggling and possibly creating a failing subgroup).

Worse, the fear of facing the penalties for failing to make AYP has encouraged schools to "balloon mortgage" their AYP schedules.[63] Specifically, rather than evenly divide the gains required to lift all children to proficiency over twelve years, states set easy gain targets in the early years and giant gains at the end. Both Ohio and Indiana have done this, and surprisingly the US Department of Education has approved their AYP plans. And, critically, requiring all children to score proficiently (in order to avoid penalties) gives schools every reason to dumb-down standards: simplify the material, lower the score needed to reach proficiency, and test scores will rise.

Sober observers recognize that it is impossible for all children in all public schools to score proficiently. Inevitably some children will have difficulties learning, some do not test well, and others will come to school low on sleep or simply have a bad day.[64] Getting, say, 90 percent of students (to say nothing of all) to read and do math proficiently is going to be very difficult.[65]

Indeed, it seems likely that most parents would be thrilled to send their children to a school where a hearty majority of children (but not all) read and do math at a proficient level. By setting the bar so high, the crafters of NCLB inadvertently created incentives for schools to cheat and have guaranteed that some good and very good schools will fall into school improvement status.[66]

Rather than require 100 percent of children to proficiency, NCLB should only require schools to get 80 percent to proficiency. This would reduce the enormity of the gains schools would have to register each year, the effects of which would be to decrease the probability that

- good schools getting results are penalized
- schools that accept large numbers of minority and immigrant children are penalized
- states "balloon mortgage" gains
- states dumb-down content and performance standards.

Annual yearly progress is an important part of raising student achievement and state standards-based reform. However, AYP is already under widespread attack, and as more and more schools are labeled failing, the idea itself will become less and less popular. As the percentage of schools labeled underperforming climbs, the believability of that label decreases. Some groups are already calling for the scrapping of AYP entirely. Political prudence suggests mollifying the anger at AYP and defanging opposition by setting a more reasonable goal. Reducing the goal to 80 percent proficiency will be controversial. Some will complain that it is an effort to abandon the most challenged children. Yet, refusing to lower the bar is even more politically risky. To quiet this charge, NCLB should be amended to create incentives for schools to increase the percentage of children learning to proficiency. For example, a school would earn additional aid for each student beyond 80 percent that scored at a proficient level. To keep states from gaming the system by low-balling their standards, participating states might be required to have had their standards benchmarked or to demonstrate a comparable performance on the NAEP examinations.

Final Step: Expand the Testing Requirements to More High-Schoolers

The testing data presented in Chapter 1 indicated that students in the United States do worse and worse the longer they stay in schools relative to children in other nations. The skills of US high school graduates, to put it charitably, are less then they ought to be. All too often, high school pupils are free to choose many of their courses (many of which are nonacademic in nature) and can earn a diploma without taking many courses in math or English.[67] The assigning of students into college preparatory and vocational education tracks continues. And, as was noted in Chapter 3, large numbers of first-year college students arrive on campus underprepared and need remedial coursework to get them up to speed.[68]

To encourage high schools to teach to higher standards, Title I should be reformed to require states to fashion exams for both entering (tenth grade) and graduating (twelfth grade) high schoolers in English and mathematics and require these students to participate in the NAEP assessments.[69] Student performance on these examinations should count toward a school's AYP. This would give high schools a strong incentive to keep twelfth-graders from experiencing the infamous "senior slump" and increase the probability that graduating students would be prepared for postsecondary schooling or training.[70]

Conclusion

Politically, raising standards to raise student achievement remains popular. Yet, using federal power directly to raise standards has proven politically problematic. Though indirect and less robust than true national standards, the present standards-raising efforts—as embodied in the 1994 and 2002 reforms of Title I—are valuable nevertheless. These reforms goad the states to put in place standards-based systems of accountability. With the federal government kept from a more direct and powerful role, the reformed Title I must serve as the main means for encouraging schools to raise education standards. Clearly, Title I can be further reworked to repair some of its present inadequacies. Small changes to the statute, more forceful federal regulatory oversight, and a zealous secretary of education will help. Raising standards through Title I's indirect mechanisms will remain a struggle for the foreseeable future. It is, however, a struggle well worth undertaking.

Notes

1. On the power of marrying policy and political analysis, see Mead, "Policy Studies and Political Science."
2. Title I, Part A, sec. 1119.
3. Ibid.
4. Title I, sec. 1112 (c)(L).
5. Title I. sec. 1116.
6. See Title I, Part B, sec. 1231.
7. On the state and local politics of school resources, see Reed, *On Equal Terms.*
8. Title I, sec. 1111(d).
9. Title I., sec.1111 (b)(2)(G).
10. Kane and Staiger, *Racial Subgroup Rules in School Accountability Systems,* paper prepared for the conference Taking Account of Accountability: Assessing Politics and Policy, Kennedy School of Government, Harvard University, June 10–11, 2002, p. 3.
11. Jennings et al., *From the Capital to the Classroom.*
12. Ryan, "The Perverse Incentives of the No Child Left Behind Act," p. 948.
13. And it is clear that states' definitions of proficient vary greatly. Olson, "'Proficient' Mark Shifts by State, Grade, Subject."
14. Emerson, "Schools May Lower Standards to Stay Off Federal Watch List."
15. Ibid. See also Wilgoren, "School Chiefs Fret over US Plan to Require Testing." See also Figlio, *Aggregation and Accountability.* On other ways for states to game the accountability system imposed by NAEP, see Goldhaber, *What Might Go Wrong with the Accountability Measures of the "No Child Left Behind Act"?*
16. Ryan, "The Perverse Incentives of the No Child Left Behind Act," pp. 944–948.
17. Heland, "Education Standards Threatened."
18. Klein et al., *The State of Math Standards, 2005*; and Stotsky and Finn, *The State of English Standards, 2005.*
19. The domain of coverage refers to the curricular area that is tested. Test items are available at http://nces.ed.gov/nationsreportcard/.
20. National Assessment Governing Board, *White Paper: Prohibition on Using NAEP to Influence State and Local Standards, Tests, and Curricula.*
21. Barton points out, "The establishment of content standards" results in "a document, likely a thick one, describing what students are to know and be able to do in all subjects and in all grades. This is not a 'curriculum.' And it is even further removed from being a set of lesson plans." Barton, "The Elementary and Secondary Education Act and Standards-Based Reform," p. 62.

22. Chapter 6 recounted the problems with the would-be national American history and English standards.

23. Title I., sec. 111(g).

24. On the substantial challenges to using NAEP as an audit of state test results and AYP, see National Assessment Governing Board, *Using the National Assessment of Educational Progress to Confirm State Test Results*; Reckase, *Using NAEP to Confirm State Test Results: An Analysis of Issues*; and Feuer et al., *Uncommon Measures*. This technical complexity affects the political capital that the secretary of education or any political actor can claim. Contrast this with a more simple moral issue: the unequal funding of schools. Here, the numbers involved are straightforward (per-capita spending per student) and the principle involved (equality) is clear.

25. National Assessment Governing Board, *Using the National Assessment of Educational Progress to Confirm State Test Results*, p. 9.

26. And this is no hypothetical situation; states have claimed test score rises but seen no rise on their NAEP scores for those same years. See Goldhaber, *What Might Go Wrong with the Accountability Measures of the "No Child Left Behind Act"?* p. 10.

27. In the case of welfare, the federal government can create punishments and force recipients off the rolls because recipients are viewed as moral agents largely responsible for their actions. Not so with education, because children are regarded as innocent and teachers are perceived as working under distressful, impoverished circumstances beyond their control. On the quicksilver nature of political power in federal politics, see Page and Shapiro, "Presidential Leadership Through Public Opinion"; and Hendrick Smith, *The Power Game*, pp. 41–84.

28. Wilgoren, "School Chiefs Fret over US Plan to Require Testing."

29. Musick, *Setting Standards High Enough.*

30. Again, conference committee chairman John Boehner (R-OH) said that NAEP would "verify the results of statewide assessments." John Boehner, *Fact Sheet on HR 1*, January 2002.

31. In author interviews, Mark Musick, Denis P. Doyle, Phyllis McClure, and Brian Jones all described this course of action as probable.

32. The bitterness over the effort to create national standards lingers, at least among some. The *Los Angeles Times* reported in autumn 2004 that the US Department of Education "destroyed more than 300,000 copies of a booklet designed for parents to help their children learn history after the office of Vice President Dick Cheney's wife [Lynne Cheney] complained that it mentioned the National Standards for History, which she has long opposed." Alonso-Zalidivar and Merl, "Booklet That Upset Mrs. Cheney Is History." Nevertheless, some respected groups are attempting to craft high school standards that they hope states will adopt. Arenson, "Study Says US Should Replace States' High School Standards."

33. Feuer et al., *Uncommon Measures.*

34. Intense squabbles have broken out over evolution theory in localities, so the federal government does have to be cautious not to dictate that schools can or cannot teach evolution or creationism.

35. Title II, section 2351.

36. Keegan et al. make an argument that norm-referenced exams can be useful. This is true, yet they do not refute the central claim here: that norm-referenced exams are not an optimal format for determining how well students are learning to standards. See Keegan et al., *Adequate Yearly Progress*, pp. 5–8.

37. Gandal, "Multiple Choices: How Will States Fill in the Blanks in Their Testing Systems?" p. 5.

38. Copies of the benchmarking reports of Texas and Maryland may be downloaded for free at http://www.achieve.org.

39. PL 103-382, Title II, section 2205(b)(2)(H).

40. PL 103-382, Title I, section 1119(a)(2).

41. On states' activities, see Keller, "States Claim Teachers Are 'Qualified,'" pp. 1, 16.

42. Jacobson, "States Criticized on Standards for Veteran Teachers," p. 11.

43. Observers have long faulted education schools for devoting too much coursework in pedagogical theory and too little in academic courses. Most recently see Steiner, *A Qualified Teacher in Every Classroom*.

44. Starks, "Substitute Teachers Hard to Find," p. A1.

45. Friel, "Making the Grade?"

46. Jennings, et al., *From the Capital to the Classroom*.

47. Thus far, two states have been penalized for failing to follow federal requirements for testing. The Department of Education cut Georgia's administrative funds by $783,000 and Minnesota's by $113,000. Prah, "Schoolhouses, Statehouses Reel from Federal Mandates."

48. Secretary Roderick Paige called officials in such states "enemies of equal justice and equal opportunity" and "apologists for failure." Paige, *Letter Released from US Secretary Paige to State School Chiefs on Implementing No Child Left Behind*. One long-term observer of federal education politics reports that the letter greatly upset a number of chief state school officers. Author interview: Denis P. Doyle, December 18, 2002. Lower-level administrators have also expressed frustration with the heavy demands of NCLB. Archer, "Survey: Administrators Vexed by Mandates," p. 3. See also Ritter and Lucas, "Puzzled States," pp. 55–61.

49. Keller, "Gov. Dean Questions the Wisdom of Accepting ESEA Money"; Danitz, "States Dubious of Federal Testing Plan"; Mendez, "Thanks But No Thanks"; Prah, "Utah Considers Opting Out of No Child Left Behind"; Borsuk, "No Child Left Behind May Not Be Enforceable"; and Dillon, "Utah Rebukes Bush."

50. On state efforts to negotiate changes to their state accountability plans, see Fast and Erpenbach, *Revisiting Statewide Educational Accountability Under NCLB*.

51. On the states' data management challenges, see Hoff, "States Need Updates for Managing Data, Analysis Concludes," pp. 1, 20. It should also be noted that the forced school choice provision is presenting school districts with significant managerial challenges. It has formed huge pools of children eligible to transfer from their schools: 30,000 children in Baltimore's schools, 125,000 in Chicago, 223,000 in Los Angeles, and 385,000 in New York City. Nationwide, the number is approximately 3.5 million and likely to grow as more states get their accountability systems in place and their definitions of AYP finalized. Rossi and Patel, "Space Crunch Lets Only 1% of Kids Leave Failing Schools"; Schemo, "Few Exercise New Right to Leave Failing Schools"; Russo, "When School Choice Isn't"; Campanile, "School Swap Looms"; Government Accountability Office, *No Child Left Behind Act*; and Hess and Finn, eds., *Leaving No Child Behind*.

52. Thirteen states actually had to cut funding for kindergarten through high school education in 2003. Prah, "Schoolhouses, Statehouses Reel from Federal Mandates."

53. Thus far, the administration has sought to appropriate far less than what was authorized. Congress has been forced to hard-bargain President Bush upward.

54. On Secretary Bell and his wall charts, see Bell, *The Thirteenth Man.*

55. This is already happening: see Olson, "In ESEA Wake, School Data Flowing Forth," pp. 1, 16–17.

56. NCLB does not explain what the federal government should do if a state's exams show its students making AYP and NAEP does not. So far, no federal guidelines have addressed this subject either. The NAGB has suggested using caution in interpreting state test results in light of NAEP. National Assessment Governing Board, *Using the National Assessment of Educational Progress to Confirm State Test Results.*

57. Kertsen, "Raising the Bar"; and Dillon, "1 in 4 Schools Fall Short Under Bush Law."

58. Robelen, "State Reports on Progress Vary Widely," pp. 1, 37.

59. Thus, former senator and ambassador Carol Moseley-Braun accused the Bush administration of setting schools up to fail as a way of getting a voucher plan in place when not all schools succeed by 2014. The education law, Moseley-Braun argued, is "part and parcel of a plan to just destroy public education." Zernicke, "Attacks on Education Law Leave Democrats in a Bind."

60. Nor does this theory make much sense. In fact, the AYP rules might retard the growth of charter schools (e.g., privately managed competitors to public schools). Entrepreneurs who hoped to open charter schools cannot escape NCLB's AYP rules. Students at a charter school must also be tested. If they do not make AYP, the charter school would fall into school improvement status and face the same penalties that an underperforming public school does.

61. Thus, the example of Abraham Lincoln Middle School in Gainesville, Florida. Before NCLB's AYP rules, Florida measured the school's success on the basis of how well students did on average. Before the new AYP measure, Lincoln Middle School rated an A. Once Lincoln was forced to break down its scores by demographics and be graded on how all groups are doing, Lincoln's rating plunged. The reason? The majority of Lincoln's black and poor children were scoring below proficiency. No longer would the school be lauded while the most-at-risk students struggled. Hall et al., *What the New AYP Tells US About Schools, States, and Public Education,* p. 2.

62. Some softening of the law has already occurred. For an overview of the changes thus far, see Center for Education Policy, *Rule Changes Could Help More Schools Meet Test Score Targets for the No Child Left Behind Act.*

63. Finn, "Adequate Yearly Progress or Balloon Mortgage?" *The Education Gadfly.*

64. Unless, of course, tests are so dumbed-down that it is impossible for any child to not score proficiently.

65. McCombs et al., *Meeting Literacy Goals.*

66. By barring struggling students from taking the tests, schools can improve their chance at making AYP. Thus, in New York City, there have been reports of low-performing students being pushed out of schools. In Chicago, three schools reworked the definition of what it means to be a high school junior in order to keep many struggling students from taking the tests and reducing the schools' chance to make AYP. See Jacob and Levitt, "To Catch a Cheat."

67. On high school course requirements, see Achieve, Inc., *The Expectations Gap—A 50-State Review of High School Graduation Standards.*

68. A recent study indicates over three-quarters of students who took the ACT had insufficient knowledge and skills in algebra, biology, and writing. ACT, Inc., *Crisis at the Core.*

69. Under the present law [Title I, sec. 1111(b)(3)(c)(v)(I)(cc)], schools must test high schoolers just once at some point between grades ten and twelve.

70. As this book was going to press, President Bush announced that he desired to expand the mathematics and readings provisions of the No Child Left Behind Act to include high school students. Fletcher and Glod, "'No Child' Expansion Is Outlined."

Acronyms

ACT	American Collegiate Test
ADA	Americans for Democratic Action
AYP	adequate yearly progress
CATS	Commonwealth Accountability Testing System
CCSSO	Council of Chief State School Officers
CTBS	Comprehensive Test of Basic Skills
EEEIA	Equity and Excellence in Education Implementation Act
ESEA	Elementary and Secondary Education Act
ESL	English as a second language
IASA	Improving America's Schools Act
IRP	Independent Review Panel
KCCT	Kentucky Core Content Test
KERA	Kentucky Education Reform Act
KIRIS	Kentucky Instructional Results Information System
LEAs	local education agencies
LEP	limited English proficient
NAEP	National Assessment of Educational Progress
NAGB	National Assessment Governing Board
NAHL	National Assessment of History and Literature
NAS	New American Schools
NASDC	New American Schools Development Corporation
NCES	National Center for Educational Statistics
NCEST	National Council on Education Standards and Testing
NCLB	No Child Left Behind Act
NEA	National Education Association
NEGP	National Education Goals Panel
NESAC	National Education Standards and Assessment Council
NESIC	National Education Standards and Improvement Council

NGA   National Governors Association
NORC   National Opinion Research Studies
OBE   outcomes-based education
OECD   Organisation for Economic Cooperation and Development
OTL   opportunity-to-learn
PISA   Programme for International Student Assessment
QSA   quality schools advocacy
SAT   Scholastic Aptitude Test
SREB   Southern Regional Education Board
TAAS   Texas Assessment of Academic Skills
TAKS   Texas Assessment of Knowledge and Skills
TEAMS   Texas Educational Assessment of Basic Skills
TEKS   Texas Essential Knowledge and Skills
TIMSS   Third International Mathematics and Science Study
TIMSS-R   TIMSS-Repeat
VNTs   voluntary national tests

Bibliography

Achieve, Inc. *Aiming Higher: Meeting the Challenges of Education Reform in Texas*. Washington, DC: Achieve, 2002.

——. *The Expectations Gap—A 50-State Review of High School Graduation Standards*. Washington, DC: Achieve, 2004.

——. *Three Paths, One Destination: Standards-Based Reform in Maryland, Massachusetts, and Texas*. Washington, DC: Achieve, 2002.

ACT, Inc. *Crisis at the Core: Preparing All Students for College and Work*. Iowa City, IA: ACT, 2004.

——. *Standards for Transitions Guide—English*. http://www.act.org/standard/.

——. *Standards for Transitions Guide—Mathematics*. http://www.act.org/standard/.

Advisory Committee on Education. *The Federal Government and Education*. Washington, DC: US Government Printing Office, 1938.

Almond, Gabriel A., and Sydney Verba. *The Civic Culture: Political Attitudes and Democracy in Five Nations*. Princeton: Princeton University Press, 1963.

Alonso-Zalidivar, Ricardo, and Jean Merl. "Booklet That Upset Mrs. Cheney Is History." *Los Angeles Times*, October 8, 2004.

American College Test website, http://www.act.org/.

American Council of Trustees and Alumni. "Losing America's Memory: Historical Illiteracy in the Twenty-first Century." Washington, DC: American Council of Trustees and Alumni, 2000.

American Federation of Teachers. *Making Standards Matter, 1998*. Washington, DC: American Federation of Teachers, 1998.

——. *Making Standards Matter, 2001*. Washington, DC: American Federation of Teachers, 2002.

Anderson, James E. *Public Policymaking: An Introduction*. Boston: Houghton Mifflin, 2000.

Anderson, Lee W. *Ideology and the Politics of Federal Aid to Education: 1958–1996*. PhD diss., Stanford University, 1997.

Andrew, John A., III. *Lyndon Johnson and the Great Society*. Chicago: Ivan R. Dee, 1998.

Angus, David L., and Jeffrey E. Mirel. *The Failed Promise of the American High School: 1890–1995*. New York: Teachers College Press, 1999.

Archer, Jeff. "Survey: Administrators Vexed by Mandates." *Education Week,* November 19, 2003.

Archibold, Douglas. *The Reviews of State Content Standards in English Language Arts and Mathematics: A Summary and Review of Their Methods and Findings and Implications for Future Standards Development.* Washington, DC: National Education Goals Panel, 1998.

Arenson, Karen. "Study Says US Should Replace States' High School Standards." *New York Times,* February 10, 2004.

Arnold, R. Douglas. *The Logic of Congressional Action.* New Haven, CT: Yale University Press, 1990.

Ashenfelter, Orley, and Cecelia Rouse. "Schooling, Intelligence, and Income in America: Cracks in the Bell Curve." Working Paper 6902. Cambridge, MA: National Bureau of Economic Research, 1999.

Associated Press. "Survey Finds Few in US Understand Science." May 2, 2002.

Axtell, James. *The School Upon a Hill: Education and Society in Colonial New England.* New Haven, CT: Yale University Press, 1974.

Bailey, Stephen K., and Edith K. Mosher. *ESEA: The Office of Education Administers a Law.* Syracuse, NY: Syracuse University Press, 1968.

Bailyn, Bernard. *Education in the Forming of American Society.* New York: Vintage Books, 1960.

———. *The Ideological Origins of the American Revolution.* Boston: Belknap Press, 1967.

Balz, Dan. "Stands on Education Cost GOP Among Women, Governors Told." *Washington Post,* November 27, 1996.

Barbour, Haley. *Agenda for America: A Republican Direction for the Future.* Washington, DC: Regnery Publishing, 1996.

Barnes, Christopher, and Chester E. Finn Jr. *What Do Teachers Teach? A Survey of Fourth- and Eighth-Grade Teachers.* New York: Center for Civic Innovation, 2002.

Barrows, Alice. *The School Building Situation and Needs.* Washington, DC: Department of the Interior, Office of Education, 1938.

Barte, Patte, et al., eds. *Dispelling the Myth: High-Poverty Schools Exceeding Expectations.* Washington, DC: The Education Trust, 1999.

Barton, Paul E. "The Elementary and Secondary Education Act and Standards-Based Reform." In John F. Jennings, ed., *The Future of Federal Role in Elementary and Secondary Education.* Washington, DC: Center on Education Policy, 2001.

———. *Parsing the Achievement Gap: Baselines for Tracking Progress.* Princeton: Educational Testing Service, 2003.

———. *What Jobs Require: Literacy, Education, and Training, 1940–2006.* Princeton: Educational Testing Service, 2000.

Baumgartner, Frank, and Bryan Jones. *Agendas and Instability in American Politics.* Chicago: University of Chicago Press, 1993.

Bell, Terrel H. *The Thirteenth Man.* New York: Free Press, 1988.

Bendiner, Robert. *Obstacle Course on Capitol Hill.* New York: McGraw-Hill, 1964.

Berliner, David C., and Bruce J. Biddle. *The Manufactured Crisis: Myths, Fraud, and the Attack on America's Public Schools.* Boston: Addison-Wesley, 1995.

Berman, Lamar T. *The Towner Sterling Bill.* New York: H. W. Wilson, 1922.

Blackford, Linda B. "Kentucky Test Scores Improve to US Average." *Lexington Herald-Leader,* August 16, 2001.

Blair, Julie. "Unions' Positions Unheeded on ESEA." *Education Week*, November 6, 2002.

Blank, Rolf K., and Ellen M. Pechman. *State Curriculum Frameworks in Mathematics and Science: How Are They Changing Across the States?* Washington, DC: Council of Chief State School Officers, 1995.

Bloom, Howard, et al. *Evaluating the Accelerated Schools Approach: A Look at Early Implementation and Impacts in Eight Elementary Schools*. New York: Manpower Research Demonstration Project, 2002.

Boehner, John A. *Fact Sheet on HR 1*. Washington, DC: House Education and the Workforce Committee, January 2002.

———. "The Unmaking of School Reform." In John F. Jennings, ed., *National Issues in Education: Goals 2000 and School-to-Work*. Bloomington, IN: Phi Delta Kappa International; Washington, DC: Institute for Educational Leadership, 1995.

Bond, Jon, and Richard Fleisher. *The President in the Legislative Arena*. Chicago: University of Chicago Press, 1990.

Boone, Richard G. *Education in the United States: Its History from the Earliest Settlements*. New York: D. Appleton, 1900.

Borsuk, Alan J. "No Child Left Behind May Not Be Enforceable, Lautenschlager Says." *Milwaukee Journal Sentinel*, May 13, 2004.

Boser, Ulrich. "Study Finds State Exams Don't Test What Teachers Teach." *Education Week*, June 7, 2000.

Boyer, Ernest L. *High School: A Report of the Carnegie Foundation for the Advancement of Teaching*. New York: Harper and Row, 1983.

Bracey, Gerald. "TIMSS Rhymes with Dim, as in Witted." *Phi Delta Kappan Online*, May 1998, http://www.pdkintl.org/kappan/kbra9809.htm.

———. "Tinkering with TIMSS." *Phi Delta Kappan Online*, September 1998, http://www.pdkintl.org/kappan/kbra9809.htm.

———. "Tinkering with TIMSS: A Response to Pascal Forgione." *Phi Delta Kappan* 80, 1 (September 1998).

Brademas, John. *Washington, DC, to Washington Square*. New York: Weidenfeld and Nicolson, 1986.

Bradford, M. E. *Founding Fathers: Brief Lives of the Framers of the United States Constitution*. Lawrence: University of Kansas Press, 1994.

Bradley, Ann. "Bingaman Would Require Annual Report Card on Goals." *Education Week*, February 7, 1990.

Breneman, David W. "Remedial Education: Its Extent and Cost." In Diane Ravitch, ed., *The Brookings Papers on Education 1998*. Washington, DC: Brookings Institution, 1998.

Breneman, David W., and William N. Haarlow. "Remedial Education: Costs and Consequences." In *Remediation in Higher Education: A Symposium*. Washington, DC: Thomas B. Fordham Foundation, 1998.

Bronner, Ethan. "Better Schools Is Battle Cry for Fall Elections." *New York Times*, September 20, 1998.

Brown, Richard D. *The Strength of a People: The Idea of an Informed Citizenry in America, 1650–1870*. Chapel Hill: University of North Carolina Press, 1996.

Buis, Anne Gibson. *An Historical Study of the Role of the Federal Government in the Financial Support of Education, with Special Reference to Legislative Proposals and Action*. PhD diss., Ohio State University, 1953.

Bush, George H.W. *Remarks by the President at Presentation of National Education Strategy*. Washington, DC: Office of the White House Press Secretary, April 18, 1991.

Business–Higher Education Forum. *America's Competitive Challenge: The Need for a National Response*. Washington, DC: Business–Higher Education Forum, 1983.

Butchart, Ronald E. *Northern Schools, Southern Blacks, and Reconstruction: Freedman's Education 1862–1875*. Westport, CT: Greenwood, 1980.

Calsyn, Chris, Patrick Gonzales, and Mary Frase. *Highlights from TIMSS: Overview and Key Findings Across Grade Levels*. Washington, DC: Government Printing Office, 1999.

Calwelti, Gordon, and Nancy Protheroe. *High Student Achievement: How Six School Districts Changed into High-Performance Systems*. Arlington, VA: Educational Research Service, 2001.

Cameron, Charles M. "Studying the Polarized Presidency." *Presidential Studies Quarterly*, December 2002.

Camilli, Gregory. "Texas Gains on NAEP: Points of Light?" *Education Policy Analysis Archives* 8, 42 (2000).

Campanile, Carl. "School Swap Looms." *New York Post*, July 15, 2002.

Campbell, J. R., C. M. Hombo, and J. Mazzeo. *NAEP 1999 Trends in Academic Progress: Three Decades of Student Performance*. Washington, DC: National Center for Education Statistics, 2000.

Caro, Robert A. *Lyndon Johnson: Master of the Senate*. New York: Alfred A. Knopf, 2002.

Carter, Samuel Casey. *No Excuses: Lessons from Twenty-one High-Performing, High-Poverty Schools*. Washington, DC: Heritage Foundation, 2000.

Ceasar, James W., and Andrew E. Busch. *Losing to Win: The 1996 Election and American Politics*. Lanham, MD: Rowman and Littlefield, 1997.

Center for Education Policy. *Rule Changes Could Help More Schools Meet Test Score Targets for the No Child Left Behind Act*. Washington, DC: Center for Education Policy, 2004.

Chaddock, Gail Russell. "Brinkmanship over National Tests Could Prompt Washington Shutdowns." *Christian Science Monitor Online*, October 20, 1997, http://www.csmonitor.com.

Chase, Bob. "Making a Difference." *Boston Review* 24, 6 (1999).

Cheney, Lynne V. "The End of History." *Wall Street Journal*, October 20, 1994.

Chira, Susan. "Prominent Educators Oppose National Tests." *New York Times*, January 29, 1992.

Chubb, John E., and Terry M. Moe. *Politics, Markets, and America's Schools*. Washington, DC, Brookings Institution, 1990.

Clinton, William J. "The Clinton Plan for Excellence in Education." *Phi Delta Kappan* 74 (October 1992).

Clopton, Paul. "Texas Mathematics Education in Transition." *Texas Education Review* 1, 3 (Fall 2000).

Clowse, Barbara Barksdale. *Brainpower for the Cold War: The Sputnik Crisis and the National Defense Education Act of 1958*. Westport, CT: Greenwood, 1981.

Clune, W. H., et al. *The Implementation and Effects of High School Graduation Requirements: First Steps Toward Curriculum Reform*. New Brunswick, NJ: Rutgers University, Center for Policy Research in Education, 1989.

Cohen, David K., and Susan L. Moffitt. *Title I: Politics, Poverty, and Knowledge*. Washington, DC: Center on Education Policy, 2000.

Cohen, Michael. "Implementing Title I Standards: Lessons from the Past, Challenges for the Future." In *No Child Left Behind: What Will It Take?* Washington, DC: Thomas B. Fordham Foundation, 2002.

Cohen, Sol. "The Industrial Education Movement, 1906–17." *American Quarterly* 20, 1 (Spring 1968).

Coleman, James S., and Thomas Hoffer. *Public, Catholic, and Private Schools: The Importance of Community.* New York: Basic Books, 1987.

Coleman, James S., et al. *Equality of Educational Opportunity.* Washington, DC: Office of Education, National Center for Education Statistics, 1964.

Coleman, James S., et al. *High School Achievement.* New York: Basic Books, 1982.

Coleman, James S., et al. *Trends in School Desegregation, 1968–1973.* Washington, DC: Urban Institute, 1975.

Coleman, James, et al. "Public and Private Schools." *Sociology of Education* 58, 2 (1985).

College Board. "10-Year Trend in SAT Scores Indicates Increased Emphasis on Math Is Yielding Results; Reading and Writing Are Causes for Concern." August 27, 2002, http://www.collegeboard.com/.

———. *What Does the SAT Measure and Why Does It Matter?* Princeton: College Board, 2002.

College Board website, http://www.collegeboard.com/.

Columbia Law Survey. *Americans' Knowledge of the Constitution.* New York: Columbia University Law School, 2002.

Commission on Chapter 1. *Making Schools Work for Children in Poverty.* Washington, DC: Commission on Chapter 1, 1992.

Congressional Quarterly. *Congressional Quarterly Almanac, 1946.* Washington, DC: Congressional Quarterly, 1946.

———. *Congressional Quarterly Almanac, 1951.* Washington, DC: Congressional Quarterly, 1951.

———. *Congressional Quarterly Almanac, 1965.* Washington, DC: 1965.

———. *Congressional Quarterly Almanac, 1983.* Washington, DC: 1983.

———. *Congressional Quarterly Almanac, 1990.* Washington, DC: 1991.

———. *Congressional Quarterly Almanac, 1993.* Washington, DC: Congressional Quarterly, 1994.

———. *Congressional Quarterly Almanac, 1996.* Washington, DC: 1997.

———. *Congressional Quarterly Annual Almanac, 1961.* Washington, DC: 1961.

———. *Congressional Quarterly Annual Almanac, 1994.* Washington, DC: Congressional Quarterly, 1995.

———. *Education for a Nation.* Washington, DC: Congressional Quarterly, 1973.

Congressional Research Service. *Annual Report Fiscal Year 2001.* Washington, DC: CRS, 2002.

Consortium for Policy Research in Education. "Putting the Pieces Together: Systemic School Reform. CPRE Policy Briefs. New Brunswick, NJ: Rutgers University, State University of New Jersey, and Eagleton Institute of Politics, 1991.

Cooper, K. J. "For Democrats a New Ball Game." *Washington Post*, January 30, 1993.

Council of Chief State School Officers. *New Tools for Analyzing Teaching, Curriculum, and Science.* Washington, DC: Council of Chief State School Officers, 2001.

———. *Trends in State Student Assessment Programs.* Washington, DC: Council of Chief State School Officers, 1996.

———. *Using Data on Enacted Curriculum on Mathematics and Science: Summary Report from Survey of Enacted Curriculum Project.* Washington, DC: Council of Chief State School Officers, 2000.

Cremin, Lawrence, ed. *The Republic and the School: Horace Mann on the Education of Free Men.* New York: Columbia University Teachers College, 1957.

Cross, Richard W., et al., eds. *Grading the Systems: The Guide to State Standards, Tests, and Accountability Policies.* Washington, DC: Thomas B. Fordham Foundation, 2004.

Cubberly, Elwood. *Public Education in the United States: A Study and Interpretation of American Educational History.* Cambridge, MA: Houghton Mifflin, 1934.

Curti, Merle. *The Social Ideas of American Educators.* New York: Charles Scribner and Sons, 1935.

Dabney, Charles W. *Universal Education in the South.* Chapel Hill: University of North Carolina Press, 1936.

Dameron, Ronald F. *An Historical Analysis of Legislators' Statements Made in Relation to Selected Federal Bills Regarding the Role of the Federal Government in Public Education.* PhD diss., Claremont Graduate School, 1966.

Danitz, Tiffany. "Education Summit Opens in New York." www.stateline.org, September 30, 1999.

———. "States Dubious of Federal Testing Plan." www.stateline.org, June 11, 2002.

Dao, James. "Gore Would Link Federal Aid to School Performance." *New York Times*, April 29, 2000.

Darling-Hammond, Linda. "National Standards and Assessments: Will They Improve Education?" *American Journal of Education* 102, 4 (1994).

David, Paul T. "Party Platforms as National Plans." *Public Administration Review* 31, 3 (May/June 1971).

Dawson, Howard. "The Federal Government and Education." *Journal of Educational Sociology* 12, 4 (December 1938).

Day, Jennifer C., and Andrea E. Curry. "Educational Attainment in the United States: March 1998 Update." Washington, DC: US Bureau of the Census, October 1998.

Delli Carpini, Michael X., and Scott Keeter. *What Americans Know About Politics and Why It Matters.* New Haven, CT: Yale University Press, 1996.

Democratic Presidential Platform. 1984. http://www.dnc.org.

Denison, Edward F. *The Sources of Economic Growth in the United States and the Alternatives Before Us.* Supplementary Paper No. 13. New York: Committee for Economic Growth, 1962.

Diegmueller, Karen. "Backlash Puts Standards in Harm's Way." *Education Week*, January 11, 1995

———. "English Group Loses Funding for Standards." *Education Week*, March 30, 1994.

Dillon, Sam. "1 in 4 Schools Fall Short Under Bush Law." *New York Times*, January 27, 2004.

———. "Utah House Rebukes Bush with Its Vote on School Law." *New York Times*, February 11, 2004.

Divine, Robert A. *The Sputnik Challenge.* New York: Oxford University Press, 1993.

Dorn, Sherman. "The Political Legacy of School Accountability Systems." *Education Policy Analysis Archives* 6, 1 (January 1998). Retrieved from http://epaa.asu.edu/epaa/v6n1.html.

Douglas, Paul H. "The Development of a System of Grants-in-Aid I." *Political Science Quarterly* 35, 2 (1920).
———. "The Development of a System of Grants-in-Aid II." *Political Science Quarterly* 35, 4 (1920).
Doyle, Denis P., and David Kearns. *Winning the Brain Race: A Bold Plan to Make Our Schools Competitive.* Oakland: ICS, 1988.
Dumeneil, Lynn. "'The Insatiable Maw of Bureaucracy': Antistatism and Education Reform in the 1920s." *Journal of American History* 77, 2 (September 1990).
Easton, David. "An Approach to the Analysis of Political Systems." *World Politics* 9, 3 (April 1957).
Eddy, Edward D., Jr. *Colleges for Our Land and Time: The Land-Grant Idea in American Education.* New York: Harper-Collins, 1957.
Edmonds, Ronald R. "Characteristics of Effective Schools." In Ulrich Neisser, ed., *The School Achievement of Minority Children: New Perspectives.* Mahwah, NJ: Lawrence Erlbaum Associates, 1986.
———. "Effective Schools for the Urban Poor." *Educational Leadership* 37, 1 (October 1979).
———. "Programs of School Improvement." *Educational Leadership* 40, 3 (1982).
"An Education Standards Bill." Editorial. *Washington Post,* August 23, 1993.
Education Trust. *Measured Progress: Achievement Rises and Gaps Narrow, but Too Slowly.* Washington, DC: Education Trust, 2004.
———. *Thinking K–16.* Washington, DC: Education Trust, 1999.
———. *Ticket to Nowhere: The Gap Between Leaving High School and Entering College and High-Performance Jobs.* Washington, DC: Education Trust, 2000.
Education Week and Pew Charitable Trust. *Quality Counts 2000: Who Should Teach?* Bethesda, MD: Education Week, 2000.
———. *Quality Counts 2001: A Better Balance.* Bethesda, MD: Education Week, 2001.
Educational Testing Service. *The Education Reform Decade.* Princeton: ETS, 1990.
Eidenberg, Eugene, and Roy D. Morey. *An Act of Congress: The Legislative Process and the Making of Education Policy.* New York: W. W. Norton, 1969.
Elam, Stanley. *How America Views Its Schools: The PDK/Gallup Polls, 1969–1994.* Bloomington, IN: Phi Delta Kappa, 1995.
Elazar, Daniel J. *The American Partnership: Intergovernmental Cooperation in the Nineteenth-Century United States.* Chicago: University of Chicago Press, 1962.
———. "Federal-State Cooperation in the Nineteenth-Century United States." *Political Science Quarterly* 79, 2 (June 1964).
Elmore, Richard F., and Robert Rothman, eds. *Testing, Teaching, and Learning: A Guide for Stats and School Districts.* Washington, DC: National Academy Press, 1999.
Emerson, Adam. "Schools May Lower Standards to Stay off Federal Watch List." *Lansing State Journal,* October 24, 2002.
Epstein, Lee, and Thomas G. Walker. *Constitutional Law for a Changing America: Rights, Liberties, and Justice.* Washington, DC: Congressional Quarterly Press, 1995.
Evers, Bill. "What Do Tests Tell Us?" *National Review,* September 17, 2001.
FairTest, the National Center for Fair and Open Testing. "The ACT: Biased, Inaccurate, Coachable, and Misused." http://fairtest.org/facts/act.html.
Farnand, Father Everest John Michael. *A Study of the Social Philosophies of Three*

Major Interest Groups Opposed to Federal Aid to Education. PhD diss., Saint Louis University, 1959.

Fast, Ellen Forte, and William J. Erpenbach. *Revisiting Statewide Educational Accountability Under NCLB: A Summary of State Requests in 2003–2004 for Amendments to State Accountability Plans*. Washington, DC: CCSSO, 2004.

Feldman, Sandra. "Passing on Failure." *American Educator* 21, 3 (Fall 1997).

Ferraro, Thomas. "Panel Backs More—and Harder—School Work." United Press International, April 26, 1983.

———. "Senate Proposal for National Education Conference." United Press International, June 6, 1983.

———. "The Sorry State of US Schools: National Education Commission's Indictment Triggers Strong Movement for School Reform." United Press International, May 25, 1983.

Figlio, David. *Aggregation and Accountability*. Washington, DC: Thomas B. Fordham Foundation, 2002.

Finn, Chester E., Jr. "Education and the Election." *Commentary*, October 2000.

———. "Making School Reform Work." *Public Interest* 148 (Summer 2002).

———. *We Must Take Charge: Our Schools and Our Future*. New York: Basic Books, 1991.

Finn, Chester E., Jr., and Marci Kanstoroom. "State Academic Standards." In Diane Ravitch, ed., *Brookings Papers on Education Policy 2001*. Washington, DC: Brookings Institution Press, 2001.

Finn, Chester E., Jr., and Michael J. Petrilli, eds. *The State of State Standards 1998*. Washington, DC: Thomas B. Fordham Foundation, 1998.

———. *The State of State Standards 2000*. Washington, DC: Thomas B. Fordham Foundation, 2000.

Finn, Chester E., Jr., and Diane Ravitch. "A Yardstick for American Students." *Washington Post*, February 25, 1997.

Fiske, Edward B. "Top Objectives Elude Reagan as Education Policy Evolves." *New York Times*, December 27, 1983.

Fitzpatrick, John Clement, ed. *The Writings of George Washington from the Original Manuscript Sources*. Washingtom, DC: US Government Printing Office, 1931–1944. Retrieved from http://etext.virginia.edu/washington/fitzpatrick/.

Fleming, Thomas. *Duel: Alexander Hamilton, Aaron Burr, and the Future of America*. New York: Basic Books, 1999.

Fletcher, Michael A., and Maria Glod. "'No Child' Expansion Is Outlined." *Washington Post*, January 13, 2005.

Foley, June, Mark Hoffman, and Tom McGuire, eds. *The World Almanac, Commemorative Edition*. New York: Pharos Books, 1992.

Free, Lloyd A., and Hadley Cantril. *The Political Beliefs of Americans*. New York: Simon and Schuster, 1968.

Friel, Brian. "Making the Grade?" *National Journal*, September 13, 2003. http://www.factiva.com.

Gamoran, Adam, et al. "Upgrading High School Mathematics Instruction: Improving Learning Opportunities for Low-Achieving, Low-Income Youth." *Educational Evaluation and Policy Analysis* 19, 4 (Winter 1997).

Gandal, Matthew. "Multiple Choices: How Will States Fill in the Blanks in Their Testing Systems?" Washington, DC: Thomas B. Fordham Foundation, 2002.

Gardner, Howard. "Paroxsyms of Choice." *New York Review of Books*, October 19, 2000.

General Accounting Office. *Title I: Education Needs to Monitor States' Scoring of Assessments*. Washington, DC: GAO, 2002.

George W. Bush for President official website, http://georgewbush.org.

Gerring, John. *Party Ideologies in America, 1828–1996*. Cambridge, UK: Cambridge University Press, 1998.

Gilreath, James, ed. *Thomas Jefferson and the Education of a Citizen*. Washington, DC: Library of Congress, 1999.

Gingrich, Newt. *To Renew America*. New York: HarperCollins, 1995.

"Gingrich Goes on the Record: Abolish the Education Department." *Education Week*, February 8, 1995.

Girotto, Jay R., and Paul E. Peterson. "Do Hard Courses and Good Grades Enhance Cognitive Skills?" Cambridge, MA: Harvard University, Program on Education Policy and Governance, 1998.

Goertz, Margaret E., and Mark C. Duffy. *Assessment and Accountability Systems in the Fifty States: 1999–2000*. Philadelphia: Consortium for Policy Research in Education, 2001.

Going, Allen J. "The South and the Blair Education Bill." *Mississippi Valley Historical Review* 44, 2 (September 1957).

Goldberg, Milton. "Education and the Economy: The Nation Remains at Risk." In Center for National Policy, *Passing the Test: The National Interest in Good Schools for All*. Washington, DC: Center for National Policy, 2000.

Goldhaber, Dan. *What Might Go Wrong with the Accountability Measures of the "No Child Left Behind Act"?* Washington, DC: Thomas B. Fordham Foundation, 2002.

Goldin, Claudia. "The Human Capital Century." *Education Next*, Winter 2003.

Goodlad, John I. *A Place Called School: Promise for the Future*. New York: McGraw-Hill, 1983.

Gore 2000, Inc. *Al Gore's Education Blue Book*. Washington, DC: Gore 2000, Inc., 2000.

Gorman, Siobhan. "Bipartisan Schoolmates." *Education Next*, Summer 2002.

Government Accountability Office. *No Child Left Behind Act: Education Needs to Provide Additional Technical Assistance and Conduct Implementation Studies for School Choice Provision*. GAO-05-7. Washington, DC: Government Accountability Office, 2004.

Graham, Hugh Davis. *The Uncertain Triumph: Federal Education Policy in the Kennedy and Johnson Years*. Chapel Hill: University of North Carolina Press, 1984.

Greene, Jay P. "The Texas Reform Miracle Is for Real." *City Journal*, Summer 2000.

Greenwald, Elissa A., et al. *NAEP 1998 Writing Report Card for the Nation and States*. Washington, DC: Office of Educational Research and Improvement, National Center for Educational Statistics, 1999.

Greenwood, Daphne T. "New Developments in the Intergenerational Impact of Education." In Walter W. McMahon, ed., *Recent Advances in Measuring the Social and Individual Benefits of Education*. Special issue of *International Journal of Education Research* 27, 7 (1997).

Grissmer, David, and Ann Flanagan. *Exploring Rapid Achievement Gains in North Carolina and Texas*. Washington, DC: National Education Goals Panel, 1998.

Grissmer, David, et al. *Improving Student Achievement: What State NAEP Test Scores Tell Us*. Santa Monica: RAND, 2000.

Gross, Martin L. *The Conspiracy of Ignorance: The Failure of American Public Schools.* New York: HarperCollins, 1999.

Grubb, W. Norton. "Reducing Inequality Through Education: Millennial Resolutions." In Center for National Policy, *Passing the Test: The National Interest in Good Schools for All.* Washington, DC: Center for National Policy, 2000.

Gutmann, Amy. *Democratic Education.* Princeton: Princeton University Press, 1999.

Hagen, Sam. *The Acts and Proposals of Congress to Aid Education from 1857–1890.* PhD diss., University of North Dakota, 1934.

Hall, Daria et al. *What the New AYP Information Tells Us About Schools, States, and Public Education.* Washington, DC: Education Trust, 2003.

Haney, Walter. "The Myth of the Texas Miracle in Education." *Education Policy Analysis Archives* 8, 41 (2000).

Hannaway, Jane, and Shannon McKay. "Taking Measures." *Education Next* 1, 3 (Fall 2001).

Hanushek, Eric, A. "The Impact of Differential Expenditures on School Performance." *Educational Researcher* 18 (1989).

———. "The Seeds of Growth." *Education Next,* Fall 2002.

Harbour, William R. *The Foundations of Conservative Thought: An Anglo-American Tradition in Perspective.* South Bend, IN: University of Notre Dame Press, 1982.

Harris, John F. "Clinton Defends National Testing Plan." *Washington Post,* September 4, 1997.

Haycock, Kati, and David Hornbeck. "Making Schools Work for Children in Poverty." In John F. Jennings, ed., *National Issues in Education: Elementary and Secondary Education Act.* Bloomington, IN: Phi Delta Kappa International; Washington, DC: Institute for Educational Leadership, 1995.

Heinsohn, A. G. *Anthology of Conservative Writing in the United States, 1932–1960.* Chicago: Regnery, 1962.

Heland, Duke. "Education Standards Threatened." *Los Angeles Times,* September 25, 2002.

Hess, David. "Bush School Bill Moves to Floor Despite Conservatives' Ire." www.nationaljournal.com, May 9, 2001.

Hess, Frederick M., and Chester E. Finn Jr. *Leaving No Child Behind? Options for Kids in Failing Schools.* Washington, DC: AEI Press, 2004.

Hess, Frederick M., and Patrick J. McGuinn. "Seeking the Mantle of 'Opportunity': Presidential Politics and the Educational Metaphor, 1964–2000." *Education Policy* 16, 1 (January-March 2002).

"High Schools Inflate Grades and Parents Are Fooled." Editorial. *USA Today,* August 30, 2001.

Hoar, George F. *Autobiography of Seventy Years.* New York: Scribners, 1903.

Hochschild, Jennifer, and Bridgett Scott. "The Polls' Trends: Governance and Reform of Public Education in the United States." *Public Opinion Quarterly* 62, 1 (1998).

Hoff, David J. "Clinton Team Pulls out Stops for Test Plan." *Education Week,* September 9, 1997.

———. "Compromise Is Next Step in Test Odyssey." *Education Week,* September 24, 1997.

———. "Goals Push for 2000 Falls Short." *Education Week,* December 8, 1999.

————. "NAEP Weighed as Measure of Accountability, President, Candidates Pursue High Stakes." *Education Week*, March 8, 2000.

————. "National Testing Plan Appears Headed for Perilous End." *Education Week*, October 14, 1998.

————. "NEA Poll Finds GOP Leaders at Odds with Their Voters." *Education Daily*, August 13, 1996.

————. "Polls Dispute a 'Backlash' to Standards," *Education Week*, October 11, 2000.

————. "To Administration's Dismay, House Passes Test Bill." *Education Week*, February 11, 1998.

Hofstadter, Richard. *Anti-Intellectualism in American Life*. New York: Vintage Books, 1963.

Holland, Robert. *Outcomes-based Education: Dumbing Down America's Schools*. Washington, DC: Family Research Council, 1994.

Horiuchi, Ellen Nobuko. *The United States Department of Education, 1981–1985: Agenda for Abolishment*. PhD diss., Arizona State University, 1990.

Hoxby, Caroline M. "Testing Is About Openness and Openness Works." *National Review*, August 20, 2001.

Huntington, Samuel P. *American Politics: The Promise of Disharmony*. Cambridge, MA: Belknap Press, 1981.

Immerwahr, John, and Jeanne Johnson. *Americans' Views on Standards: An Assessment by Public Agenda*. New York: Public Agenda, 1996.

Izumi, Lance T. *They Have Overcome: High Poverty, High Performing Schools in California*. San Francisco: Pacific Research Institute, 2002.

Jacob, Brian A., and Steven D. Levitt. "To Catch a Cheat." *Education Next*, Winter 2004.

Jacobson, Linda. "States Criticized on Standards for Veteran Teachers." *Education Week*, January 5, 2005.

Jeffrey, Julie Roy. *Education for Children of the Poor: A Study of the Origins and Implementation of the Elementary and Secondary Education Act of 1965*. Columbus: Ohio State University Press, 1978.

Jencks, Christopher. *Who Gets Ahead? The Determinants of Economic Success in America*. New York: Basic Books, 1979.

Jencks, Christopher, and Meredith Phillips. "Aptitude or Achievement: Why Do Test Scores Predict Educational Attainment and Earnings?" In Susan E. Mayer and Paul E. Peterson, eds., *Earning and Learning: How Schools Matter*. Washington, DC, and New York: Brookings Institution and Russell Sage Foundation, 1999.

————. *The Black-White Test Score Gap*. Washington, DC: Brookings Institution, 1998.

Jennings, John F. "Opportunity to Learn or Opportunity to Lose." *Education Week*, November 26, 1997.

————. *Why National Standards and Tests? Politics and the Quest for Better Schools*. Thousand Oaks, CA: Sage, 1998.

Jennings, John F., et al. *From the Capital to the Classroom*. Washington, DC: Center on Education Policy, 2003.

Joftus, Scott, and Ilene Berman. *Great Expectations? Defining and Assessing Rigor in State Standards for Mathematics and English Language Arts*. Washington, DC: Council for Basic Education, 1998.

Johnson, Donald B., and Kirk H. Porter, eds. *National Party Platforms 1840–1972*. Urbana: University of Illinois Press, 1975.

Johnson, Lyndon B. *The Vantage Point: Perspectives of the Presidency 1963–1969.* New York: Holt, Rinehart, and Winston, 1971.

Johnson, Robert C. "In Texas District, Test Scores for Minority Students Have Soared." *Education Week*, April 5, 2000.

Jones, Charles O. *Clinton and Congress, 1993–1996.* Norman: University of Oklahoma Press, 1999.

Jones, Lyle V., and Ingram Olkin. *The Nation's Report Card: Evolution and Perspectives.* Bloomington, IN: Phi Delta Kappa International, 2004.

Jorgenson, Dale W., and Zvi Griliches. "The Explanation of Productivity Change." *Review of Economic Studies* 34, 3 (June 1967).

Jorgenson, Lloyd P. *The State and the Non-Public School, 1825–1925.* Columbia: University of Missouri Press, 1987.

Just for the Kids. *Promising Practices: How High-Performing Schools in Texas Get Results.* Austin, TX: Just for the Kids, 2000.

Kaestle, Carl F. *Pillars of the Republic: Common Schools and American Society, 1780–1860.* New York: Hill and Wang, 1999.

Kaestle, Carl F., and Marshall S. Smith. "The Federal Role in Elementary and Secondary Education, 1940–1980." *Harvard Educational Review* 52, 4 (1982).

Kane, Thomas J., and Douglas O. Staiger. *Racial Subgroup Rules in School Accountability Systems.* Paper prepared for the conference, Taking Account of Accountability: Assessing Politics and Policy, Kennedy School of Government, Harvard University, June 10–11, 2002.

Kantor, Harvey. "Work Education and Vocational Reform: The Ideological Origins of Vocational Education, 1890–1920." *American Journal of Education* 94, 4 (August 1986).

Kaye, F. B., ed., and Bernard Mandeville, author. *The Fable of the Bees: or, Private Vices, Public Benefits.* 2 vols. Oxford, UK: Clarendon Press, 1924.

Kearns, David T., and James Harvey. *A Legacy of Learning: Your Stake in Standards and New Kinds of Public Schools.* Washington, DC: Brookings Institution, 2000.

Keegan, Lisa Graham, et al. *Adequate Yearly Progress: Results, Not Process.* Washington, DC: Thomas B. Fordham Foundation, 2002.

Keller, Bess. "Gov. Dean Questions the Wisdom of Accepting ESEA Money." *Education Week*, May 1, 2002.

Kelly, Alfred H., et al. *The American Constitution: Its Origins and Development*, vol. 2. New York: W. W. Norton, 1991.

Kelman, Steve. "The Japanization of America." *The Public Interest* 98 (Winter 1990).

Kentucky Department of Education. *Results Matter: A Decade of Difference in Kentucky's Public Schools, 1990–2000.* Frankfort: Kentucky Department of Education, 2000.

Kertsen, Denise. "Raising the Bar." *Government Executive*, January 2005.

Kildee, Dale. "Enacting Goals 2000: Educate America." In John F. Jennings, ed., *National Issues in Education: Goals 2000 and School to Work.* Bloomington, IN: Phi Delta Kappa International; Washington, DC: Institute for Educational Leadership, 1995.

Kindleberger, Charles P. *Economic Response: Comparative Studies in Trade, Finance, and Growth.* Cambridge, MA: Harvard University Press, 1978.

Kingdon, John. *Agendas, Alternatives, and Public Policies.* New York: Addison-Wesley, 1995.

Kirschten, Dick. "The Politics of Education." *National Journal*, July 9, 1983.

Klein, David, et al. *The State of Math Standards, 2005.* Washington, DC: Thomas B. Fordham Foundation, 2005.

Kliebard, Herbert M. *Schooled to Work: Vocationalism and the American Curriculum, 1876–1946*. New York: Teachers College Press, 1999.

Klingemann, Hans-Dieter, et al. *Parties, Platforms, and Democracy*. Boulder, CO: Westview, 1994.

Knox, Samuel. "An Essay on the Best System of Liberal Education." In Frederick Rudolph, ed., *Essays on Education in the Early Republic*. Cambridge, MA: Belknap Press, 1965.

Kohn, Alfie. *The Case Against Standardized Testing: Raising the Scores, Ruining the Schools*. Portsmouth, NH: Heinemann, 2000.

———. "The Case Against Tougher Standards." http://www.alfiekohn.org.

———. "Standardized Testing and Its Victims." *Education Week*, September 27, 2000, http://www.edweek.org.

Kolb, Charles. *White House Daze: The Unmaking of Domestic Policy in the Bush Years*. New York: Free Press, 1994.

Koretz, Daniel M., et al. *The Perceived Effects of the Kentucky Instructional Results Information System (KIRIS)*. Santa Monica: RAND, 1996.

Kosar, Kevin R. *National Education Standards and Federal Politics*. PhD diss., New York University, 2003.

Kozol, Jonathan. *Savage Inequalities: Children in America's Schools*. New York: Crown, 1991.

Kursch, Harry. *The United States Office of Education: A Century of Service*. New York: Chilton, 1965.

Labovitz, I. M. *Aid for Federally Affected Schools*. Syracuse: Syracuse University Press, 1963.

Lachman, Seymour P. *The Church-State Issue as Reflected in Federal Aid to Education Bills, 1937–1950*. PhD diss., New York University, 1964.

Lake Snell Perry, with John Deardourff. "Report on Findings from Seven Focus Groups." In *Passing the Test: The National Interest in Good Schools for All*. Washington, DC: Center for National Policy, 2000.

Langley, Lawrence D., and Neal Peirce. *The Electoral College Primer 2000*. New Haven, CT: Yale University Press, 2000.

Lasswell, Harold. *Politics: Who Gets What, When, How*. Cleveland, OH: Meridian, 1958.

Lawson, Millicent. "Feds' Position on National Tests on Fast Track." *Education Week*, August 6, 1997.

Lee, Gordon C. "Learning and Liberty: The Jeffersonian Tradition in Education." In Lawrence A. Cremin, ed., *Crusade Against Ignorance: Thomas Jefferson on Education*. New York: Teachers College Press, 1961.

———. *The Struggle for Federal Aid, First Phase: A History of the Attempts to Obtain Federal Aid for the Common Schools 1870–1890*. New York: Teachers College Press, 1949.

Lee, Valerie E., and Julia B. Smith. "Social Support and Achievement for Young Adolescents in Chicago: The Role of School Academic Press." *American Educational Research Journal* 36 (1999).

Lieberman, Robert C. "Ideas, Institutions, and Political Order: Explaining Political Change." *American Political Science Review* 96, 4 (December 2000).

Lightfoot-Clark, Regina. "Opposition to Vouchers May Be Dissipating." *Education Daily*, August 27, 1996.

Linn, Robert L. "Assessments and Accountability." *Educational Researcher* 29, 1 (2000).

Loveless, Tom, and Paul DiPerna. *How Well Are American Students Learning?* Washington, DC: Brookings Institution, 2004.

————. *How Well Are Students Learning? Focus on Math Achievement.* Washington, DC: Brookings Institution, 2000.

Lowi, Theodore J. "American Business, Public Policy, Case Studies, and Political Theory." *World Politics* 16 (July 1964).

Luntz, Frank, and Jennifer Laszlo-Mizrahi. "American Voters Overwhelmingly Give High Stakes Test an 'F'." *American Association of School Administrators,* July 2000.

Lusi, Susan Follett. *The Role of State Departments of Education in Complex School Reform.* New York: Teachers College Press, 1997.

Lynch, Richard L., and Kelvin F. Cross. *Measure Up! Yardsticks for Continuous Improvement.* Cambridge, MA: Blackwell Business, 1995.

McAndrews, Lawrence J. *Broken Ground: John F. Kennedy and the Politics of Education.* New York: Garland, 1981.

McClellan, B. Edward, and William J. Reese. *The Social History of American Education.* Urbana: University of Illinois Press, 1988.

McCombs, Jennifer Sloan, et al. *Achieving State and National Literacy Goals: A Long Uphill Road.* Santa Monica: RAND, 2004.

McCormack, William. *The Struggle to Secure Federal Aid for Education, 1959–1960.* PhD diss., University of California, 1961.

McDonnell, Lorraine M., and Craig Choisser. *Testing and Teaching: Local Implementation of New States Assessments.* Los Angeles: UCLA/National Center for Research on Evaluation, Standards, and Student Testing, 1997.

McKnight, Curtis C., et al. *The Underachieving Curriculum: Assessing US Mathematics from an International Perspective.* Urbana: Board of Trustees, University of Illinois, 1987.

McNeil, Linda. *Contradictions of School Reform: Educational Costs of Standardized Testing.* New York: Routledge, 2000.

Macchiavelli, Niccolo. *The Discourses.* Edited by Bernard Crick. London: Penguin Books, 1983.

————. *The Prince.* Edited by Daniel Donno. New York: Bantam Books, 1981.

Madsen, David. *The National University: Enduring Dream of the USA.* Detroit: Wayne State University Press, 1966.

Malsberger, John W. *From Obstruction to Moderation: The Transformation of Senate Conservatism, 1938–1952.* Selinsgrove, PA: Susquehanna University Press, 2000.

Martin, Don T. *The Public Statements of Presidents Truman and Eisenhower on Federal Aid to Education.* PhD diss., Ohio State University, 1970.

Marx, Paul. "Why We Need the SAT." *Chronicle of Higher Education,* June 7, 2002.

Massel, Diane, et al. *Persistence and Change: Standards-Based Reform in Nine States.* Philadelphia: CPRE, University of Pennsylvania, 1997.

Mayer, William G. *The Changing American Mind: How and Why American Public Opinion Changed Between 1960 and 1988.* Ann Arbor: University of Michigan Press, 1992.

Mead, Lawrence M. *The New Politics of Poverty.* New York: Basic Books, 1992.

————. "Policy Studies and Political Science." *Policy Studies Review* 5, 2 (1985).

Mehrens, William A., and Irvin J. Lehmann. *Measurement and Evaluation in Education and Psychology.* Orlando: Holt, Rinehart, and Winston, 1991.

Meier, Deborah. "Educating a Democracy: Standards and the Future of Public Education." *Boston Review* 24, 6 (December 1999).

Meranto, Philip. *The Politics of Federal Aid to Education in 1965: A Study in Political Innovation*. Syracuse: Syracuse University Press, 1967.

Metropolitan Life Company. *Metropolitan Life Survey of the American Teacher, 2000: Are We Preparing Our Students for the 21st Century?* New York, Metropolitan Life Company, 2000.

Michaelis, John U. *An Appraisal of the Lanham Act School Program with Special Reference to the Problem of Federal Control over Public Education*. PhD diss., University of Maryland, 1943.

Michel, Robert. *Political Parties: A Sociological Study of the Oligarchical Tendencies of Modern Democracy*. New York: Collier Books, 1962.

Miller, Julie A. "Administration Readies Reform Bill." *Education Week*, March 24, 1993.

———. "Administration Says It Lacks Funds to Support Goals Panel." *Education Week*, September 4, 1991.

———. "Buoyed by Senate Vote, Ford Backs off Deal on School Choice." *Education Week*, March 4, 1992.

———. "Bush Administration Is Seeking to Block Congressional Alternative to America 2000." *Education Week*, August 5, 1992.

———. "Bush's School Plan Is 'Lamar's Baby,' Participants Agree." *Education Week*, June 5, 1991.

———. "Conservatives Succeed in Killing Omnibus Education Bill." *Education Week*, November 7, 1990.

———. "Democrats' Objections Spur E. D. to Delay Reform Bill." *Education Week*, March 31, 1993.

———. "Election 1992: Candidates' Education and Related Policies at a Glance." *Education Week*, October 21, 1992.

———. "Legislation to Create National System of Standards, Assessments Comes Under Fire." *Education Week*, March 25, 1992.

———. "Most of Bush Plan Would Need Congressional Nod, Lawmakers Say." *Education Week*, May 15, 1991.

———. "Democrats Stress Party's Historic Role with Set of Six Key Goals for Schools." *Education Week*, September 27, 1989.

Milner, Henry. *Civic Literacy: How Informed Citizens Make Democracy Work*. Ontario: University of British Columbia Press, 2002.

Mirel, Jeffrey. *The Evolution of the New American Schools: From Revolution to Mainstream*. Washington, DC: Thomas B. Fordham Foundation, 2001.

Mitchell, William A. *Federal Aid for Primary and Secondary Education*. PhD diss., Princeton University, 1948.

Mollison, Andrew. "US Falling Behind in Educating Workers." *Atlanta Journal-Constitution*, March 28, 2001.

Molnar, Alex. "Comment." In Diane Ravitch, ed., *The Brookings Papers on Education Policy 2001*. Washington, DC: Brookings Institution, 2001.

Moo, G. Gregory. *Power Grab: How the National Education Association Is Betraying Our Children*. Washington, DC: Regnery Publishing, 1999.

Moore, Stephen, ed. *Restoring the Dream: The Bold New Plan by House Republicans*. New York: Time Books, 1995.

Morrison, Robert G. "An Exercise in Government-Approved Truth." *Education Week*, June 5, 1996.

Moss, Michael, and Michael Puma. *Prospects: The Congressionally Mandated Study of Educational Growth and Opportunity*. Cambridge, MA: Abt Associates, 1995.

Mullis, I. V. S., et al. *The State of Mathematics Achievement: NAEP's 1990 Assessment of the Nation and the Trial Assessment of the States*. Washington, DC: Department of Education, Office of Educational Research and Improvement, June 1991.

Mulroy, David. "Reflections on Grammar's Demise." *Academic Questions* 17, 3 (2004).

Munger, Frank J., and Richard F. Fenno. *National Politics and Federal Aid to Education*. Syracuse: Syracuse University Press, 1962.

Murphy, Jerome. "The Education Bureaucracies Implement Novel Policy: The Politics of Title I of ESEA, 1965–1972." In Allan Sindler, ed., *Politics and Policy in America*. Boston: Little, Brown, 1973.

Murphy, John P. *Congress and the Colleges a Century Ago: A Political History of the First Morrill Act, Other Congressional Support for Educational Purposes, and the Political Climate of the United States as It Involved Education Prior to 1862*. PhD diss., Indiana University, 1967.

Musick, Mark. *Setting Standards High Enough*. Atlanta: Southern Regional Education Board, 1996.

National Assessment Governing Board. *White Paper: Prohibition on Using NAEP to Influence State and Local Standards, Tests, and Curricula*. Washington, DC: NAGB, May 18, 2002.

National Assessment Governing Board, Ad Hoc Committee on Confirming Test Results. *Using the National Assessment of Educational Progress to Confirm State Test Results*. Washington, DC: National Assessment Governing Board, 2000.

National Assessment of Chapter 1 Independent Review Panel. *Reinventing Chapter 1: The Current Chapter 1 Program and New Directions*. Washington, DC: US Department of Education, February 1993.

National Center for Education Statistics. "International Mathematics and Science Assessments: What Have We Learned?" January 1992, http://nces.ed.gov/pubs/92011.html.

———. "NAEP 1998 Civics Report Card Highlights." Washington, DC: National Center for Educational Statistics.

National Commission on Excellence in Education. *A Nation at Risk: The Imperative for Educational Reform*. Washington, DC: NCEE, April 1983.

National Commission on the High School Senior Year. *Raising Our Sights: No High School Senior Left Behind*. Princeton, NJ: Woodrow Wilson National Fellowship Foundation, October 2001.

National Geographic Society. *Roper Geographic Survey 2002*, http://geosurvey.nationalgeographic.com.

National Governors Association. *The Debate on Opportunity-to-Learn Standards*. Washington, DC: National Governors Association, 1993.

National Science Board Commission on Precollege Education in Mathematics, Science, and Technology. *Educating Americans for the 21st Century*. Washington, DC: 1983.

National Science Foundation. *Decade of Achievement: Educational Leadership in Mathematics, Science and Engineering*. Washington, DC: National Science Foundation, 1992.

NEA/Greenberg Quinlan Research. *Education Poll*. Washington, DC: February 2000.

Nessler, Ulrich. "Rising Test Scores and What They Mean." In Ulrich Nessler, ed., *The Rising Curve: Long-Term Gains in IQ and Related Measures*. Washington, DC: American Psychological Association, 1998.

Neustadt, Richard E. *Presidential Power.* New York: John Wiley and Sons, 1960.

New Standards Project. *Listening to the Public.* Pittsburgh: National Center on Education and the Economy and the Learning Research and Development Center at the University of Pittsburgh, 1993.

New York City Board of Education. *Chancellor's 60-Day Report: A Report on the CTB-Mathematics Test (CTB-M) Administration in New York City, June 2000.* New York: New York City Board of Education, 2000.

Newmann, F. M. "Beyond Common Sense in Educational Restructuring: The Issues of Content and Linkage." *Educational Researcher* 22, 2 (1993).

Nie, Norman H., Jane Junn, and Kenneth Stehlik-Berry. *Education and Democratic Citizenship in America.* Chicago: University of Chicago Press, 1996.

Niemi, Richard G., et al. *Trends in Public Opinion: A Compendium of Survey Data.* New York: Greenwood, 1989.

Nye, Joseph S., Jr. "Limits of American Power." *Political Science Quarterly* 117, 4 (Winter 2002–2003).

Office of Educational Research and Improvement, Department of Education. *Highlights from TIMSS: Overview and Key Findings Across Grade Levels.* Washington, DC: Office of Educational Research and Improvement, 1999.

Ohanian, Susan. *One Size Fits Few: The Folly of Educational Standards.* Portsmouth, NH: Heinemann, 1999.

Olson, Lynn. "Bills to Scrap NESIC Likely to Hold Sway." *Education Week,* February 8, 1995.

———. "K-12 and College Expectations Often Fail to Mesh." *Education Week,* May 9, 2001.

———, "Undo School Programs, Heritage Urges." *Education Week,* December 7, 1994.

Olson, Lynn, and Julie Miller. "Congress Set to Fight over Panel Overseeing Goals." *Education Week,* September 5, 1990.

Onuf, Peter S. "The Founders' Vision: Education in the Development of the Old Northwest." In Paul H. Mattingly and Edward W. Stevens Jr., eds., ". . . Schools and the Means of Education Shall Forever Be Encouraged." Athens: Ohio University Libraries, 1987.

Orfield, Gary, and Johanna Wald. "The High Stakes Testing Mania Hurts Poor and Minority Students the Most." *The Nation,* June 5, 2000.

Organisation for Economic Cooperation and Development (OECD). *Education at a Glance, 1996.* Washington, DC: OECD, 1996.

———. *Education at a Glance—OECD Indicators.* Washington, DC: OECD, 2001.

———. *Learning for Tomorrow's World: First Results from PISA 2003.* Washington, DC: OECD, 2004.

———. *Knowledge and Skills for Life: First Results from the PISA 2000.* Washington, DC: OECD, 2001.

Page, Benjamin I., and Robert Y. Shapiro. "Presidential Leadership Through Public Opinion." In George C. Edwards III, Steven A. Shull, and Norman C. Thomas, eds., *The Presidency and Public Policy Making.* Pittsburgh: University of Pittsburgh Press, 1985.

Paige, Roderick. *Dear Colleague Letter Regarding the Implementation of the No Child Left Behind Act.* Washington, DC: Department of Education, July 24, 2002.

———. *Letter Released from US Education Secretary Paige to State School Chiefs on Implementing No Child Left Behind Act.* Washington, DC: Department of Education, October 23, 2003.

Pangle, Lorraine Smith, and Thomas Pangle. *The Learning of Liberty: The Educational Ideas of the Founders.* Lawrence: University Press of Kansas, 1993.

Peers, Reverend Benjamin O. *American Education: Or, Strictures on the Nature, Necessity, and Practicability of a System of National Education Suited to the United States.* New York: John S. Taylor, 1838.

Perkins, Robert, et al. *The High School Transcript Study: A Decade of Change in Curricula and Achievement, 1990–2000.* Washington, DC: National Center for Education Statistics, 2004.

Perkinson, Henry J. *Two Hundred Years of American Educational Thought.* Lanham, MD: University Press of America, 1987.

Petersen, Paul E., and Martin R. West, eds. *No Child Left Behind? The Politics and Practice of School Accountability.* Washington, DC: Brookings Institution, 2003.

Phelps, Richard P. "Why Testing Experts Hate Testing." Washington, DC: Thomas B. Fordham Foundation, 1999.

Phi Delta Kappa. *The 29th Annual Phi Delta Kappa/Gallup Poll of the Public's Attitudes Toward Public Schools.* Bloomington, IN: Phi Delta Kappa, 1998.

Phillips, Gary W. "Statement on Long-Term Trend Writing NAEP." Washington, DC: NCES, April 11, 2000.

Pianin, Eric. "Deal on National Testing Crumbles Under Pressure." *Washington Post,* October 31, 1997.

———. "Hill Negotiators Compromise on Plan for National Student Tests." *Washington Post,* October 30, 1997.

Pianin, Eric, and Rene Sanchez. "Compromise Reached on Testing Plan." *Washington Post,* November 6, 1997.

Piche, Dianne M., et al. *Title I in Midstream: The Fight to Improve Schools for Poor Kids.* Washington, DC: Citizens Commission on Civil Rights, 1999.

Pitsch, Mark. "Chapter 1 Formula Plan Hot Topic in States, Districts." *Education Week,* November 3, 1993.

———. "E. D. Officials Begin Marketing Proposal to 'Reinvent' ESEA." *Education Week,* September 29, 1993.

———. "Education Aide Leaves 27-Year Legacy of Quiet Influence." *Education Week,* September 28, 1994.

———. "Former Secretaries Urge Abolishing E. D." *Education Week,* February 1, 1995.

———. "GOP Begins Reign, Makes Changes in Panel." *Education Week,* January 11, 1995.

———. "House Panel Launches Series of Hearings on National Standards." *Education Week,* March 29, 1995.

———. "New Committee Chairman Outlines Agenda, Basks in the Spotlight." *Education Week,* November 23, 1994.

———. "School-Choice Plan Could Endanger Entire Bush Proposal." *Education Week,* June 19, 1991.

———. "Sharply Divided House Panel Amends 'Goals 2000.'" *Education Week,* July 14, 1993.

———. "Supporters Worry That Goals 2000 Changes Hurts Standards Efforts." *Education Week,* May 8, 1996.

———. "To Placate Conservatives, Measure Alters Goals 2000." *Education Week,* May 1, 1996.

Pitsch, Mark, and Julie A. Miller. "Down to Work: Congress Sets a New Course." *Education Week,* January 11, 1995.

Pomper, Gerald M. *Elections in America.* New York: Longman, 1980.

————. *Elections in America: Control and Influence in Democratic Politics.* New York: Dodd, Mead, 1968.

Porter, Andrew C. "A Curriculum out of Balance: The Case of Elementary School Mathematics." *Educational Researcher* 18, 5 (1988).

————. "Defining and Measuring Opportunity to Learn." In National Governors'Association, *The Debate on Opportunity-to-Learn Standards.* Washington, DC, 1993.

————. "External Standards and Good Teaching: The Pros and Cons of Telling Teachers What to Do." *Education Evaluation and Policy Analysis* 11, 4 (1989).

————. "National Standards and School Improvement in the 1990s: Issues and Promise." *American Journal of Education* 102, 4 (August 1994).

————. "The Effects of Upgrading Policies on High School Mathematics and Science." In Diane Ravitch, ed., *Brookings Papers on Education, 1998.* Washington, DC: Brookings Institution, 1998.

Powell, Arthur G., et al. *The Shopping Mall High School: Winners and Losers in the Educational Marketplace.* Boston: Houghton Mifflin, 1985.

Prah, Pamela M. "Schoolhouses, Statehouses Reel from Federal Mandates." *Stateline,* December 8, 2003, http://www.stateline.org.

————. "Utah Considers Opting Out of No Child Left Behind." *Stateline,* December 30, 2003, http://www.stateline.org.

Presidential Transition Team, Education, Labor, and Humanities Cluster. *Report of the K–12 Transition Team to Incoming Assistant Secretary for Elementary and Secondary Education.* White Paper, 2003.

President's Commission on Educational Excellence for Hispanics. *Creating Educational Excellence: Hispanics Achieving Educational Excellence* Washington, DC: 2000.

Preston, Mark, and Susan Crabtree. "Parties Vie for Edge on Education." *Roll Call,* May 6, 2002.

Price, Hugh Douglas. "Race, Religion, and the Rules Committee: The Kennedy Aid-to-Education Bills." In Alan F. Westin, *The Uses of Power: Seven Cases in American Politics.* New York: Harcourt, Brace, and World, 1962.

Public Agenda and *Education Week. Reality Check 1999,* http://www.edweek.org/sreports/qc99/pub-agn.htm.

————. *Reality Check 2001.* New York and Bethesda: Public Agenda and Education Week, 2001.

————. *Reality Check 2002.* New York and Bethesda: Public Agenda and Education Week, 2002.

————. *Survey Finds Little Sign of Backlash Against Academic Standards or Standardized Tests.* October 5, 2000, http://publicagenda.org.

Public Education Network and *Education Week. Accountability for All: What Voters Want from Education Candidates.* Washington, DC, and Bethesda: Public Education Network and Education Week, 2002.

Rakove, Jack. "Ambiguous Achievement: The Northwest Ordinance." In Jack Rakove, ed., *The Northwest Ordinance: Essays on Its Formulation, Provisions, and Legacy.* Lansing: Michigan State University Press, 1989.

————, ed. *Madison: Writings.* New York: Library of America, 1999.

Ravitch, Diane. "The Coleman Reports and Education." In Aage B. Sorenson and Seymour Spilerman, eds., *Social Theory and Social Policy: Essays in Honor of James A. Coleman.* New York: Praeger, 1993.

————. "Dumbing Down the Public: Why It Matters." Hoover Institution online, http://www.hoover.stanford.edu.

———. "Education After the Culture Wars." *Daedalus,* Summer 2002.

———. "National Tests: A Good Idea Gone Wrong." *Washington Post,* August 26, 1997.

———. "The History Lesson in Bush's School Plan." *New York Times,* January 17, 2001.

———. *Left Back: A Century of Failed School Reform.* New York: Simon and Schuster, 2000.

———. *National Standards in American Education: A Citizen's Guide.* Washington, DC: Brookings Institution, 1995.

———. *The Troubled Crusade: American Education 1945–1980.* New York: Basic Books, 1983.

———, ed. *Debating the Future of American Education: Do We Really Need National Standards and Assessments?* Washington, DC: Brookings Institution, 1995.

Ravitch, Diane, and Chester Finn Jr. *What Do Our 17-Year-Olds Know? A Report on the First National Assessment of History and Literature.* New York: Harper and Row, 1987.

Reckase, Mark D. *Using NAEP to Confirm State Test Results: An Analysis of Issues.* Washington, DC: Thomas B. Fordham Foundation, 2002.

Reed, Douglas S. *On Equal Terms: The Constitutional Politics of Educational Opportunity.* Princeton: Princeton University Press, 2001.

Reich, Robert B. *The Work of Nations: Preparing Ourselves for 21st-Century Capitalism.* New York: Alfred A. Knopf, 1991.

Reid, Karla Scoon. "From Worst to First." *Education Week,* April 11, 2001.

Reiman, Richard. *The New Deal and American Youth: Ideas and Ideals in a Depression Decade.* Athens: University of Georgia Press, 1992.

Richard, Alan. "State Chiefs' Group Readies for New Direction." *Education Week,* November 21, 2001.

Richard, Carl J. *The Founders and the Classics: Greece, Rome, and the American Enlightenment.* Cambridge, MA: Harvard University Press, 1994.

Ritter, Gary W., and Christopher J. Lucas. "Puzzled States." *Education Next* 3, 4 (Fall 2003).

Robelen, Erik W. "Bush Leading Republicans in New Direction." *Education Week,* April 5, 2000.

———. "Bush Touts Spending He Never Proposed." *Education Week,* September 29, 2004.

———. "GOP, Democrats Vie for Education Bragging Rights." *Education Week,* June 5, 2002.

———. "McCain's Views on Schools Becoming Clearer." *Education Week,* February 16, 2000.

———. "States Sluggish in Execution of 1994 ESEA." *Education Week,* November 28, 2001.

———. "States, Ed. Dept. Reach Accords on 1994 ESEA." *Education Week,* April 17, 2002.

Robinson, William Harry. *An Analysis of the Relationship Between Federal Education Legislation and Identifiable Economic, Political, or Social Crises in the United States.* PhD diss., Drake University, 1977.

Rochfert, David A., and Roger W. Cobb, eds. *The Politics of Problem Definition: Shaping the Policy Agenda.* Lawrence: University Press of Kansas, 1994.

Rossi, Rosalind, and Julie Patel. "Space Crunch Lets Only 1% of Kids Leave Failing Schools." *Chicago Sun-Times,* August 24, 2002.

Rossiter, Clinton. *The First American Revolution*. New York: Harvest Books, 1956.

Rotherham, Andrew. *Towards Performance-Based Federal Education Funding*. Washington, DC: Progressive Policy Institute, April 1999.

Rothman, Robert. "Educators, Analysts Hail Strategy as Bold Departure." *Education Week*, April 24, 1991.

———. "Efforts to Create National Testing System Move into High Gear." *Education Week*, July 31, 1991.

———. "Group Urges 'Hitting the Brakes' on National Test." *Education Week*, January 29, 1992.

Rothstein, Richard. *The Way We Were? The Myths and Realities of America's Student Achievement*. New York: Twentieth Century Fund, 1998.

Rudalevige, Andrew. "No Child Left Behind: Forging a Congressional Compromise." In Paul E. Petersen and Martin R. West, eds., *No Child Left Behind? The Politics and Practice of School Accountability*. Washington, DC: Brookings Institution, 2003.

Rudolph, Frederick. *The American College and University: A History*. New York: Knopf, 1957.

———, ed. *Essays on Education in the Early Republic*. Cambridge, MA: Belknap Press, 1965.

Rush, Benjamin. "Plan for the Establishment of Public Schools." In Frederick Rudolph, ed., *Essays on Education in the Early Republic*. Cambridge, MA: Belknap Press, 1965.

Rushing, Dorothy Marie. *Attitudes and Actions of the First Six Presidents of the United States Concerning Higher Education*. PhD diss., University of North Texas, 1981.

Russo, Alexander. "When School Choice Isn't." *Washington Monthly*, September 2002.

Ryan, James E. "The Perverse Incentives of the No Child Left Behind Act." *New York University Law Review* 79 (2004).

Sack, Joetta L. "Money Woes Hitting Home for School." *Education Week,* June 5, 2002.

———. "Smith to Leave the Education Department in January." *Education Week*, November 17, 1999.

Sacks, Peter. *Standardized Minds: The High Price of America's Testing Culture and What We Can Do to Change It*. Cambridge, MA: Perseus, 1999.

Sanchez, Rene. "Senate Backs Modified Plan for National Student Tests." *Washington Post*, September 12, 1997.

Sandham, Jessica L. "States Slowing Spending for Public Schools. *Education Week*, September 6, 2001.

Schattschneider, Elmer E. *The Semi-Sovereign People: A Realist's View of Democracy*. New York: Holt, Rinehart, and Winston, 1960.

Schemo, Diane Jean. "Few Exercise New Right to Leave Failing Schools." *New York Times*, August 28, 2002.

———. "Many Summer Classes Cut, Casualty of Revenue Decline." *New York Times*, June 7, 2002.

Schlafly, Phyllis. "The Clinton Master Plan to Take over Education." February 19, 1997, http://www.eagleforum.org.

Schmidt, William H., et al. *Why Schools Matter: A Cross-National Comparison of Curriculum and Learning*. San Francisco: Jossey-Bass, 2001.

"Schools Rank First as Spending Priority." *New York Times*, August 25, 1999.

Schultz, Theodore. "Capital Formation by Education." *Journal of Political Economy* 68 (December 1960).

Schwartz, Robert B., and Marian Robinson. "Goals 2000 and the Standards Movement: The Limits of Federal Policy Building in a National Education Strategy." In Diane Ravitch, ed., *The Brookings Papers on Education Policy, 2000*. Washington, DC: Brookings Institution, 2000.

Sizer, Theodore R. *Horace's Compromise: The Dilemma of the American High School*. Boston: Houghton Mifflin, 1984.

Skrla, Linda, et al. *Equity-Driven, Achievement-Focused School Districts: A Report on Systemic School Successes in Four Texas School Districts Serving Diverse Student Populations*. Austin: University of Texas, 2000.

Slawson, Douglas James. *The Attitudes and Activities of American Catholics Regarding the Proposals to Establish a Federal Department of Education Between World War I and the Great Depression*. PhD diss., Catholic University of America, 1981.

Smith, Darrell Hevenor. *The Bureau of Education: Its History, Activities, and Organization*. Baltimore: Johns Hopkins University Press, 1923.

Smith, Gilbert E. *The Limits of Reform: Politics and Federal Aid to Education, 1937–1950*. New York: Garland, 1982.

Smith, Hendrick. *The Power Game: How Washington Works*. New York: Ballantine, 1984.

Smith, Marshall S. "Education Reform in America's Public Schools: The Clinton Agenda." In Diane Ravitch, ed., *Debating the Future of American Education: Do We Need National Standards and Assessments?* Washington, DC: Brookings Institution, 1995.

Smith, Marshall S., and Jennifer O'Day. "Systemic School Reform." In Susan Fuhrman and Betty Malen, eds., *The Politics of Curriculum and Testing: The 1990 Yearbook of the Politics of Education Association*. London: Taylor and Francis, 1990.

Smith, Rogers M. "Should We Make Political Science More of a Science or More About Politics?" *PS: Political Science and Politics* 35, 2 (June 2002).

Spillane, J. P. "State Policy and the Non-Monolithoic Nature of the Local School District: Organizational and Professional Considerations." *American Educational Research Journal* 35, 1 (1998).

Sroufe, Gerald E. "Politics of Education at the Federal Level." In *Politics of Education Yearbook, 1994*. London: Taylor and Francis, 1994.

Sroufe, Gerald, and Marcia Knutson. *OIA Info Memo, May 1993*. Washington, DC: American Educational Research Association, 1993.

Starks, Kimberly. "Substitute Teachers Hard to Find; Many Lack Degrees." *Chattanooga Times Free Press*, July 18, 2004.

Stecher, Brian M. "Consequences of Large-Scale, High-Stakes Testing on School and Classroom Practice." In Laura S. Hamilton et al., *Making Sense of Test-Based Accountability*. Santa Monica: RAND, 2002.

Stecher, Brian M., and Sheila I. Barron. *Quadrennial Milepost Accountability Testing in Kentucky*. CSE Technical Report 505. Los Angeles: RAND/National Center for Research on Evaluation, Standards, and Student Testing, Center for the Study of Evaluation, 1999.

Stecher, Brian M., and K. J. Mitchell. *Portfolio-Driven Reform: Vermont Teachers' Understanding of Mathematical Problem Solving*. CSE Technical Report 482. Los Angeles: UCLA/National Center for Research on Evaluation, Standards, and Student Testing, Center for the Study of Evaluation, 1995.

Stecher, Brian M., et al. *The Effects of Standards-Based Assessment on Classroom*

Practices: Results of the 1997–98 RAND Survey of Kentucky Teachers of Mathematics and Writing. Los Angeles: UCLA/National Center for Research on Evaluation, Standards, and Student Testing, 1998.

Stedman, Lawrence. "The Achievement Crisis Is Real: A Review of the Manufactured Crisis." *Education Policy Analysis Archives* (Arizona State University), January 23, 1996, http://epaa.asu.edu/.

———. "An Assessment of the Contemporary Debate over US Achievement." In Diane Ravitch, ed., *The Brookings Papers on Education Policy, 1998.* Washington, DC: Brookings Institution, 1998.

Stevenson, Harold W., and Shinying Lee. "An Examination of American Student Achievement from an International Perspective." In Diane Ravitch, ed., *Brookings Papers on Education, 1998.* Washington, DC: Brookings Institution, 1998.

Stotsky, Sandra, and Chester E. Finn Jr. *The State of English Standards, 2005.* Washington, DC: Thomas B. Fordham Foundation, 2005.

Sufrin, Sidney C. *Administering the National Defense Education Act.* Syracuse: Syracuse University Press, 1963.

Sundquist, James L. *Dynamics of the Party System: Alignment and Realignment in the United States.* Washington, DC: Brookings Institution, 1983.

Swain, Martha H. "The Harrison Education Bills, 1936–1941." *Mississippi Quarterly* 31, 1 (Winter 1977–1978).

Swift, Fletcher Harper. *A History of Public Permanent Common School Funds in the United States, 1795–1905.* New York: Henry Holt, 1911.

Swint, Henry L. *The Northern Teacher in the South, 1862–1870.* Nashville: Vanderbilt University Press, 1941.

———. "Rutherford B. Hayes, Educator." *Mississippi Valley Historical Review* 39, 1 (June 1952).

Symcox, Linda. *Whose History? The Struggle for National Standards in American Classrooms.* New York: Teachers College Press, 2002.

Takahira, Sayura, et al. *Pursuing Excellence: Initial Findings from the Third International Math and Science Study.* Washington, DC: National Center for Educational Statistics, 1998.

Takahira, Sayura, Patrick Gonzales, Mary Frase, and Laura Hersh Salganik. *Pursuing Excellence: A Study of US Twelfth-Grade Mathematics and Science Achievement in International Context.* Washington, DC: Government Printing Office, 1998.

Task Force on Education for Economic Growth of the Education Commission of the States. *Action for Excellence.* Washington, DC: Task Force on Education, 1983.

Taylor, Howard C. *The Educational Significance of the Early Federal Land Ordinances.* New York: Teachers College, 1922.

Teles, Steven M. "Paradoxes of Welfare-State Conservatism." *Public Interest* 141 (Fall 2000).

Texas Education Agency webpage, http://www.tea.state.tx.us/.

Thernstrom, Stephan, and Abigail Thernstrom. *America in Black and White: One Nation Indivisible.* New York: Simon and Schuster, 1997.

Thomas, Norman C. *Education in National Politics.* New York: David McKay, 1975.

Tiedt, Sidney W. *The Role of the Federal Government in Education.* New York: Oxford University Press, 1966.

Traub, James. "The Class War over School Testing." *New York Times Magazine,* April 7, 2002.

Treat, Payson Jackson. *The National Land System, 1785–1820*. New York: E. B. Treat, 1910.

Tucker, Marc S., and Judy B. Codding. *Standards for Our Schools: How to Set Them, Measure Them, and Reach Them*. San Francisco: Jossey-Bass, 1998.

Twentieth Century Fund Task Force on Elementary and Secondary Education Policy. *Making the Grade*. New York: Twentieth Century Fund Task Force, 1983.

Tyack, David B. *The One Best System: A History of American Urban Education*. Cambridge, MA: Harvard University Press, 1974.

———. *Turning Points in American Educational History*. Waltham, MA: Blaisdell, 1967.

Tyack, David B., Thomas James, and Aaron Benavot. *Law and the Shaping of Public Education, 1785–1954*. Madison: University of Wisconsin Press, 1987.

U.S. Congress, House of Representatives, Committee on Economic and Educational Opportunities. *Hearing on the Proper Federal Role in Education Policy*, 104th Cong., 1st sess., January 12, 1995. Washington, DC: Government Printing Office, 1995.

U.S. Congress, House of Representatives, Subcommittee on Elementary, Secondary, and Vocational Education, Committee on Education and Labor. *Aid to Elementary and Secondary Schools*, 89th Cong., 1st sess., Washington, DC: Government Printing Office, 1965.

———. *Goals 2000: Educate America Act, Report to Accompany H.R. 1804*, April 1993. Washington, DC: Government Printing Office, 1991.

———. *Hearings*, 102nd Cong., 1st sess., March 12, 14, 1991. Washington, DC: Government Printing Office, 1991.

———. *Hearings on HR 6: The Role of ESEA Programs in School Reform*, 103rd Cong., 1st sess., February 2, 4, 1993. Washington, DC: Government Printing Office, 1993.

———. *Hearings on HR 6: Assessment*, 103rd Cong., 1st sess., February 18, 1993. Washington, DC: Government Printing Office, 1993.

———. *Hearings on HR 6: Reform Proposals for Chapter 1*, 103rd Cong., 1st sess., February 25, 1993. Washington, DC: Government Printing Office, 1993.

———. *Hearings on Reauthorization of HR 6: The Elementary and Secondary Education Act of 1965*, 103rd Cong., 1st sess., March 4, 18, 23, 31, April 21 and 27, 1993. Washington, DC: Government Printing Office, 1993.

———. *Hearings on Reauthorization of HR 6: The Elementary and Secondary Education Act of 1965*, 103rd Cong., 1st sess., May 13, 25, June 10 and 30, 1993. Washington, DC: Government Printing Office, 1993.

———. *Hearings on H.R. 1804—Goals 2000: Education America Act*, 103rd Cong, 1st sess., April 22, 1993. Washington, DC: Government Printing Office, 1993.

———. *Hearings on H.R. 3130: Improving America's Schools Act of 1993*, 103rd Cong., 1st sess., September 23, 1993. Washington, DC: Government Printing Office, 1993.

———. *Oversight Hearings on the Report of the National Council on Education Standards and Testing*, 102nd Cong., 2nd sess., February 4, 19, and March 18, 1992. Washington, DC: Government Printing Office, 1992.

U.S. Congress, House of Representatives, Subcommittee on Oversight and Investigations, Committee on Economic and Educational Opportunities. *Hearing on Education Standards*, 104th Cong., 1st sess., March 22, 1995. Washington, DC: Government Printing Office, 1995.

————. *Hearing on Reexamining Old Assumptions,* 104th Cong., 1st sess., January 26, 1995. Washington, DC: Government Printing Office, 1995.

U.S. Congress, Senate, Committee on Labor and Human Resources. *Examining the Need to Improve National Education Standards and Job Training Opportunities,* 103rd Cong., 1st sess., February 24, 1993. Washington, DC: Government Printing Office, 1993.

————. *Hearing on the Administration's Education Reform Proposal,* 102nd Cong., 1st sess., April 23, 1991. Washington, DC: Government Printing Office, 1991.

U.S. Congress, Senate, Subcommittee on Appropriations, Committee on Appropriations. *Goals 2000,* 104th Cong., 1st sess., September 12, 1995.Washington, DC: Government Printing Office, 1995.

US Department of Education. *Guidance on Standards, Assessments, and Accountability.* Washington, DC: Government Printing Office, 1997.

————. *Highlights from TIMSS.* Washington, DC: Department of Education, 1999.

————. *Improving America's Schools Act of 1993: Reauthorization of the Elementary and Secondary Education Act and Amendments to Other Acts.* Washington, DC: Department of Education, September 13, 1993.

US Office of the Federal Register. *United States Statutes at Large.* Washington, DC: GPO. http://memory.loc.gov/ammem/amlaw/lwsl.html.

Verba, Sidney, et al. *Voice and Equality: Civic Voluntarism in American Politics.* Cambridge, MA: Harvard University Press, 1995.

Viadero, Debra. "Against Odds, School Propels Its Students to College." *Education Week,* May 16, 2001.

————. "Schooled Out of Poverty." *Education Week,* December 13, 2000.

————. "Testing System in Texas Yet to Get the Final Grade." *Education Week,* May 31, 2000.

Vinovksis, Maris. *The Development and Demise of the National Education Goals,* forthcoming.

Viteritti, Joseph P. "Agenda Setting: When Politics and Pedagogy Meet." *Social Policy* 15 (Fall 1984).

————. "Blaine's Wake: School Choice, the First Amendment, and State Constitutional Law." *Harvard Journal of Law and Public Policy* 21 (1998).

————. *Choosing Equality: School Choice, the Constitution, and Civil Society.* Washington, DC: Brookings Institution, 1999.

Vogel, Ezra F. *Japan as Number One: Lessons for America.* Cambridge, MA: Harvard University Press, 1979.

Wahlberg, Herbert J. *Spending More While Earning Less.* Washington, DC: Thomas B. Fordham Foundation, 1998.

————. "Uncompetitive American Schools: Causes and Cures." In Diane Ravitch, ed., *Brookings Papers on Education Policy, 1998.* Washington, DC: Brookings Institution, 1998.

Walsh, Julie M. *The Intellectual Origins of Mass Parties and Mass Schools in the Jacksonian Period: Creating a Conformed Citizenry.* New York: Garland, 1998.

Wang, Jianjun. "A Content Examination of the TIMSS Items." *Phi Delta Kappan* 80, 1 (September 1998).

Ward, Annie M., and Mildred Murray-Ward. *Assessment in the Classroom* (Boston: Wadsworth, 1999.

Warren, Donald R. *To Enforce Education: A History of the Founding Years of the United States Office of Education.* Detroit: Wayne State University Press, 1974.

Weaver, Samuel Horton. *The Truman Administration and Federal Aid to Education.* PhD diss., American University, 1972.

Webb, Norman L. *Alignment of Science and Mathematics Standards and Assessments in Four States.* Research Monograph No. 18. Washington, DC: Council of Chief State School Officers, 1999.

Weisman, Jonathan. "Businesses Sign on to Bush Plan, but Many Also Raising Concerns." *Education Week,* May 8, 1991.

Weiss, A. R., et al. *The Next Generation of Citizens: NAEP Civics Assessments, 1988 and 1998.* Washington, DC: National Center for Educational Statistics, 2001.

Wesley, Edgar B. *Proposed: The National University of the United States.* Minneapolis: University of Minnesota Press, 1936.

Whittington, Dale. "What Have 17-Year-Olds Known in the Past?" *American Education Research Journal* 28 (1991).

Wildavsky, Aaron. *Speaking Truth to Power.* Boston: Little, Brown, 1979.

Wilgoren, Jodi. "School Chiefs Fret over US Plan to Require Testing." *New York Times,* July 7, 2001.

Wills, Garry. *A Necessary Evil: A History of American Distrust of Government.* New York: Simon and Schuster, 1999.

———, ed. *The Federalist Papers.* New York: Bantam, 1988.

Wilson, James Q. *The Moral Sense.* New York: Free Press, 1993.

Winfield, Unda F., and Michael D. Woodard. "Where Are Equity and Diversity in America 2000?" *Education Week,* January 29, 1992.

Winship, Christopher, and Sanders D. Korenman. "Economic Success and the Evolution of Schooling and Mental Ability." In Susan E. Mayer and Paul E. Peterson, eds., *Earning and Learning: How Schools Matter.* Washington, DC, and New York: Brookings Institution and Russell Sage Foundation, 1999.

Wise, Lauress. *Impact of Exclusion Rates on NAEP 1994 to 1998 Grade Four Reading Gains in Kentucky.* Washington, DC: National Center for Educational Statistics, 1999.

Wixson, Karen K., and Elizabeth Dutro. *Standards for Primary-Grade Reading: An Analysis of State Frameworks.* Ann Arbor: University of Michigan, Center for the Improvement of Early Reading Achievement, 1998.

Wolfe, Barbara, and Samuel Zuvekas. "Nonmarket Outcomes of Schooling." In Walter W. McMahon, ed., *Recent Advances in Measuring the Social and Individual Benefits of Education.* London: Elsevier Science, 1997.

Wolfe, Charles. "New US Education Law Seen as Flawed." *Lexington Herald Leader,* June 6, 2002.

Wood, Gordon S. *The Creation of the American Republic, 1776–1787.* New York: W. W. Norton, 1993.

Woronoff, Jon. *World Trade War.* New York: Praeger, 1984.

Zernicke, Kate. "In Two Years, Mt. Vernon Test Scores Turn Around." *New York Times,* May 23, 2001.

———. "Why Johnny Can't Read, Write, Multiply, or Divide." *New York Times,* April 15, 2001.

Zuckman, Jill. "Elbowing Democrats Aside, Bush Unveils School Plan." *Congressional Quarterly Weekly,* April 20, 1991.

———. "House Panel Moves on National Test." *Congressional Quarterly Weekly,* June 1, 1991.

———. "Small Panel, Big Goals." *Congressional Quarterly Weekly,* July 6, 1991.

Index

About the Book

In the past fifteen years, presidents from two parties, supported by parents and civic leaders, have tried—and generally failed—to increase student achievement through federal policymaking. Supposedly pathbreaking legislation to "leave no child behind" has hardly made a dent in the problem. What is going on? Kevin R. Kosar delves into the political maneuvering behind the crafting of federal education standards policy.

Drawing on a wealth of evidence, Kosar makes a strong case for vigorous federal action to raise standards. Then, turning to the "real world" of Washington, DC, he shows how politics has thwarted smart policy—and how we are left with the present reforms, which talk tough but deliver little. He concludes with sober proposals for education policies that, while not aiming at perfection, have a chance of surviving political attacks from both the right and the left.

Kevin R. Kosar is an analyst in the Congressional Research Service at the Library of Congress.